PRAISE FOR *RALPH COULD HAVE BEEN A SUPERSTAR*

"Rich Vivone has produced an enjoyable book and a valuable resource for those wanting to understand politics and governance in Alberta. He translates over two decades of engagement in Alberta politics - 19 years publishing *Insight into Government* - into a fast-paced and highly readable account of how Ralph Klein reshaped the Alberta political scene and left a legacy that continues to influence the character of Alberta politics and government.

In 12 stand-alone essays, Vivone combines a dose of memoir with a serious journalistic attempt to look back and understand politics and governance during the Klein era. The essays delve into public policy (health and children's policy), explore Alberta political culture (media, political apathy and fear) and examine the challenges of governing in an energy-dominated political economy. But, above all, they strive to understand the politics of Ralph Klein and his governments.

A keen observer of major political events, Vivone also manages to discover insights into politics in the subtle and apparently mundane events and conversations that occur just outside the spotlight of mainstream journalistic coverage - the result is a perfect compliment to other journalistic and academic analysis of the Klein era."

  - Steve Patten, Associate Professor of Political Science,
    University of Alberta

"For nearly 20 years Rich Vivone was the original embedded independent reporter covering Alberta politics. His inside-the-action vantage point presents a unique 360-degree view of the day-by-day events of Alberta politics before, during and after the Klein years.

This collection of essays is an impressive effort and covers a lot of territory while maintaining an easy-to-read style. Through it all, Rich Vivone's telling observations deliver real insight into where the Alberta Progressive Conservative government has taken Alberta and where they may direct Alberta into the future.

There are too few books covering this important period of Alberta politics; *Ralph Could Have Been a Superstar* is a wonderful addition to that small collection."

  - Jim Wachowich, Legal counsel to the Consumers' Coalition of Alberta

"In his approach to Alberta politics, Vivone is the perfect 'critical friend' - at the core, respectful and even affectionate, but unrelentingly straightforward, analytical and honest as well. He pulls no punches: Alberta's Auditors-General 'have become sheep,' Alberta's government has often relied on 'fear and intimidation', and the climate at times has been one where 'the fear was palpable, the silence pervasive'. But clearly the criticism is to help us to understand, and to improve - and we should listen closely if we care about democracy and the public interest.

Perhaps the most helpful and unusual aspect of the book is that Vivone goes beyond simply analyzing the problems, and actually suggests solutions to the big political questions facing Albertans. His suggestions are thoughtful, principled and well-argued, and should be debated across the province by people who are tired of the anaemic political culture that has characterized Alberta for too long."

   - Larry Booi, Board Chair, Public Interest Alberta

"From his unique perspective as a political insider, Rich Vivone offers a vivid analysis of how Ralph Klein became Alberta's most controversial premier, how he transformed the province and where he fell short. In a clear, accessible style, Vivone also delivers a critique of Alberta's place on the national stage and the entrenchment of one-party dominance. Vivone's book is provocative and important reading for those who want to understand where Alberta is today."

   - Sheila Pratt, Feature Writer, Edmonton Journal

"Rich Vivone gives us a very revealing look at the Klein years and also a glimpse into Alberta's longest-serving and in some ways enigmatic Premier, himself. It is a 'must-read' for anyone that is interested in Canadian politics and who wants to better understand the domination of the Conservative party in Alberta, and its significant influence within Confederation.

What will Ralph Klein's legacy be to Alberta and within Canada, and how will Alberta's longest-serving Premier be remembered? Rich Vivone's extremely revealing book paves the way to the answers; and these answers are important to every Canadian."

   - Gary McPherson, Former Chair,
   Premier's Council on the Status of Persons with Disabilities

"There is for many an inexplicable delight in political pratfalls and kicks in the pants. Rich Vivone's *Ralph Could Have Been a Superstar* provides lots of these. Ralph Klein and other key Alberta political actors provide plenty of slips and trips, while Vivone delivers some great boots. Vivone's punts are swift but not savage; yet, they leave no doubt about what the author thinks of the policies and actions of Alberta's parliamentary political elites and, too, of the province's timid press.

Any thought that *Ralph Could Have Been a Superstar* is moribund stuff - the reminiscing about old battles of mostly retired political warriors - can be put immediately to rest by cheating and reading the final chapter first. This crowning piece is an open letter to the current premier, Ed Stelmach. Vivone distills his indictment of Klein, opining that with so much political power 'he achieved so little when he could have achieved so much', then challenges Stelmach to not fail in the same way.

Vivone's passions and political values are in full display in the final chapter in which he offers policy prescription in three key areas: the role of government, the political process, and the place of Alberta in Confederation. Required reading for the last chapter is the previous chapters, which provide essential historical perspective; they are the meal to the dessert.

It is impossible to predict what lasting contribution this book will have in telling the tale of the Klein years. One thing is certain though, for anyone with an interest in Alberta provincial politics, it is a good read."

- Edward C. LeSage Jr., Professor Emeritus, University of Alberta

RALPH COULD HAVE BEEN A SUPERSTAR

TALES OF THE KLEIN ERA

Rich Vivone

Patricia
Publishing Inc.
Kingston, Ontario, Canada

PUBLISHED BY
Patricia Publishing Inc.
851 Lotus Avenue
Kingston, ON K7K 0A6

CREDITS
Original cover photo copyright © Gunther Ruppel
Page design by Patricia Publishing Inc.
Printed and bound in Canada by Custom Printing

Library and Archives Canada Cataloguing in Publication

Vivone, Rich, 1941-
    Ralph could have been a superstar : tales of the Klein era / Rich Vivone.

Includes bibliographical references and index.
ISBN 978-0-9812954-0-4

    1. Alberta--Politics and government--1971-.
2. Klein, Ralph, 1942-. 3. Politicians--Alberta.
4. Legislators--Alberta. I. Title.

FC3675.2.V59 2009   971.23'03   C2009-904315-7

This book is for
Patricia
who made it possible

and for the
grandchildren
Bailey, Freya, Grayson, Mackenzie,
Michael, Mikayla, Parker, Stephanie

CONTENTS

ACKNOWLEDGEMENTS

The book culminates two decades of political journalism in Alberta. It would not have happened without the help of many friends, all of who encouraged me and, in some cases, pitched in when the task of publishing my own work seemed so formidable. All authors writing their first book should have so many friends. They gave their help generously and without expectation. Mere written words cannot fully express my appreciation to them. I must, however, try to write words give tribute to their generosity.

My wife, Pat, was a constant support from start to finish. She took over publishing, marketing and distribution. Her dedication to helping make this book a publishing success allowed me to concentrate on the book itself. Without her, *Ralph Could Have Been a Superstar* still sits on my computer. Because of her efforts, you have this book to read.

Peter Johnston of PSC Consulting has been a friend since our university years at the University of Alberta in the 1960s when he worked in Photo Directorate and I worked at *The Gateway*. When I was publishing *Insight into Government*, Peter took care of all my technological problems. He did the website for this book with the same patience, wisdom and competence.

Gunther Ruppel, another long-time friend in Edmonton and a fellow retiree, rescued us by designing the cover. He patiently listened to our ideas and translated them into a series of concepts that became a terrific cover.

Ian Gray worked with me at *Insight into Government* for more than a decade. No member of the Alberta Legislature Press Gallery knew provincial politics as well as Ian. His sources were impeccable. One of Ian's best pieces - Dr. Death or Dr. Dud - is reproduced in this book exactly as he wrote it. Ian's work contributed to other essays as well.

Christine and Paul Silveira are good friends in Kingston. When the business aspects of publishing the book overwhelmed us, they gave direction and encouragement on setting up a business in Ontario, managing it, and effectively using the internet for marketing and sales.

Danielle and Martin McCarron, also good friends in Kingston, generously allowed us to piggy-back on their business for packaging and distribution. They made it possible for this book to get from their warehouse into your hands within a reasonable time and at affordable costs.

Lisa Sansom of Kingston, who has an unbelievable understanding of the written word, read the manuscript and offered suggestions to make it more readable, sensible and grammatically correct.

Kevin Kuchinski did solid research work at the Alberta Legislature Library, digging into files for documents from as far back as the 1970s. Kevin got the facts on some events reported in the essay on scandals and scandalous behaviour.

Finally, a number of trusted sources insisted on remaining anonymous. Some of these sources work in places where they saw and heard plenty, generously shared what they knew, and trusted me to use the information intelligently. As insiders, they gave me the benefit of their knowledge of the Premier's Office, the people in it, the people who influenced it, and the way decisions were made. They generously read early drafts of essays and contributed information I otherwise did not have access to.

To all of you, thank you. Without the help of each and every one of you, this book doesn't happen.

While I had so much help, the words in this book are mine. Any errors are my responsibility alone.

INTRODUCTION

I came west as a mildly curious student in 1964, intending to earn an undergraduate degree from the University of Alberta in Edmonton and to get a taste of life. I had no grand scheme for my adult life. I had minimal skills in everything other than spending my parents' hard-earned money, a skill at which I had become quite proficient.

Why Alberta? Not because of oil or a dream of big money, but for a more practical reason. Alberta was about halfway between Vancouver and Winnipeg, two cities in which my family had relatives. In Edmonton, there was no chance I would live with relatives. In Edmonton, more than 2,000 km from my hometown of Nipigon, in Northwestern Ontario, and at least 1,000 km from the nearest relatives, I was a kid finally on my own. In Edmonton, I had the freedom to fully enjoy a university life.

I came to love Alberta. My escape became my home. I lived in Alberta for 42 years. I came with nothing but the values my parents instilled in me and I left as a mature adult with a lifetime of memories and friendships.

Alberta changed me forever. I am who I am largely because of the people I met in Alberta, the skills I developed, and the work I did. The friends I met at the University of Alberta in the 1960s remain friends to this day, scattered as they are around the country. I traveled the province from east to west, north to south, both in my work and on my own. I met and worked with too many people to count but not too many to remember.

I became a journalist, then a politician's assistant, and combined the two into a 19-year career publishing *Insight into Government*, the first political newsletter in the province to analyze public policy and certainly one of the most successful.

The Gateway was the student newspaper at the University of Alberta. Reading *The Gateway* while waiting for an economic class to begin, a fellow sitting in the row behind asked me what I thought about the student newspaper. Naive, cocky and critical, I launched into a two-minute critique based on my limited knowledge of journalism. After listening politely, he introduced himself as *The Gateway's* news editor - Al Broemling - and he was my introduction to journalism. He told me that if I thought the newspaper could be improved, I should come to the office and help make it a better publication.

Several years later, I was the Editor-In-Chief. My first real job after graduation was in daily journalism, as Sports Editor of the *Red Deer Advocate*.

David King, a university friend, introduced me to partisan politics. David, the Conservative MLA for Edmonton Highlands, was appointed Minister of Education in 1979. A year later, he asked me to join his staff. I told him that I had little interest in politics generally, had no taste for partisan politics, and had no experience in provincial affairs other than a short stint as the Communications Director of the Government of Alberta's Department of Recreation, Parks & Wildlife in 1975.

David was aware of my background but he insisted that he needed help and asked me to think about it. I worked with him for five years, developed a passion for politics, public policy and the political process that continues to this day.

After David lost in Edmonton Highlands in 1986, he and I set up a consulting company and created a political newsletter called *Insight into Government*. We soon learned that political consulting and political journalism were incompatible. The newsletter was split from the consulting arm and I went with it.

Insight into Government became my passion and my professional life. I published it for 19 years until my retirement in 2005. The newsletter brought me a career some people can only dream of, a career that excites and stimulates every minute of every day. I couldn't wait to get to work every morning. If that wasn't enough, I was my own boss.

Covering provincial politics day by day with eyes and ears experienced in a political environment, I saw through the fog and the follies to write about what was really going on. I wrote more than I could ever have imagined. In covering the Klein era over 14 years, I published 536 issues with 3,200 pages of original work and wrote about three million words. The Getty era, including three years with Klein as Environment Minister, required another million words. This book is based on that total body of work.

A year into retirement and living in another province, I continued to follow Alberta politics. Through the wonders of modern communications, I was still reading the *Edmonton Journal* and the *Calgary Herald* most mornings, just as I did when I was publishing *Insight into Government*.

Eighteen months ago, an old Alberta friend called.

"When's the book coming out?"

"What book?" I asked.

"The book you are writing."

"I'm not writing a book."

"Why not? I don't know anyone better to do it," he said. "It would be a shame to let all that knowledge go to waste. Somebody has to write about what happened here for 15 years. You're the only guy who wrote about it from start to finish. Why don't you at least think about it?"

Until that phone call, I didn't consider myself capable of writing a book. The commitment is huge and, so early in retirement, I lacked the motivation to do anything but eat, read, bike and travel.

Yet my friend's question kept nagging me: "When's the book coming out?"

I began to think about a book. Surprisingly, I learned that few books had covered the Klein era from start to finish. The Parkland Institute at the University of Alberta produced an academic treatment called the *Return Of The Trojan Horse: Alberta and the New World (Dis)Order*. Liberal leader Kevin Taft wrote *Democracy Derailed*. Both are helpful, valuable books but I waited in vain for a street-smart book with an independent voice. Three others had been written previously, one of them eight years ago and two others some 15 years before.

I decided to give it a try.

How does one write a book? I had no idea. There was so much to the Klein era, and the Getty era before that - the political eras I wrote about in *Insight into Government* - that one book couldn't possibly cover it all.

I decided on a perspective that looked at Ralph Klein's administration: the people in it, its policies and how they impacted the province. There was a story that had to be told but how could the massive volumes of information be organized into a relevant, readable document?

A flood of memories came back about events, conversations, and arguments. As I re-read copies of *Insight into Government* and sorted through my memories, the themes of the book slowly organized themselves into the 12 essays that follow. Each is written to be read independently.

Insight into Government readers used to tell me that they read the newsletter backwards, meaning they read the gossipy, speculative "Talk In The Corners" on the back page first. Then they flipped back to the front and read it normally, from front to back. Similarly, if I wrote the essays well, you should be able to read any essay at any time, in any order, and each should tell a different story.

The story of Ralph Klein the endless campaigner is well known. Part of his pitch was that he knew people better than other politicians because he did not suffer from what he called "dome disease", a condition that builds a myopic view in politicians who spend too much time in the Legislature Building listening to bureaucrats. Klein's remedy: "Get out from under the dome" and talk to voters to learn what they want.

The pitch was seductive. He became popular and earned the people's trust. Re-election became easy.

One form of myopia leads to another. If politicians hanging around the Legislature Building weren't in tune with voters, politicians hanging around with voters weren't in tune with the Legislature Building.

While Klein was not in the Legislature, who was writing the dozens of laws debated in the Legislative Assembly every Spring and mostly ignored by the media? Who was making the political decisions while Klein was away being a populist?

In assessing Klein's career as Premier of Alberta from 1992 through 2006, it struck me that he saw the province through one eye - the eye of a populist. If his other eye had been opened, the eye that saw how to convert the wishes of a population into public policy, he might have been a great Premier. He could have been a superstar amongst political leaders in Canada. The key words are "could have been". He had the trust and the popularity to do almost anything he wanted and still survive.

The record shows that while his fiscal achievements early in his career were significant, the rest of the record is bare. He utterly failed at health reform and economic diversification. He did little for culture, recreation or the arts. He failed to build his own legacy.

He could have done so much more; he could have been a political superstar.

Readers will notice that many sources are not identified. As with political reporting elsewhere, sources demanding anonymity are a fact of life in Alberta politics:

nobody talks provincial politics to a journalist for attribution. Talking "on the record" is distinctly un-Albertan.

Politicians, senior bureaucrats and observers of the political scene will talk to media guys like me - but they don't want to be identified. In essence, they offer candour in exchange for anonymity. So many conversations began with this qualifier: "You didn't hear this from me, but ...." or "Don't quote me but ..."

Not surprisingly, I found that when names were not used, sources were talkative. Comments for attribution, rare as they were, usually were inane, innocuous and meaningless.

Writing this book was one experience, getting it published was another.

While still a concept in the summer of 2008, I contacted a publisher with a history of doing political books. He was immediately interested, and traveled to my retirement home in Kingston, Ontario, to discuss a deal. We came to a verbal agreement on theme and time. Two months later, while I was working up a draft of the manuscript, he told me that his company had changed his mind.

"Why?" I asked. "You haven't seen my work yet."

"I made some calls to Alberta," he said. "The general consensus is that Albertans want to forget about Ralph Klein as quickly as possible. We don't see a market for a book on Klein. Sorry."

A sample was sent to a publisher in Alberta. Similar answer: "We've been there, we've done that, Klein was a mistake, time to move on." Just like that, the publisher says Albertans can dismiss one era of political history by pretending it didn't happen.

I had heard this argument before. When *Insight into Government* began publishing in 1986, numerous friends said from the start that there was no market for a weekly political newsletter and that I was wasting my time and money. I stubbornly went ahead, betting that they were wrong. Now under another publisher, *Insight into Government* is still going strong 23 years later.

This book is another gamble. This time, I am betting against those who say that Albertans want to forget Ralph Klein.

Rather than continue to search for a publisher, my wife and I set up our own company to publish this book.

I believe Albertans will read an interpretation of the Klein era from an independent political analyst who was there from the beginning. I believe Albertans care about their modern political history, and the man called Ralph, who was a large part of it. I believe it so strongly that I'm putting my money where my mouth is.

1

RALPH KLEIN
HE COULD HAVE BEEN A SUPERSTAR

Ralph Klein still perplexes me. I covered Alberta politics through my newsletter **Insight into Government** *for 19 years. Klein was Premier for 13 of those years and Environment Minister for another three. He was as perplexing to me at the start late in 1989 as he was when I published my last newsletter in June 2005. As I write this in 2009, he still perplexes me. What did voters find so comforting in this man? Why were his last 10 years so unproductive? Was he as smart as so many voters thought or a mediocre talent who happened to be Premier when energy prices rebounded and oil sands investment went through the roof?*

"One searches for a deep philosophical or metaphysical meaning in the Klein phenomena, for a mystical connection explained by psychobabble but finds only Ralph. He is not a fiery orator or even a dynamic speaker. He hasn't a definable political, social or economic philosophy. He has no formal leadership or management skills. He's just indefinable, trustworthy Ralph."

- Insight into Government, March 1994

From 1993 through 2001, Ralph Klein was Alberta's political maestro. He wrote the right songs and sang the tunes Albertans wanted to hear. They listened to him, especially the folks throughout the rural regions of the province, in Calgary and in parts of Edmonton. He delivered the political theatre they wanted and he was rewarded by massive re-elections in 1997 and 2001. Then his popularity and the trust and respect that came with performance began to decline. By 2006, his own political party, tired of his antics and reluctant to trust him with another election, dumped him.

Ralph Klein, who had ruled the province for 14 years, was sent packing. What happened? Where did the teflon man go wrong? Like all good stories, the end starts at the beginning.

I was there when Ralph Klein walked into the Legislature in 1989 as a rookie minister in the Conservative Government headed by Premier Don Getty. I saw Klein rise quickly, surprisingly winning the Conservative Party leadership in 1992 and successfully completing one of the toughest deficit-cutting programs in Canadian political history.

With the deficit eliminated and the provincial debt under control, Ralph Klein's star dimmed. He tried to sing the same simple song again and again - debt is bad, we must get rid of it, stick with me because I'm the guy to do it. His fans were no longer listening.

The rise and decline of Ralph Klein is a unique story in Alberta provincial politics. This man, who easily gained people's trust and confidence, struggled as the head of a government with huge money to manage. He was fine when he knew exactly what to do - cut the deficit - but when faced with reforming and rebuilding the province's political institutions to lead it into the 21st century, he was lost. Yet, the cracks in his political armour had started to appear years earlier.

To me, publisher of a political newsletter devoted strictly to provincial politics, I had wondered what all the fuss was about the first time I met him in 1989.

A STAR IS RELEGATED TO THE BASEMENT

I was looking for Ralph Klein. The short, paunchy, Columbo-like former Mayor of Calgary - a politician with a reputation for talking fast, drinking hard and winning elections handily - had been appointed as Alberta's Environment Minister and I was eager to meet him.

Klein was Premier Don Getty's star recruit in 1988, enticed into provincial politics by a prized seat at the cabinet table. Getty's popularity was in free-fall and he wanted Klein, not because the Conservatives needed him badly, as much as to prevent Klein from running as a Liberal. There were ample rumours about a Ralph Klein/Laurence Decore alliance to lead the Liberals and Getty was going to make sure that if Klein entered provincial politics, it would be as a Conservative.

Getty won. Surely Getty would make Klein a populist centerpiece of the newly-elected Conservative Government.

I found Klein and his sidekick, Rod Love but they weren't where I expected to find them. Their office was buried in the west wing of the Legislature Building's dimly lit basement. No office is further from the Premier's Office; no office is further from the Legislature Building's main entrance than Klein's new office. Unless you work in the basement of the Legislature Building, the only reason to go into the basement's west wing is to use the washroom. Why wasn't this fresh new face, in a government that badly needed freshness, located on the main floor where he would be visible?

There are those who claim that a basement office in the Legislature has nothing to do with status and everything to do with space limitations. To which I must answer: which star newcomer has ever been promoted to the basement?

Getty's reason for burying this well-known character in the basement, I learned, was that Klein couldn't keep his mouth shut around reporters. Before he had walked into the Legislature Building as a Conservative MLA for the first time, Klein had already annoyed Getty by talking to reporters about Getty's offer of a cabinet post which, given Getty's penchant for secrecy, was not wise. Klein's reward: the basement.

With all the subtlety of a jackhammer, Getty had told the media that this Klein character, so friendly, open and popular with the reporters that Getty detested, was just another face in his cabinet. The final slap: on Getty's first List of Precedents after the 1989 election that, in effect, suggests the relative influence of each minister, Klein was buried at the bottom of the last page. Not an auspicious start to a new political career.

Having found the office, Rod Love didn't waste time with me. I had been forewarned that he didn't engage in small talk, that he was aggressive and blunt. Love didn't disappoint. Seconds after shaking hands, he looked me straight in the eye and said: "Edmonton reporters think Ralph's stupid. You probably think he's stupid too." Was this a classic case of lowering expectations?

The truth is that I rarely thought about Ralph Klein until he won a seat in the Legislative Assembly. I knew the Mayor of Calgary only by what I read in the newspapers: he was popular, loose-lipped and often engaged his tongue before he engaged his mind. Calgarians loved him, he drank too much at the St. Louis Hotel, Calgary police sometimes drove him home after a night at the St. Louis, and his "eastern creeps and bums" harangue gave him a national profile. I had heard and read about him, was curious about the manner in which he conducted himself in political office, but I had not met him.

HE LOOKED AS COMFORTABLE IN A SUIT AS COLUMBO

Early in the 1980s, Klein was a breath of fresh air in Calgary, a city laden with money, suspicious of municipal politicians, and inflicted with entitlement. His ability to win elections was impressive. As for Klein's record as mayor, few could tell me whether he did anything memorable not directly connected to the 1988 Olympic Winter Games. He certainly didn't mind spending money and didn't appear to be concerned with Calgary's mounting capital debt. Otherwise, Klein was another colourful politician lucky enough to be mayor of the host city in an Olympic year.

Did I think Klein was stupid? Why would Love even utter the word? Getty's cabinet already had more than its fair share of stupidity and didn't need any more. I didn't know enough about the man or the politician to decide. In the ten seconds it took to walk from Love's office into Klein's office, I asked myself why anyone would think Ralph Klein is stupid. I was anxious to find out.

A newsletter publisher talks to a politician for one reason: to get information. In a first meeting with new ministers, my single purpose is to determine whether they are worth a second interview. Most of them either had nothing interesting to say or wouldn't tell a newsletter publisher anyway. New ministers often appeared to be stunned at how far they had risen so quickly, were intimidated by their sudden influence and were terrified to make a mistake. It wasn't difficult to get a sense of whether a new minister would be open to frank talk. If ministers won't talk, what's the point of being with them? If an interview becomes a political game of words and evasions rather than an adult conversation, why waste my time?

I had spent five years working in a minister's office, sitting in meetings with powerful politicians, and learned to recognize the essence of successful ministers; work ethic, an ability to get to the guts of complex issues, and a willingness to delegate. I had long lost an automatic awe of people in powerful positions. Instead, I look for the little things that separate the good from the mediocre: a twinkle in the eye, a tinge of sincerity when a politician says "good to see you", a quiet confidence, a willingness to listen, respect for people with a differing view, and that most rare quality of all: grace.

Only five minutes into the interview and I noticed how unremarkable Ralph Klein was even when I had few expectations. His face was round and deeply lined. He had that after-shower glow and his hair was slick, foppish and fashionable: just the right length to suit the style of 1989. He was well-dressed, as ministers usually are because of the generous clothing allowance that comes with the job. I would learn over the years that although Klein was dressed in expensive, tailored suits, he didn't wear a suit well - he wore it like Columbo. He always had the look of a man who felt more comfortable in jeans.

Klein's shirt was freshly laundered, his tie straight and his suit jacket hung over his chair. He smiled, shook hands and offered a seat.

He knew neither who I was nor the newsletter I published. Because I was curious about him, I assumed that he might be curious about a media guy he hadn't met before. I was wrong: he showed no interest in me or my work.

Pages of notes were piled neatly on the table in front of him and when I asked a question, he glanced at the notes before responding. Occasionally he made eye contact. He was relaxed and disarming, unlike some ministers who behave as if they want to be somewhere else, anywhere but in a room with a reporter. Yet Klein talked in a monotone of his plans for environment.

The interview was over in a half hour and I was disappointed. Klein did not make a good first impression. His response to every question came from notes. For a journalist, a politician reading notes prepared by someone else - Rod Love most likely - is disappointing. A politician reading from a script is never a good interview. It suggests the man either isn't capable of thinking for himself, doesn't know what he thinks, or fears blurting out something he doesn't want to see in print. I wanted to know what Klein was thinking, not his assistant or anyone else.

After Klein became Premier in 1992, all Conservative MLAs would use such notes - they became known as Talking Points - in interviews with reporters. They were spewing the latest government line rather than explaining their own views. Every Conservative MLA was saying the same thing, in some cases using the same words, about new policies. They rarely told reporters what they personally thought about the policies or how the new policies would affect their constituents. Talking Points devalued political discourse.

When my first interview with Klein was over, I wasn't sure whether Klein was worth a second interview. I saw nothing to indicate whether he was either smart or stupid. He had demonstrated only an ability to read. I also suspected that Rod Love might be more open about what I needed - policy information - than Klein.

Charisma is a curious animal. A person either has charisma, or doesn't. There is no middle ground. Charisma is like pornography: difficult to define or describe, but easily recognizable. Charisma has nothing to do with education or social class. Charisma begins in the school yard and, like a good education, stays with you for the rest of your life. Charismatic people dominate a room; they make a room more interesting by being in it; they attract attention without obvious effort; they know how to handle attention. Charisma masks personal and political faults. Charismatic people rarely try to impress. And a charismatic person has the unique ability to make every person they meet feel more important.

I saw no evidence of charisma in Klein in that first meeting in 1989. At first glance, he was another minister sitting in his chair reading his notes waiting for the meeting to start. No polite small talk; he patiently waited for my questions as I scanned the tiny office. Klein seemed no different from the politicians I talked with often. Ralph Klein, it seemed to me, was the kind of guy I could have a beer with and not feel intimidated - if he put his notes away. Premier material? The more relevant question was whether Klein, who had a reputation for being thin-skinned and overly sensitive to criticism, could handle the often-controversial Environment portfolio.

HE WASN'T AFRAID TO CHALLENGE HIS OWN PREMIER

Time would show that there was more to Ralph Klein than he showed me in that first interview. He certainly wasn't a morning person.

"Ralph drank a lot from the time he came to the Legislature and he usually showed it when he arrived. He was hung over. It took time for him to get going," I was told. "Most of the time, we didn't know what to expect. Like everybody else, we underestimated him."

In the months that followed, Klein proved to be a politician with a flair for entertaining a small crowd, especially in Question Period.

He sat in the second row in the Legislative Assembly, well-groomed, well dressed in a dark, slimming three-piece suit encasing his thick body, ready for his new adventure. He had already achieved well beyond anything he could have imagined as a reporter in Calgary 10 years ago.

Klein took a keen interest in his work. From a very good source: "In Environment, Ralph was on top of his game. He had his ear to the ground and he knew what Albertans wanted. He knew what would sell."

Getty's economic diversification strategy encouraged pulp mills for the north and northwest regions of the province. All had serious environmental implications. Klein found a middle ground between environmentalists against everything that smacked of economic development and the pro-development forces that cared only for economic growth. He wasn't afraid to challenge his own Premier, a Premier hell-bent on diversifying a struggling provincial economy by building a forestry industry in northern Alberta.

When the New Democrats attacked in the Legislative Assembly, Klein came back hard. He came into the Assembly well prepared. He was fast on his feet and as fast with his mouth. Love told me that in preparing Klein for Question Period, he and a few others would pepper Klein with "the dirtiest, nastiest questions we could think of" and when Klein walked into Question Period, he knew he could deal with anything the New Democrats could throw. And he was not above a little humour, a welcome relief from the snore that the Assembly had become.

After several months of watching Klein in Question Period, it was clear that he was a politician with ambition, that he was worth watching for no other reason than his entertainment value, and that he had greater things in mind for himself. Unlike most ministers, he enjoyed the cut and thrust of Question Period. He was enjoying partisan politics. He was being noticed and he loved the attention. Curiously, as Premier, Klein loathed Question Period and having to account for himself.

On the eve of the Conservative leadership race in September 1992, I reported: "Ralph Klein still stands out as a lone ranger in the Conservative caucus. I still hear questions about his ability to be part of a team. I still hear comments about him being an intellectual lightweight and a buffoon. Some of it may be accurate ... but Klein is a populist and easily the most popular populist in the Legislature. Rarely do I find someone who doesn't like him."

In 1990, reports of Ralph Klein the Environment Minister showing up regularly at constituency meetings throughout rural Alberta began to spread. Nothing unusual about that - ministers travel to constituencies all the time to spread the government's message and to curry favour with backbench MLAs. What was unusual: Klein was accepting every speaking engagement that came his way, and there were plenty. Perhaps, I thought, he was too willing to be seen everywhere across the province. Was he up to something? He certainly wasn't doing all this to explain his environmental policies. I already knew Klein wasn't a policy man.

His purpose became clear in September 1992. When Premier Don Getty announced his retirement in September, the Conservative leadership race was on and Klein was ready - he was one of the first to declare. His campaign team was ready. All Klein had to do was convince a skeptical public that, despite his reputation for booze, fun and a loose tongue, he was a serious candidate.

THE FIRST CANDIDATES' FORUM AND EDMONTON HIGHLANDS

With roots reaching back into the 19th century, Edmonton Highlands is one of Edmonton's oldest neighbourhoods. A number of its buildings - the McGrath Mansion, the Holgate Mansion, and the Hibbard Block - are designated as historic sites. The Highlands Historical Foundation with its walking tour of historic homes is active.

The rich who were attracted to Highlands in the 19th century left after World War II for the more prestigious Glenora area in the west end of the city. Highlands became a working class neighbourhood with small bungalows built in 1940s and 1950s. These were people who got their hands dirty, who were always employees rather than employers. Some were teachers, some worked for the provincial government, some ran small local businesses. Many were retired. People came to Highlands and stayed there. Until recently when many of the retired went into nursing homes, Highlands was one of the most stable neighbourhoods in the city; very few houses went on the real estate market.

Edmonton Highlands is a walking community where neighbours talk over fences, walk their dogs and stroll up and down Ada Boulevard to appreciate the mansions and gaze at the North Saskatchewan River. The Highlands Historical Society distributed its newsletter throughout the neighbourhood.

The Avenue Community Hall on 118th Avenue in a working class neighbourhood on the northern boundary of the Highlands riding was a small, intimate hall more accustomed to community league events than political debates. My business office was located four blocks south on 66th Street. I knew the neighbourhood and the people who lived in it.

In late October 1992, about 500 locals crowded into the small room at this community hall to hear the leadership candidates speak of their ideas for a revamped Conservative Party. There were the usual entourages traveling with the candidates but the majority in this room was curious folks from the Highlands neighbourhood - my neighbours - who hadn't seen many of the nine candidates in person before, and with good reason: after the Edmonton Highlands riding elected New Democrat Pam Barrett in the 1986 provincial election, Conservative politicians avoided the riding. For the next decade, the Conservatives had a difficult time finding a candidate to contest elections.

I didn't know what to expect from my neighbours as the nine leadership candidates filed into the Alberta Avenue Community Hall. My neighbours were working class people hit hard by rising unemployment in the city. Don Getty's Conservative Government hadn't been good to the Highlands community. Labour strife at Gainer's meat packing plant less than a mile north on 66th Street inflicted serious damage on the community. To the residents of Edmonton Highlands, Gainer's wasn't a newspaper story or distant labour violence reported on the late night television news; Gainer's was an employer in their neighbourhood. Getty tried to intervene with a loan guarantee but eventually sold the plant to Burns Foods who closed it and moved operations out of the province. Over 1,000 jobs were lost.

Some of my neighbours had lost the money they invested in the Principal Group. The investment company declared bankruptcy, part of the blame resting with unenthusiastic regulation by the Conservative Government. After Getty had pumped about $2 billion into struggling private businesses, he had little money left to help working people like those who lived in Highlands.

When the population of school-aged children began to decline in the 1980s, the Conservative Government allowed two local public schools to be closed, schools that were also used for community events. No Conservative politician bothered to come to the riding to explain. The citizens of Edmonton Highlands certainly weren't happy with the Getty Government and voted accordingly.

That evening in October, five of Getty's ministers, all vying for Getty's job, were finally going to speak to the community. Who could blame these citizens for thinking that they were typical politicians: they showed up only when they wanted something.

The crowd was somber but polite and attentive as candidate after candidate talked of everything except what the residents of Highlands expected to hear, namely what the provincial government might do to help their community. The candidates talked of cleaning up government - the government they were part of - but didn't accept responsibility for its actions. They railed at excessive spending, the need for balanced budgets and other esoteric political topics but not a word about local concerns.

Political audiences in Alberta are remarkably polite, even when they are insulted twice on the same night by the same people. The residents of Highlands were insulted when no local concerns were addressed and again when speeches were over and the mikes simply turned off. No chance for questions or debate. The candidates had come to talk, not to listen. The crowd stood around, talking amongst themselves about what had happened.

WHO IS THE REAL RALPH KLEIN?
Watching Ralph Klein in that the Alberta Avenue forum, I couldn't believe he was the same guy who stood out in the cut-and-thrust of Question Period.

Klein was not particularly effective in a controlled medium such as a podium despite having the television reporter's commanding voice and a decade of experience. In delivering speeches, he tended to be monotone and stuck to reading his notes. Fifteen years after his political career began in Calgary, Klein was dull and boring on the podium.

It still surprises me that an experienced politician can't get up in public and, without reading notes written by someone else, whip off a 10-minute speech on a familiar issue of public policy and do it forcefully and confidently. Klein kept his head down and plowed through his speech, word for word. He offered a litany of vague promises and ambiguous statements. He talked of "Ralph-style politics" which could mean anything you wanted it to mean. He said that one of the government's serious fiscal problems was inaccurate revenue projections (he said the energy industry should be consulted to help determine energy revenues in the government's annual budget), and he said policy would rise up from the streets rather than descend from the Legislature. He said nothing about huge spending cuts should he win.

I began to wonder which Ralph Klein was the real one - the boring, scripted character in that first interview in 1989, or the colourful, fun-loving character who swapped barbs with opposition MLAs in the Legislative Assembly, or the serious, ambitious politician who bored the crowd at this forum.

When the speeches were finished and everyone stood around wondering what to do because there was no discussion, I saw the first signs of Klein's raw personal drawing power.

Rather than leave after a suitable interval as some of the other candidates did, Klein hung around the rest of the evening, talking to anyone who wanted to talk to him. As the evening wore on, I noticed that more and more people drifted to him. He listened attentively and knew how to draw people into the conversation. When he talked with people, he wasn't another stuffy politician telling them how the world was, but a regular guy bantering on a personal level about regular things. Klein talked with people, always paying close attention to the person talking to him. He stayed after the last candidate left, and then stayed later. Klein broke the mould of politicians who run in, do their thing, thank the host, and run out the door to their next function.

It was apparent that he liked to be with people and paid attention to them. He had a unique ability to make people feel that he cared about what they said. And he wasn't a famous football player like Don Getty, or a big shot like Peter Lougheed, or from a wealthy family like Liberal leader Laurence Decore. He didn't travel surrounded by a team of advisors. Klein was just ... himself. After two decades of Lougheed and Getty, people liked the difference. As Albertans would learn over time, that was both good and bad.

For most of us regular working people, Don Getty, Peter Lougheed and Laurence Decore wouldn't be seen in our neighbourhoods unless they were looking for votes. Ralph Klein, on the other hand, could be a neighbour.

The Alberta Avenue forum was Klein's only appearance in Highlands during the leadership race and the provincial election that followed six months later.

It wasn't enough to change their minds. Ralph-style politics without action and commitment didn't work with these people. He didn't talk about their concerns; he talked about what was wrong about the Getty Government and the need to make things right. Despite sitting in Getty's cabinet for three years, he accepted no responsibility for what had gone on. Everything could be blamed on others.

As I walked home with one of my neighbours, he told me that Klein confused him. Oh? He said that about a year earlier, on a short-lived CBC television debate program, Klein debated former Getty cabinet minister Marvin Moore. Moore had become a critic of Getty's spending habits. Getty turned down CBC's invitation to appear with Moore but Klein quickly filled in, and ably defended Getty's fiscal program. A year later, Klein was attacking the record of the same Premier he had defended earlier. That perplexed my neighbour.

Accordingly, Highlands and the riding to its north both elected Liberals in 1993. Highlands returned a New Democrat in 1997, another New Democrat in the 2000 by-election, and the same New Democrat in 2001, 2004 and 2007. During Klein's 14-year premiership, Edmonton Highlands didn't elect a single Conservative.

HE PAID LITTLE ATTENTION TO POLICY

"Ralph-style politics" worked better in other ridings. Farmers in particular took to him and his political style.

"The reason farmers liked him so much is that he was visibly comfortable around them," a source said. "In my view, Ralph was insecure in himself, a shy man who was more comfortable in a bar than in a board room. When he spoke to well-heeled crowds, he had trouble. He had to be coached. That's where Rod Love was so important. He made sure that Ralph was always prepared."

And Klein was being prepared for a run at the Conservative Party leadership. The plan was simple: get outside the cities and away from the inquisitive urban media, cater to small town reporters and editors who will be grateful he came to town and took the time to talk to them. Rural weekly newspapers are more influential in their communities than any city newspaper and Klein spent time with local reporters wherever he went.

By appearing at constituency meetings in rural Alberta for three years, Klein earned the support of every Conservative MLA in rural Alberta. Their support would be the difference in the leadership race and in the provincial general election that followed. A party that wins a majority of Alberta's 35 rural seats in the 83-seat legislative Assembly has the makings of a majority government before a vote is counted in the cities.

As would become his standard practice before provincial general elections, Klein didn't offer a substantive platform in the leadership race. Klein was an advocate of one of the timeless strategies in politics: the KISS principle - Keep It Simple, Stupid. He had little interest in policy and paid scant attention to details. He subscribed to the theory that the more a politician explains, the greater the probability that someone will disagree. Better to stick to a few firm, unshakable beliefs. He was all about basic fiscal reform.

Promising little would become a Klein staple. In the elections in 1997, 2001 and 2004, he promised only "more of the same". It was up to voters to decide what he meant.

Early in the Conservative leadership race, the so-called Leduc high school speech - why would a serious leadership candidate unveil his entire platform to a class of bored high school students south of Edmonton? - explained little except that the government should be smarter at revenue forecasts, balance the budget within four years, demand that balanced budgets be the law, pursue private sector partnerships, and reorganize government into core services such as health, education and infrastructure. Not a word about salary cuts, education cuts, health service cuts, health regionalization or any other measures that would be taken when he became the Premier.

By omission, the Leduc speech warned of a departure from the Lougheed and Getty governments in which the provincial government was a proponent of cultural, social and economic policy and encouraged an activist and diverse political community. Klein's idea of government had little role in the social or cultural sectors of the province. It cared little for libraries, the arts, human rights or using the power of government to direct economic activity. He didn't even mention them.

Nonetheless, he won the race in December 1992. He finished second on the first ballot, a single vote behind Nancy Betkowski, but through aggressive campaigning the following week, he won easily on the second ballot.

Campaigning for the provincial general election in the spring, Klein relished the attack, and avoided issues that would make him a target. He believed that divisive issues such as abortion could wreck a political career and he wasn't going to let that happen to his career. His position: abortion is a matter between a woman, her doctor and God. If he believed anything else, he wasn't saying. He became popular not by imposing his own ideas but on figuring what voters wanted and giving some of it back to them.

Clinging to the KISS principle, Klein hammered three principles over and over again: debt is bad; low taxes are good; government is spending too much money. He repeated them so often that people began to believe him.

Remarkably, with a few ideas, Klein convinced voters demanding change that he represented change. Despite being an integral part of the Getty Government that created a problem, Klein passed himself off as the solution. He said he could be trusted to do what he said he would do and voters generally agreed. Klein sold himself during the election campaign rather than the tough medicine he promised. He looked directly into a television camera and convinced viewers that the election was about trust and only trust. He said he would set an example by taking the first salary cut. A portion of each cabinet minister's salary was sliced by a meager 5% - the cut was part of Nancy Betkowski's leadership platform - but 5% is hardly what he had in store for the health, education and infrastructure budgets.

Then Klein cancelled the lucrative, controversial MLA pension plan that gave retired politicians up to $80,000 annually starting the minute they left political office, regardless of their age. Astonishingly, a loophole allowed cabinet ministers dumped on the backbench to collect part of their pension while still sitting in the Legislative Assembly.

Public anger over the pension plan was palpable. Klein's caucus balked at the wholesale cancellation of the plan - MLAs who were part of the Lougheed and Getty governments threatened to take the matter to court if they lost their pensions - but a compromise was finally reached to cancel it for all MLAs elected in 1989 and afterwards.

Voters appreciated the sacrifice to win the 1993 election but by the 1997 election, when the novelty of governing wore off, Conservative MLAs wondered what they had done to themselves. Some started to complain that when they retired they had no pension to rely on.

Five years later, on a hot August afternoon when the province was enjoying a rare warm summer, the Legislative Assembly's Member Services Committee, chaired and driven by Legislature Speaker Ken Kowalski, set up not a pension plan but a very lucrative severance package that would see people like Klein and Shirley McClellan walk away with more than $500,000 in hand. While the Conservatives bragged about canceling the pension plan in 1993, nothing was said about the new benefits. My newsletter was the first to explain in detail what MLAs had done for themselves.

Insight into Government reported that when the rich, controversial MLA pension plan was scrapped in 1992, it was replaced by a simple severance package based on years of experience to a maximum 12 years. No MLA, regardless of salary, would get more than $137,000 on retirement under the old plan. The new severance plan has no limits. Each MLA gets three months salary for every year served, without limit. Under the new severance package, retired MLAs were walking out of the Legislature Building clutching cheques for hundreds of thousands of dollars. Some cheques were over a half million dollars.

HEY BUDDY, GOT A SMOKE?

The consummate salesman, Klein knew how to sell himself. After the generous MLA pension plan was cancelled, a photo appeared on the front page of the *Edmonton Journal* in the spring of 1993 that further cemented his "everyman" image. There was the new Premier of Alberta, suitcase in hand, waiting in line at the Air Canada counter at Edmonton International Airport like any other impatient traveler. He was flying to Ottawa to see the Prime Minister and he was flying economy, just like everyone else concerned about the cost. A voter could relate to that. Peter Lougheed and Don Getty never stood in line at the airport. They flew on government-owned jets, a practice Klein would come to appreciate and enjoy years later.

In Ottawa, Klein quickly ingratiated himself to the eastern media who always had a soft spot for ambitious politicians from Alberta. Always the entertainer, he seduced that national media effortlessly: he bummed a cigarette from a reporter during a news conference outside the Prime Minister's residence at 24 Sussex Drive. Although national reporters knew little about him, they loved the image he projected. After years of Pierre Trudeau and Brian Mulroney, Klein was refreshing.

The symbolism of Klein's actions cannot be underestimated. Albertans bought the example, the personality and the message in its entirety. Polls heading into the June 1993 election reported that Klein had restored Conservative support to over 40%, about 15 points higher than when Don Getty left six months earlier. Klein was ready to call an election.

Insight into Government assessed the new guy as the June election approached: "From the first day of the Tory leadership race last fall, Klein began to distance himself from Don Getty and the Conservative Party. Klein has gone so far as to wipe out all references to the Conservative Party in campaign literature. It is now Ralph's Party. Albertans don't have a Premier, they have Ralph, a street-smart, folksy, jolly front man who, by his own admission, likes to be wound up and pointed in the right direction. People love it, so far. Klein has taken a thoroughly discredited government and given it new life. Whether it has a heart and a head is another matter."

LAURENCE DECORE AND THE LIBERAL PARTY

Laurence Decore's Liberals were the alternative in 1993. While Getty was the Premier, Decore polled well. In the summer of 1992, polls still gave him a 15-point lead. No matter how you looked at it, the Liberals were an attractive alternative when compared to the Getty Government and its miserable record. However, no poll between 1990 and late 1992 measured Decore against a leader other than Getty because there was no indication that Getty might leave anytime soon. Decore polled well because Albertans were angry at Getty, because voters were ready to vent their frustrations on the Getty Conservatives, and because the Liberals were the only alternative.

Political history says that a majority of Albertans won't vote Liberal, federally or provincially. Jack Horner of the Horner family, a Conservative institution on the farmlands in central east Alberta, couldn't get elected as a Liberal well before the National Energy Program. Occasionally, a Calgary or an Edmonton seat will go

Liberal for a term, but in the rest of the province, the Liberals usually came up dry.

Klein's election victory in 1993 was dubbed "the miracle on the prairies." The win was impressive but not so impressive to achieve "miracle" status. The first reason is that Decore and the Liberals weren't going to win seats in rural Alberta - perhaps two or three seats - but definitely not more. Against Getty, maybe the Liberals would do slightly better. Against a Conservative alternative led by Klein, not likely. Most farmers would sooner stay home than vote Liberal. The other alternative: the New Democrats. They do well to win 10% of the popular vote, most of it concentrated in North Edmonton.

No matter what rural Albertans thought about the Conservatives under Getty, Klein started the 1993 campaign leading to the provincial election with a significant advantage over the Liberals in rural Alberta. There was little reason to believe that he wouldn't lose the Conservative rural vote as long as he didn't screw up in a major way.

Secondly, Laurence Decore suffered two bouts with cancer. Cancer is a terrifying disease. All other things being equal, given the choice between a healthy politician and one susceptible to cancer, most voters will go with the healthy guy.

Thirdly, Decore lost critical support when, midway through the June campaign, he denounced abortion clinics as "repugnant." The careless outburst cost him the pro-choice vote in his own party and the female New Democrat vote in Edmonton that was leaning his way.

Why Decore suddenly took off on abortion clinics is mystifying because the election had nothing to do with abortion. Klein wisely avoided unwinnable political positions. Decore, a strong Catholic, tried to explain the abortion comments when the fallout became apparent: "I was having a very good day. Everything was going well - and then I let my emotions get the best of me. There's no other way I can explain it."

To win, the Liberals had to be much better than the Conservatives. They weren't. To win, Decore had to perform better than Klein. He didn't. Decore lost the election as much as Klein won it.

Klein was a successful leader and a good campaigner. How good? Would Klein have been as successful had he joined the Liberals after the Olympics in 1988? He came close to joining the Liberal Party. In *King Ralph: The Political Life and Success of Ralph Klein,* author Don Martin says Klein would have joined the provincial Liberals except that his wife persuaded him otherwise. Perhaps - but Klein may have been smart enough to know that with Laurence Decore as leader, the Liberals were fixed for at least another provincial election. If Decore beat Getty in the next election, he would have been Premier for at least four years, probably longer. Would Klein want to play second fiddle for so long? It would make more sense to go with a tired, threatened Premier who could be gone after an election and run for the leadership of that party. The risk of joining the Conservatives was great but the reward was much greater.

We will never know whether Klein was capable of building a new Liberal Party from the floor up, whether he had the skills to attract quality people and give them purpose and direction. Based on his record as leader of the Conservative Party, the evidence is not encouraging.

THE CAMPAIGNING DIDN'T END AFTER THE ELECTION

After an election, winning politicians usually stop campaigning and start to do what they promised to do - govern. Klein didn't play the game - campaigning was his business and he was good at it. The details of governing and administration were for others. He was tireless. In December 1993, six months after the election and shortly after an exhaustive three-week trade mission in Asia, Klein delivered four speeches in one week, made six other public appearances, and did an open-line radio program. His poll numbers continued to climb despite cuts to programs that people had come to expect and rely on, programs such as education, health and seniors programs.

Writing in my newsletter, I reported: "He has another habit that would drive an opponent dizzy: he shows up at political functions and sometimes stays for three or four hours." A year after the June 1993 election, Klein showed up at a political fundraiser for Stan Woloshyn, Conservative MLA for Stony Plain who had crossed the floor in February 1993.

One of my newsletter subscribers was at the function. He called the next morning. "You won't believe this," he said. "Ralph Klein - the Premier - was at Stan's party last night. He stayed the whole evening and had a few beers with the guys. Imagine, the whole evening. Joe Clark (Conservative MP for Yellowhead) used to come and stay for an hour. Great guy, that Ralph."

A similar story came from the small rural community of Legal where Klein had been campaigning. He stopped at the local bar and had a beer with the boys. After Lougheed and Getty, Klein seemed to be from another planet.

POWER IS AN APHRODISIAC

In 1993, the new Premier launched the Government of Alberta into a debt reduction scheme that attracted attention across the country, and even drew applause from the *Wall Street Journal*, that bastion of elitist corporate capitalism. Klein's supporters were ecstatic at their boy being compared to the conservative ideologue in the White House. Ronald Reagan had promised and delivered change - smaller government, lower taxes - and, oddly, wasn't concerned as the U.S. government debt soared. Reagan and British Prime Minister Margaret Thatcher spread the Conservative gospel in the 1980s - government wasn't the solution, it was the problem.

With hard work, good planning and considerable luck, Alberta's deficit was gone in a year. The luck came in the form of rising energy royalties. In the first full fiscal year under Klein and Provincial Treasurer Jim Dinning, energy royalties rose $630 million and another $560 million in the second year. Other revenues were increasing, bringing total revenues under Klein after two years to almost $2 billion more than in Getty's last term. While spending cuts got all the attention, added revenues ate more than half the deficit.

Klein's staff was beside themselves at the attention from a prominent American institution such as the *Wall Street Journal*. They loved the attention - Rod Love sidled up to me in the Legislature shortly after the *Wall Street Journal* story appeared and said: "Everybody is watching us." Klein and his people were starting to think that they were much smarter than they were. Power, as Henry Kissinger said, is the ultimate aphrodisiac.

Klein formed a cabinet, set out a plan based on pieces from at least six other sources espoused by the likes of Reform leader Preston Manning, Sir Roger Douglas of New Zealand, Liberal leader Laurence Decore, Conservative candidate Nancy MacBeth and the Chief Deputy Minister in the Getty Government. All of them talked of smaller government and spending cuts.

Klein began to hack, hack and hack some more. No program was sacred. As Love described it, "We went hunting where the ducks are." Health, education and social services were the big programs, eating up over 60% of all government spending. All of them would suffer a hefty bite by 1995. Welfare took a heavy hit. The retail liquor business was privatized.

Everything was about money and the deficit. Values, culture, and tradition did not matter; all that mattered was money. Every decision would be based on its affordability or, as the vernacular changed later, on its "sustainability". Reducing all decisions to a single criteria made governing easy. Money and affordability were matters that everyone understood. Try to explain to a voter that a program was dumped because of its cultural or social values and you might get an argument. To claim that the program must go because there is no money is a different argument.

Who convinced Klein that deficits had to be eliminated quickly even if it meant slashing essential public services? Certainly not the band of flagrant spenders who sat with him in Getty's cabinet - Peter Elzinga, Ken Kowalski, Peter Trynchy - and who now constituted his inner circle. If Marvin Moore, a cabinet veteran, convinced Klein, that was different because Moore was a true fiscal conservative who saw deficits as a sign of irresponsible management and bad politics and wasn't afraid to say so long before they became a public issue. Maybe it was the small group of influential businessmen in Calgary - the fabled kitchen cabinet - that included Art Smith and Scobey Hartley. Maybe he read the polls. Or maybe Klein looked at the Conservative Party's financial contributors, saw all those big corporations and the big bucks they gave, and saw the light.

What did Klein know about privatization? He had never worked for a corporation or run a company. Yet he thought he knew the economics of privatization. He lectured Liberal leader Nancy MacBeth in the Legislature: "It stands to reason: when you have competition, prices tend to go down … Competition, good solid competition, always without exception brings about lower prices." Economic principles and practice should be so simple and predictable.

Klein had swallowed the ideology of business and the ideology of the right: government is the problem, not the solution. When he privatized the provincial government's retail liquor stores and recklessly deregulated an extremely complex electricity industry, he operated on the simple premise that competition and free markets resolve complex matters. Later, when meeting with the *Edmonton Journal's* editorial board, Klein admitted that he didn't understand the electricity industry or the deregulation scheme. If he didn't, who in the Conservative caucus did?

Where did Klein discover conservative ideology? He had no education in economics so he must have learned it from the Calgary crowd and they pedaled it to him as a way to cut government's costs and invigorate the economy.

The certainty of ideology makes governing easy because ideologues have pat answers to every problem. For right wingers, the answers are always lower taxes, less regulation, and smaller government. The bottom line is the ultimate performance measure. If they don't work, blame the left wingers. The themes of right wing ideology would dominate Klein's agenda until members of his own party ran him out of office.

He's at his best running against something

What did Klein know about public finances? He wasn't overly concerned in his previous political life as Mayor of Calgary. The city's capital debt was huge, principally from costs of beautifying the city and building light rail transit for the Olympics.

While Klein was spending generously in Calgary, the new Reform Party was raging against debt and deficits. Liberal leader Laurence Decore picked up on Reform's platform in 1989, repackaged it as "Alberta's Biggest Problem: The System Itself", and made it the base of his platform. Now Klein, as Premier of Alberta, who had rarely uttered the words "debt" and "deficits" before, was a strong proponent of fiscal management and deficit elimination at any cost. He didn't get tough until others got tough, and then he got tougher. He was focused and had something to say that meant something. He was confident that he was reading the public correctly.

Was Alberta's deficit really out of control? Deficit spending is not good public policy if it persists too long but Alberta had been running deficits for less than a decade. The size of the deficit was no big deal and, one might argue, deficits should be expected in the midst of a recession and low energy prices. Energy prices would turn around, as they always do, and the recession will end, as it always does. Prudent fiscal management was a matter of competence and a sense of reality, not panic at the first sign of trouble.

Did Klein personally believe that Alberta was in dire financial straits? Or did he need something to run against? I learned later that Klein is at his best when running against something, anything. Without a real or perceived enemy - either people or public policy - Klein is just another tired politician hanging on because the pay is good and he doesn't know anything else. The enemy in 1993 had been the policies of his former boss, Don Getty, the man who invited Klein into the Conservative Party.

Klein and Treasurer Jim Dinning - both in Getty's cabinet for at least three years - started to blame "the previous government" as the source of all Alberta's fiscal troubles. Getty and company - minus Klein and Dinning of course - let spending get out of control. The new guy made sure voters knew who was responsible; the new guy made sure everyone knew who could clean up the mess. No one plays the "blame game" as well as Ralph Klein. Everything bad that happens is always the fault of others.

When his repeated promised health reform didn't happen, he blamed the federal government for its restrictive definition of essential services. As late as January 2008, he was still blaming the feds. What he did not say was that the Government of Alberta's provincial health insurance plan paid about $2 billion a year for services not required under the Canada Health Act.

When his efforts to lay the foundation for private health services in Alberta were not warmly accepted, he blamed the media and left wing interest groups.

HE KNOWS ONLY 10% OF WHAT'S HAPPENING IN HIS OWN GOVERNMENT
Klein wasn't around the Legislature to make decisions. Jack Davis, Klein's Chief Deputy Minister before moving to the Calgary Health Authority in 1999, told me that Klein "knew only 10% of what was going on in government but you have to believe that it is the most important 10%."

Davis's assessment may have been optimistic. In 2009, Klein told *Alberta Views* magazine that "in politics, there is little time to consider policy."

While the Conservative caucus was doing the grunt work in the Legislature, Klein was selling the package because that's what he does best. His message is always short and simple. Call it the economy of speech. The rules: keep the speech simple - make three points at most; don't explain because people might argue the details; repeat the messages until people believe them. The old sales trick: tell the customer what you are going to tell him, then tell what you want him to hear, then wrap up by telling him what you just told him.

How is this for simplicity: we must balance the budget, we won't raise taxes, which leaves us with what? You got it, friend: we must cut spending.

Klein promised a reward if you stuck with him: "A better Alberta with balanced budgets, declining debt, low taxes, high investment and steady employment." What could be more simple?

How to make the plan work? In September 1994, Klein described his strategy to the St. John's Board of Trade: "Go fast, target the big three spenders (health, education and social programs), be honest, be consistent and keep it simple." The strategy came straight out of *Unfinished Business* by Sir Roger Douglas of New Zealand.

Even when the cuts began to be felt in schools, hospitals and homes, Klein seemed to be above it. Bettie Hewes, the popular Liberal MLA from Edmonton Goldbar, told me the story of a group of senior citizens who came to her office angry about cuts to the Government of Alberta's seniors programs. She said some were crying because they couldn't support themselves without their government money and pleaded with her to do something.

Hewes told them that she was in opposition and while she couldn't change the seniors' benefits program she could make the Conservatives aware of how the cuts were affecting seniors. She added as an afterthought: "If you don't like what this government is doing to you, you should consider voting for another party that is against such changes." Hewes paused for a moment as she told the story, and continued: "They glared at me and got up to leave the office. 'Vote against Ralph', one admonished her. 'Not on your life sister!'"

Hewes fiddled with the spoon beside her coffee while her story sunk in. Then she laughed and shrugged her shoulders: "How do you fight something like that?"

We will never know how long Klein would have survived had the spending cuts lasted through another election. His spending cuts lasted three years, ending a year before the Conservatives began to prepare for the 1997 election. At the end of Klein's third year, the $3.4 billion deficit had turned into a $1 billion surplus. There was no need for further cuts. By the time the impact of the cuts began to be felt, Klein was already through another election and had begun to spend like no Premier before him.

Given Klein's agenda in 1993, his first term went as well as he could have imagined. All his ducks had been in order and he shot them down, one by one. The budget was balanced, debt reduction had begun and the role and structure of the provincial government had been changed to a business model. Albertans appeared to be happy with him and the job he had done. The pain had been short and now it was over.

The Conservatives won re-election easily.

Klein's first term would be his only good term.

SEARCHING FOR A FUTURE

With the deficit gone and debt reduction underway in 1997, Klein sought a new agenda for the second term. There was no easy answer. He soon learned that building a new, sleek Government of Alberta is more difficult than ripping apart an old, tired Government of Alberta. Rebuilding a province requires foresight, imagination, thought, intelligent allocation of resources, and achievable goals; destroying meant hunting where the ducks are, shooting straight and reloading quickly.

In the first term the agenda was clear and straightforward - say "no" to every request for money or leniency. Klein looked for a similarly simple and clear plan for the second term. He did what he does best - give the job to others.

The Growth Summit, an elite government-appointed discussion group, was told to write a plan for the future. Following a summer of mini-summits across the province, the idea was to have the main group come together for two days in late September and deliver a workable plan the government could relate to.

The Summit was another example of Klein's political cunning. Rather than give the chair to a well-known Conservative supporter and open himself to opposition attack, he handed it to Mike Percy, a retired Liberal MLA, and now Dean of the School of Business at the University of Alberta. Not content with one Liberal, he went for another. Klein convinced Bettie Hewes, another Liberal MLA, to chair a discussion group. Some Liberals didn't appreciate Percy because he was too friendly with the Conservatives but nobody questioned Hewes' loyalty to the Liberal cause. Liberal criticisms of the Growth Summit and everything that came out of it were instantly muted.

Percy came into provincial politics in 1993 with Laurence Decore as leader and left in 1997 with Grant Mitchell as leader. He and Mitchell, I was told, didn't see eye to eye on fiscal policy. Mitchell was a Liberal and Percy was a fiscal conservative. The more I listened to him, the more I realized that he could have written the four Dinning budgets exactly as Dinning wrote them.

Rumors began to surface that Percy was considering crossing the floor to the Conservative side. Because Percy was personally friendly with some of the Conservatives, it may have been more than a rumour.

I was in Treasurer Jim Dinning's office late one afternoon in 1996 asking about a story I had heard from one of his friends in Calgary claiming that Dinning would retire at the end of this term. Passing through the Legislature rotunda on the way to Dinning's office in the west wing of the main floor, I passed Percy talking to reporters. I stopped to listen. He was criticizing a government policy, as good opposition MLAs should do.

Dinning was toying with my question about his retirement, as he always did when he didn't want to come clean. Before he finished, Paul Taylor, his assistant, came through the open door followed by Percy. Sporting a mischievious grin, Percy said offhandedly to Dinning: "I took it easy on you today."

Taylor, always serious, looked at Percy: "Why don't you stop the nonsense, Mike. Come and join us." Percy laughed nervously, looked sideways at me and quickly left the room. He retired a year later, at the same time as Dinning.

Klein had put a lot of faith in the Growth Summit. The concept was floated early in the spring of 1997, principally, I thought, to delay public sector demands for money until after the March election.

In January 1997, nurses and teachers were both involved in negotiations with the Conservative Government under Klein. The situation was risky for the Conservatives despite the popularity of its deficit reduction scheme. If thousands of nurses and teachers were on the picket lines during an election, a government, no matter how popular, will pay a price.

In that context, the Growth Summit was clever business. It looked more like a slick political ploy to delay legitimate bargaining until the campaign was over. If Percy as chair of the Growth Summit could convince teachers, nurses and other public sector groups to participate, a potential campaign wart could be avoided.

The United Nurses of Alberta didn't bite. They took the government to the brink in the spring - the nurses correctly figured that the Conservatives wouldn't risk losing votes and possibly seats over a nurses' strike - and negotiated a nice contract. Teachers and other public sector groups put themselves at the mercy of the Growth Summit and a re-elected Conservative Government.

After the 1997 provincial election in which the Conservative Government was handily re-elected, it waited patiently for the Growth Summit to spell out a new plan. That's not what the Conservatives got.

Insight into Government summarized the report:

"Put 100 sensible people with radically different views of the world together in a room for two days and any guru of group dynamics and group behaviour will guarantee that nine times out of ten, the extreme views are tamed and everyone eventually agrees on the only thing they can agree on: platitudes that can mean anything and everything they want them to mean. Everybody goes home happy; nobody goes home mad; but nobody gets what he or she came for. That's precisely what happened at the Growth Summit this week in Edmonton. The seven sectors arrived with expensive shopping lists just in case the vault was open. The Business & Industry Sector asked for $1 billion on new spending and tax breaks and the social economy group wanted the entire vault.

"Specifics? The Summit administration will work on the 240 specific proposals for the next month and deliver them to the Tory Government, which, in turn, will go into its private caucus discussions. Some proposals will appear in next spring's Throne Speech or budget but most will not. Until the budget in late February or early March, the real outcome of the Growth Summit won't be known.

"What should you expect? The Premier insists the vault will not be opened, at least not all the way. Until the day the Summit opened, Treasurer Stockwell Day clung to 1% annual increases over three years. Give this government credit: like the astute politicians they are, they set low expectations. Then, with impeccable timing, they went out the next day and pumped $110 million into health and education and suggest more is coming."

TWO TRAINS RUNNING IN OPPOSITE DIRECTIONS

Klein couldn't hide his disappointment at the Growth Summit. If he needed to place blame, he could blame himself. In establishing parameters for the Growth Summit, he wanted widespread involvement. The trouble, as management consultants know, is that the greater the involvement, the more mediocre the outcome. The best results come from a small group of like-minded people working on a well-defined problem.

At the Growth Summit's conclusion, I was standing at the back of the room, as was my habit, watching the proceedings. Klein, co-chair of the Summit with Percy, had been put in an awkward position, I thought. Summit participants had worked for two strenuous days putting together a plan and now the Premier, who hadn't spent time in discussions (he rarely participated in serious open discussions anywhere at any time) and with the media in full view, was asked to respond.

He sat by himself on a chair in front of a room full of people who expected him to know what they had been doing and respond intelligently. He didn't have a day or two with his advisers to review the Summit's work and come up with a speech he could read. He was asked to comment on a plan that recommended a ton of spending, the very thing he had fought for four years.

It became clear very quickly that the Growth Summit's train of thought and Klein's train of thought weren't on the same track. They were heading in opposite directions. His reaction foretold of the way he would respond to the many public consultations that followed - he was stumped when he didn't get what he expected.

Over the next four years, time and time again, Klein would exhibit the same inability to deal with a reconstruction agenda. His mind was always on money ("sustainability" was the new mantra) rather than on the general merits of an argument in the context of a growing province with a resource-based economy. He thought only about a proposal's costs.

He complained that he expected the Growth Summit to give him a more detailed agenda - a way to cut administration and "allocate current resources". He didn't appreciate a gigantic shopping list, which is what they gave him.

Oddly, in one of those thoughts that came out of nowhere, he lamented that local police didn't buy vehicles in volume to save money (they did) and that communities throughout the province have separate economic development offices. If they got together, they would save money, he suggested.

He said that his 62-member caucus would decide as a group what flies and what doesn't. I noted in the newsletter that the Premier should get what he wants "but genuflection is neither a caucus trait nor a caucus rule." Some Conservatives had been complaining about the Growth Summit all along, insisting that it was usurping what they believed was their job - deciding who gets the money.

Klein left promising that the Summit's recommendations would be reflected in the next year's Throne Speech.

KLEIN FOUND HIS AGENDA IN AN OLD ADVERSARY - NANCY

The first budget after the Growth Summit was balanced and reasonable. Spending was up marginally, with health and education getting the bulk of the increase. The personal income tax rate was cut 1.5% to bring it under the Ontario rate and return bragging rights to Alberta as the lowest personal tax rate in the country. If the Growth Summit and its demands for big spending drove the budget, it was well disguised.

The signature bill for the 1998 Spring Session, the first bill introduced by the government, usually dictates how bold the government will be. Of all the issues begging for action, the Klein Government decided on the Protection Of Children Involved In Prostitution Act.

Klein and the caucus had kept the lid on spending despite the Growth Summit. They were still without a clear, focused agenda. That is, until Nancy MacBeth won the Liberal leadership two months later, in April 1998. Only in Alberta: the leader of the Conservative Party had been a Liberal and the leader of the Liberal Party had been a Conservative.

Klein, the political animal who loved to vanquish his enemies, had an issue he could deal with, and this one was personal. No way would the new Liberal leader, whom he had beaten once, do better a second time. It was not a coincidence that Conservative spending took off in the next budget. Klein did what all politicians do under duress – spend, spend, and spend more. Jim Dinning was gone and with him went clear thinking and a coherent strategic plan.

By the end of Klein's second term in 2001, and two budgets after MacBeth became the Liberal leader, the dedicated fiscal conservative had launched a spending spree that would have made a free-spending Liberal blush. In the three budgets after MacBeth won the Liberal leadership, these hard-bitten fiscal conservatives increased spending by $5.5 billion, or up 38%. More surprising, his Treasurers in the second term were both hard-bitten fiscal hardliners – Stockwell Day and Steve West. Day pinned a loonie on his lapel to remind himself that he was spending taxpayer's money. He spent like he accused Liberals of spending. Same for West. The money couldn't be shoveled out of the Legislature fast enough. Health spending went up 80%, education up 62% and social services up 28%.

If the Government of Alberta had a spending problem from 1987 through 1993, how could the 1997-2001 binge be described? What had changed so terribly to demand such massive spending? Few asked; few complained.

Despite abandoning his savings principles, Klein still talked as if he was fighting the deficit in the first term. Ever the campaigner with his mind still mired in the successes of the first term, he continued to talk about balanced budgets, low taxes, debt reduction and the Alberta Advantage. He was seeing things from his customary post - the street level - when he should have been looking at the province and its condition from 30,000 feet up - "blue-skying", as the vernacular of the day described the visioning concept.

Looking for an easy answer to complex problems, Alberta's very own summit series continued. Despite the disappointing outcome of the Growth Summit, other summits followed: Health Summit, Gaming Summit, Justice Summit, Future Summit and an endless procession of consultations on various aspects of public policy. Few areas were untouched by a public consultation.

Governing is complex. Not surprisingly, none of the summits came up with easy answers that didn't include large injections of government money. The more the summits dug into issues, the more complex they became. Affordability was merely the tip of the proverbial iceberg. Questions were asked about the long-term implications of taking programs in a certain direction, about government's role in social and cultural life including the morality of a quickly escalating government-sanctioned gambling industry. Competing arguments and counter arguments were on the table. Simple matters of affordability had suddenly become terribly perplexing. Unable to agree on many of the critical issues, participants wrapped everything in a tidy package and dumped the reports in the government's lap.

Klein's caucus, dominated by rural MLAs who see everything through the prism of simple rural life, argued over the recommendations they had received from the various consultations and couldn't agree either. Policy debates became a matter of geography. As long as the rural guys had money to take back to their constituencies and their pictures in the local newspapers handing out cheques, they were happy. They cared little for the cities.

Edmonton MLAs fought for money for their community. Calgarians did the same. Klein gave no direction. His long-time advisor Rod Love had returned to Calgary to set up his own business. Dinning was in the private sector in Calgary. Without their focus and strategic minds, Ralph Klein was floundering.

Leadership of a province, so simple when the agenda was defined exclusively by money, was becoming, shall we say, rather complex and unfamiliar. Not that Albertans were unhappy; they weren't. They were waiting for the second chapter of the Klein Revolution, a master plan similar to the one in the first term, a scheme to restore services and programs without breaking the bank.

Little did Albertans suspect at the time - Klein didn't either - that his productive work and his credibility in developing new policies and programs had begun a slow, steady decline that would continue until he involuntarily retired in 2006.

PETER ELZINGA AND THE BOMB SQUAD

One reason for Klein's demise, I believe, is rarely mentioned: he didn't have friends he could trust with his political life. In high corporate or political office, loyalty and trust are everything. Trusted friends are critical to a political leader; they provide the tough, honest advice so essential in high office. Without sound advice from trusted allies, a political leader will flounder, unable to determine the best course of action when the issues become complex and the solutions indistinguishable. As the new Conservative Premier in 1992, Klein brought only one trusted friend from Calgary to administer his office, to be a trusted sounding board, to hold the leader's interests first. He had only Rod Love.

People who were linked to Klein in Calgary - Sherrold Moore, Jack Donohue, Art Smith and Scobey Hartley - were successful in their own right and had little interest in political shenanigans in the Legislature Building. None were Klein's personal friends. All became Klein's friends - FORK: Friends of Ralph Klein - after he became famous as mayor and powerful as Premier. They saw Klein the politician as a person they had to know rather than a person they wanted to know.

Hartley, a Texan who did well in the energy industry in Calgary, was close to Klein. As legend has it, Hartley called Klein from a fishing boat off Campbell River in the spring of 1993 and told him that if the MLA pension plan wasn't eliminated before the coming election, the Conservatives wouldn't win.

Hartley told me that Klein worked so hard that he sometimes needed "down time" at the fishing lodge near Prince Rupert owned by a group of Alberta businessmen. "What do you guys do out there?" I asked. "Trying to drink B.C. dry of vodka," he said.

Shortly after Love quit the Legislature and returned to Calgary, I saw Hartley in the Legislature Building and asked him if he was looking for work in the Premier's office. In his Texas drawl, he said: "Are you nuts?"

Premier Klein formed an office, not of loyal allies who helped him get elected in Calgary, but of men he met in the Conservative caucus after winning a Conservative seat in 1989. After his first Chief of Staff, Rod Love, left to return to Calgary in 1998, Klein had trouble replacing him. Peter Elzinga, a veteran of federal and provincial politics, had to be talked into the job. Klein and Elzinga met in the Conservative caucus in 1989 and they liked to party together. Four of Getty's cabinet ministers - Klein, Elzinga, Ernie Isley and Steve West - were called the Glenlivet Four. "They could polish off a 26'er before supper and then head straight for the bar and the peanuts," I was told.

Insight into Government reported: "Elzinga is one of four key people who drive the Klein Government. He retired prior to the 1993 provincial election and was appointed executive director of the Alberta Progressive Conservative Party. In our view, Elzinga's influence comes from his personal friendship with Klein and from his role as a key organizer in both the Tory leadership campaign and the provincial general election. Public expressions of Elzinga's influence occurred on December 5, 1992 and June 15, 1993. On December 5, Klein won the Tory leadership on the second ballot and in his acceptance speech, Klein thanked only a few people, including Elzinga. That raised eyebrows, particularly from people who had little good to say about Elzinga's achievements in the ministries of Agriculture (1986-89) and Economic Development & Tourism (1989-93). Rightly or wrongly, Elzinga shared the blame for the failed loan guarantees approved and issued while he was in cabinet and a member of the influential Priorities Committee. The more notable expression of Elzinga's influence occurred on the June 15 election night. When the victorious Klein entered Heritage Park in Calgary to celebrate his greatest political achievement, Elzinga was at his side. Put them all together, and it is clear that Peter Elzinga and Ralph Klein are very close and that Klein trusts his judgment. That association guarantees that Elzinga has a huge role in the governing of this province."

Elzinga was a cautious political moderate who, some of my sources believe, was closer to Klein than Rod Love.

"Love and Elzinga played different roles," I was told. "Rod challenged Klein, debated him to make sure he knew what he was doing. Elzinga didn't bother - he did things himself."

Klein had great confidence in Elzinga, trusted his judgment and could count on his personal loyalty. Not many know it, but Elzinga was Klein's enforcer. Klein never, ever had to discipline his people. When a minister or backbencher stepped out of line, Elzinga came down hard. When Deputy Premier Ken Kowalski behaved as if he were the Premier, Elzinga fired Kowalski. Because he had federal and provincial experience and never lost an election, Elzinga had status with everybody in the Conservative caucus and a very extensive network across the province. Elzinga knew people in places that Klein didn't know existed.

Unlike Rod Love, Elzinga was not a hard-nosed strategic thinker but relied on his own common sense. He was a likable, gregarious fellow who rewarded his friends, chose assistants for cabinet ministers and leaked stories to his favourite media people.

He was a politician, first for 12 years as a federal Conservative MP for Sherwood Park and two terms as a provincial Conservative MLA, also for Sherwood Park. Elzinga knew that information is power and built a network of people who owed him throughout the Legislature Building. This network kept him informed on what ministers were doing. He had an interesting habit of always showing up behind Klein on election night, particularly when Klein was speaking to a television audience.

I often talked to groups about lobbying the provincial government. At one session, I was describing an approach that included talking to Conservative MLAs individually. One participant, from Sherwood Park, got up and told the group that the approach I was describing was the "hard way." He advised the group to call Peter Elzinga rather than talk to politicians. "He always solves my problem right away."

The reason Elzinga could solve problems is because he worked himself into a position where he could do what he said. Months after he became Premier Klein's Chief of Staff after Love returned to Calgary in December, 1997, Elzinga went straight to Klein's weakness - he didn't know what was happening in the government he led. To win the Conservative leadership in 1992, Klein had relinquished too much power to the Conservative caucus and its rural core, and hence compromised the ability to control the political agenda. With Klein spending so much time campaigning and Love gone, who was taking care of business in the Legislature Building? Who was keeping ambitious, aggressive Conservatives in line?

For those few months early in 1998, it became clear that no one was in charge. Unexpected trouble would soon follow.

In March 1998, Justice Minister Jon Havelock introduced the infamous Institutional Confinement & Sexual Sterilization Compensation Act. The bill was a direct response to the Leilani Muir case in which a victim of the Social Credit Government's sexual sterilization policy sued the provincial government. Havelock's response: revoke the right of sterilization victims to legal remedies, and should the bill be challenged, include the Constitution's notwithstanding clause to eliminate the challenge.

Public reaction was swift and thoroughly negative. Klein withdrew the act less than 24 hours after it was introduced in the Legislative Assembly. The greater question was how this bill got so far without anyone in the Premier's office noticing, or if the bill was noticed, no one had the sense to see its political dangers. The bill was a complete embarrassment to Premier Klein and his government.

Not long afterwards, a new committee was formed in the Premier's office. It wasn't listed on any of the organizational charts, didn't report to anyone, and didn't keep records. The committee became known as the Bomb Squad and its singular purpose was to detect potentially troublesome political bombs before they got into the decision-making process, before they were put on the cabinet agenda, and before the Conservative caucus saw them. This committee didn't write policy but ministers proposing policy had to run it through the committee first.

Organizational experts know that whoever controls the input, effectively controls the output. With this committee, chaired by Elzinga and made up of people Elzinga could demote if they got out of line (i.e. the Conservative caucus chair, the Finance Minister, the Government House Leader, the Chief Deputy Minister and the Deputy Premier), Elzinga controlled the government's agenda.

One contact working in the Legislature described the committee to me this way: "This was the committee that did the first screening for bombs. It made sure potential bombs were completely defused. Nothing got past this committee if they did not like it. I think you get the picture - this was not just control, it was total control out of the Premier's office. Ralph was the velvet glove; his office was the iron fist. Everybody didn't like it but that didn't matter. I remember one cabinet retreat where a minister took a run at this committee and Klein shot him down quickly by saying that this was his personal advisory committee on policy. He said nothing further and there was complete silence in the room. Not another word was said about the committee from then on."

Another source in the Premier's office: "It was the most powerful committee ever - everything else was the tail on the donkey."

And another: "The existence of this committee is not unusual in Premier's offices across the country. The work of this committee however was different. It was more than a policy coordinating committee, it made policy decisions. Klein's cabinet got its back up when they learned that policy decisions were being made before they got to cabinet."

Had this committee existed before the sterilization bill was introduced, there would have been no sterilization bill.

The Bomb Squad met in the Legislature Building every Monday morning at 8 a.m. Klein never came to work that early, so he never attended a meeting. He didn't have to - Elzinga was looking after Klein's interests.

STEVE WEST - THE NUMBER TWO GUY

When Elzinga had enough, Steve West, the worst possible choice for a job demanding a strategic brain and sound political judgment, got the job. Klein, with no other friends to turn to, wanted West so badly that he included a six-figure severance package as part of the contract. West lasted barely a year. He was fired a day after the 2004 election. Not one to appreciate the political acumen of women, West berated the women around Klein once too often. Colleen Klein couldn't tolerate his behaviour and Premier Klein fired him, personally - the only person Klein fired himself.

West was deeply hurt by the firing but he got no sympathy. He got a dose of the medicine he had been handing out for a decade and he couldn't handle it. It was West who had swiftly and unsympathetically fired a host of senior bureaucrats and literally decimated the Transportation and Economic Development departments.

Ian Gray, a veteran newsman with excellent contacts in the Legislature, wrote a gutsy piece for *Insight into Government* (September, 2004) on West's performance as a political adviser. It was entitled "Dr. Death or - Dr. Dud?" Here is that piece, verbatim:

"Steve West has been called many things. Back in Don Getty's government, as an MLA and cabinet minister, West was known as Genghis Khan for his hard-charging style in both his political and personal life. As a senior minister in the Ralph Klein administration, the Vermilion veterinarian was dubbed 'Dr. No' or 'Dr. Death' by public servants in the departments he headed, departments that were invariably much smaller when West left them.

"One thing West hadn't been called, was a failure. Until now. When West returned to the Legislature last February 26, replacing Peter Elzinga as Klein's Chief of Staff, all manner of things were predicted about his tenure. The Premier predicted that the Liberals would see their 'rear-ends pucker' with West in charge. He warned that West will keep his ministers' 'feet to the fire,' especially if they try to 'backdoor' him.

"In the seven months that have passed, it is the Tories who 'pucker' at West's name and the flaming feet belong to Klein. Perhaps that's why he puts his feet in his mouth so often - to quench them. Some Conservative politicians and staffers are worried about their Premier's performance these days: the increasing belligerence, the perceived arrogance and a general sense of disengagement with the job. And they're blaming West. Klein has always been something of a political chameleon, taking on the colour of those around him. He was at his most flamboyant and daring with Rod Love as Chief of Staff. Love could be seen directing Klein at media scrums - a nod meant answer the question, a headshake meant dodge it.

"With the cunning Peter Elzinga as top aide, Klein reached his peak as the 'tiny Teflon Premier' - political mud did not stick. During West's short tenure, Klein has been embroiled in one gaffe after another and has seen his personal popularity ratings drop significantly for the first time. There's no indication that West has lost Klein's confidence. The knives are being unsheathed elsewhere, however, and not only by nervous Edmonton Tories.

"The most common view is that West is an example of the Peter Principle, that he's reached his level of incompetence. The argument is that West never really had to run anything before. He moved into a department, slashed it and moved on, leaving others to deal with the fallout. One senior Tory says that in cabinet, rather than the confident alpha male approach you'd expect, West seems perplexed. The

'Sherpa' role doesn't suit West the way it did Elzinga, the theory goes, and the Premier's in-your-face attitude may reflect West's own frustration.

"Another opinion is that West lacks Elzinga's Machiavellian ability for multilevel communication both internally and externally. Elzinga was known to personally spin reporters with the story he wanted put out, something West would never stoop to.

" 'Steve never had a job where he needed friends before,' is the way another Tory operative puts it. It's also said that West lacks an agenda. It's well known that he's itching to build his first cabinet, to put his stamp on Executive Council and to reduce its numbers. Klein and Elzinga put the boots to talk of a pre-election shuffle.

"Apart from cutting cabinet, nobody seems to know what West expects to achieve. It was suspected that he was brought on to ramrod health care reform. But despite Klein's recent pronouncements that he intends to push ahead with reform, there are doubts to what a lame-duck Premier with a lame-duck Chief of Staff can achieve. There are still Tories who defend the Chief of Staff. One of them, while acknowledging the grumbling, suggests it originates with Edmonton area MLAs who are not finding the same level of happiness at the doors they did prior to the last election. Regardless of that sentiment, if Tory election losses in Edmonton area ridings are more than the brass can bear, a scapegoat will be required and West may fit the bill. Should that time come, who will tell West to his face that's he's fired?"

Peter Kruselnicki, the one-time Deputy Provincial Treasurer and a Klein acquaintance at best, was handed the job after several others turned it down. Kruselnicki had gone to New Zealand and was back in Alberta within a year. Klein needed help; Kruselnicki needed a job.

The man Klein really wanted was Robert Day, a long-time Tory operative who handled government relations for TransCanada Pipelines. Day had experience in the Legislature as assistant to David Carter, a former Speaker of the Legislative Assembly. The Premier's wife badly wanted Day as her husband's Chief of Staff but Klein couldn't talk him into the job. When I asked Day why he turned Klein down, he told me that as a lobbyist, one of his strengths was anonymity. "If I take the Chief of Staff job, I lose anonymity forever. It would have to be my last job and because Ralph won't be around much longer, I can't accept that."

Klein's media friends turn on him

In August 2002, my wife and I were driving north to Edmonton on Highway 2. As we approached Red Deer, words scrawled on a grain storage bin caught my eye.

"Stop the car," I said. "I have to see what I think I saw with my own eyes."

We got out of the vehicle and walked back about 20 yards to read the writing on the bin. There in big capital letters: "Ralph Kline (sic) is the oil industry's pimp."

Political language in Ralph's World doesn't get much rougher. This was personal. Had the sign appeared in downtown Edmonton, it would have been written off as just another angry interest group. But smack in the middle of rural Alberta?

The grain bin was the beginning.

The same year, students and teachers protesting the 2002 budget paraded a sign around the Legislature grounds claiming that "Ralph drank away our future."

Then Klein's media friends turned on him.

Through my newsletter, I reported in September 2002: "*Edmonton Sun* columnist Neil Waugh was one of the Premier's loyal fans. Year after year, he wrote nothing but good news about the Premier. No more. In recent months, Waugh's columns have become critical of government spending and performance. A recent column expounded on the unhappiness of MLAs elected in 2001 and the lack of leadership.

"Waugh's counterpart at the *Calgary Sun*, Paul Jackson, is another who has treated the Premier very well. Even Jackson has fallen off the wagon. In a column published July 9, Jackson says Klein has stayed too long and the tarnish has set in. He says Klein is out of touch and his saving grace is that opposition is so fragmented and uninspiring it offers no real alternative - yet.

"Separately, these incidents are small but when you put them together, they start to add up. Five years ago, any of these incidents would have been political heresy. No longer."

In March 2002, a newspaper cartoon depicted a red-nosed Ralph Klein sitting at a bar surrounded by wet circular stains left by beer bottles. The caption read: Lord Of The Rings. Five years earlier, the cartoon would have gone straight to the shredder. That day, it got wide circulation. A copy arrived on *Insight into Government's* fax machine.

Later in the same month, at an Oilers-Flames hockey game in Edmonton, the teletron flashed an inebriated fan on a rant, part of which included a reference to the Premier and his drinking habit. Fans roared. It recalled hockey fan reaction when then Premier Peter Lougheed attended a Canada Cup game in Edmonton in 1984. When he was introduced, the booing was instantaneous. Lougheed retired a year later.

In May 2003, Art Smith, one of Klein's closest political friends, told Don Martin of the *Calgary Herald* that Klein should retire before the 2005 election and that he should shuffle his cabinet before he retires.

Finally, my *Insight into Government* newsletter conducted annual reader surveys on the popularity and effectiveness of the Premier and his cabinet ministers. These elementary surveys asked readers to list their top three political performers and three worst performers. The surveys weren't scientific but certainly sampled the mood of readers who came from all sectors of the province, both public and private. Klein always came off poorly. In the 2002 survey, he didn't rank in the top 10 performers but was third in the worst performers. Two years later, in the 2004 survey, he didn't make the top 10 list again, but rose to second on the worst performers list.

Readers hammered him: "He has lost interest, become arrogant and can't come up with any plan for the future. He is doing what Jean Chretien did, disengaging except to meddle, ignoring scandal, playing games with election timing and his own retirement, perpetuating a bad system where the power is increasingly concentrated in the Premier's office. Where's the leadership? What was the common touch has evolved into arrogance."

Count the reasons for the disenchantment. Start with the night of the 2001 election when he slurred to a national television audience: "Welcome to Ralph's World." This was not the first time he had embarrassed himself in public and it wouldn't be the last. In November 2001, Klein embarrassed himself with his drunken act in a homeless shelter in Edmonton.

Klein swore off booze in December after the incident at the homeless shelter but the damage had been done and he had done it to himself.

Alcohol never brings good things. Voters will tolerate politicians with drinking problems as long as the drinking doesn't affect their performance. Klein had embarrassed himself on election night but he also embarrassed the province and the people who voted for him.

Liquor had been part of his routine from the beginning. When he moved into the Premier's office, he brought a beer fridge with him.

Alcohol would play no small role in his political demise.

THE DEMON ALCOHOL

The first time I saw Klein outside the Legislature Building was in a pub. It was 1990. I had gone to Cliff Claven's pub at the foot of the 105th Street hill, about two blocks from the Legislature Building, to talk to Rod Love about developments with the proposed Alberta Pacific pulp mill in northern Alberta. Given Getty's determination to build a forestry industry, did the government have the guts to reject the huge Alberta Pacific project if an independent environmental impact study came back negative?

Love took me away from the table where he was sitting with three Alberta Environment officials and an *Edmonton Journal* reporter to a seat near the south window. While Love was talking, I looked over his shoulder and saw Klein cross the street heading towards the pub. The bartender saw him too: "Ralph's coming. Two rum and coke." It was 4 p.m.

I'm no prude. I like an occasional drink. I also come from a family with a history of alcoholism and know that alcohol and trouble are soul mates. Alcohol doesn't make a person more productive. I know of no one who admires or respects people who regularly drink to excess. Klein's reputation for booze had trouble written all over it. As always, trouble would be just a matter of time. Some reporters thought that boozing with Klein was smart because he might drop a tidbit of information. That's like seducing an inebriated girlfriend.

Later, Klein admitted to drinking the equivalent of a bottle of wine a day. In 2001, he celebrated an election victory with a boozy appearance on national television. Later that year, *Insight into Government* reported: "One of the first changes in the Legislature Building after Klein became Premier in 1992 was to lift the liquor ban the minute they controlled the place. Under Lougheed and Getty, liquor was forbidden. Liquor followed Klein and his staff on the road. When Klein and his staff traveled out of province, stories filtered back about 'buckets full of Bloody Marys in their hotel rooms'."

If Klein wasn't drinking, he found other ways to embarrass the province. He walked out of a First Ministers' Health meeting in Ottawa to gamble in a casino in Hull. He was flying corporate jets to the hunting lodge he jointly owned near Prince Rupert. He had come a long way from the media-astute politician photographed carrying his luggage and waiting in line at an Air Canada counter.

Other things changed, change that indicated a lack of respect for tradition. Without respect for institutions, there is no respect for the people who built them.

Dress codes were lowered. Under Lougheed and Getty, all Legislature staff were expected to dress appropriately all the time. Under Klein, casual dress was acceptable. Ministers dressed in bright shorts and Hawaiian shirts showed up at meetings. Jeans and sneakers were acceptable.

Walking through the Legislature one summer afternoon, I walked right into Rod Love wearing bright summer shorts. "You wouldn't wear those things in here when Lougheed was Premier," I told him. "Yeah, but Lougheed isn't here anymore," he replied.

Ties between the Klein regime and the Getty and Lougheed regimes would be so brittle that efforts to hold a reunion on the 25th anniversary of the Conservative Party winning the government in 1971 fizzled. Another attempt in 2001 to celebrate the 30th anniversary found no takers either. The Getty/Lougheed people didn't want to be in the same room as the Klein people, the people who addressed them disrespectfully in public as "the previous administration."

In the months and years that followed, there would be persistent talk that Klein would retire sooner than later. He didn't. He won another election, in 2004, and appeared to be ready to settle in for another term or two, or as long as people would have him.

UNRAVELING OF A PREMIER

The enormous political capital Klein earned his first and second terms was being squandered in the third term. As it turns out, the focus and determination of the first term were an aberration in his career. After the first term, he couldn't recreate the interest, the energy and the focus. Although tackling everything at once worked in the destruction phase, it was mind-numbing in the construction phase. In the first term, he knew what people wanted; after the first term, people wanted to know what he wanted - and he couldn't answer.

In September 2003, in the midst of the chaos brought by the discovery of mad cow disease on a northern Alberta ranch, Klein was in Montana to meet with U.S. state governors. When asked about the mad cow situation, Klein said "a self-respecting rancher would not have taken the animal to slaughter but would have shot, shoveled and shut up." That was the advice of a Premier of a province with a serious mad cow situation: shut your eyes and the monster will go away. In other words, Alberta doesn't deal with tough problems, it ignores them. Rather than test for mad cow disease, Alberta wanted to ship the animals to the U.S. Ralph Klein's smart-assed, off-the-cuff cracks were no longer so funny.

When Klein was asked about the causes of global warming, Klein sarcastically replied: "Dinosaur farts." *Alberta Views*, a political/cultural magazine published in Calgary, still uses the comment to promote subscriptions.

In March 2006, in a fit of anger in the Legislative Assembly, he threw a Liberal policy book at a young Legislature intern who had delivered it to him. It made national headlines. So did a bout of nastiness in an altercation with Liberal MLA Laurie Blakeman who dared to challenge him in a committee meeting. Klein still hadn't exhausted his ability to embarrass himself.

Always there was his crude use of language. Some say that Klein masterfully dealt with that crude "eastern creeps and bums" harangue when he was Mayor of Calgary by squarely facing the media in eastern Canada. His crude, abusive language, however, was not an isolated incident. Mark Lisac, in his book *The Klein Revolution*, writes that Klein referred to him as an "asshole". Klein called Liberal leader Laurence Decore "a rat" in the Legislative Assembly. He called Liberal MLA Grant Mitchell "stupid" several times. Klein accused Mitchell and Liberal MLA Laurie Blakeman of calling him "a liar" when they did not. He made crude jokes about Prime Minister Jean Chretien's intelligence. In 2002, at the height of the Kyoto Protocol controversy, Klein told a Calgary audience that "When I talk to the Prime Minister, it is not a very intelligent conversation."

When the premiers of other provinces raised taxes rather than lower them as Klein promised to do in Alberta, he called them "brainless" and "cowardly" in a speech to the Fraser Institute in 1995.

Meanwhile, the Conservative Government was running on autopilot. Nothing remotely interesting or innovative was coming out of it. They had as much power and money as any government would need or could handle, but the leadership wasn't there. Voters didn't seem to mind; Klein kept getting good poll numbers –

not quite as good as in the early years - but certainly good enough. The opposition wasn't a threat. After the debacle that Nancy MacBeth had wreaked on the Liberal Party in 2001 election, Klein appeared to be as unassailable as ever. There was no alternative to the Conservative Party. Without an alternative they could support, Albertans didn't bother to vote. Thousands of Conservative supporters, unhappy with Klein but not about to vote Liberal, stayed home. Participation in the 2004 election plunged to 44%.

Klein might have been accused of shameful behaviour once, perhaps twice - maybe even three times. But, eventually, enough is enough. Albertans may not have lost trust in Klein but they were losing their patience with his behaviour.

Sensing the end, Klein promised to retire in 2008. It wasn't good enough. Resentment and anger within his own party at a leader who had lost interest, and a government that had no direction, started to boil over. Looking for an agenda to deal with health reform, environment, infrastructure and a struggling post-secondary education system, they got vague rhetoric about taxes, debt and the economy. If voters weren't going to deal with him, the Conservative Party membership would.

The party constitution calls for a leadership review after each election, including the 2004 election. In the past, the review was meaningless. Not this time.

Shortly before the Conservative convention, the once friendly *Calgary Herald* turned on him. In a toughly-worded editorial, it said: "Good leaders know when it is time to go. Klein evidently does not. Having missed the obvious chance to fade out with the last of the Centennial fireworks, he postponed his departure until late. We say this with sadness, not anger, but two years of ill-tempered indecision at the top is too long for Alberta to wait. This is not Ralph's World anymore. There is important work to be done and somebody better suited to it than Klein should occupy the Premier's office. Since voters cannot express an opinion until 2008, it must then fall to party members to perform the unpleasant task of walking their leader to the door. When the party reviews Klein's leadership on March 31, they will have their opportunity."

The Conservative Party sent him a hard right to the jaw. He got a slight majority in the leadership review vote, which sent a powerful signal that he was done. He talked himself into staying until September.

Jeffrey Simpson, a *Globe & Mail* columnist, dubbed Klein's final months as the end of the "bozo era".

WHAT WAS HIS PUBLIC APPEAL?

The Klein era was over. He went out with a whimper rather than a bang. In four terms and 14 years, he had but one truly successful term and that was the first term. Deficit elimination and debt retirement will be his legacy, and both got their start in the 1993/97 term. After that, it was merely government as usual; a team of accountants could have done the same work.

A source insists that the end of the Klein era was the day Peter Elzinga left the Premier's office in February 2003. "Klein trusted Elzinga completely. When Peter left, Klein's interest in being Premier of Alberta left with him. You have to remember that by 2003, Klein has spent a decade as Premier and he was getting bored. Familiar faces were moving around - Love to Calgary, Elzinga to a more private life, Stockwell Day to federal politics, Marvin Moore back to Grande Prairie, and some of his ministers to the private sector - and Klein is forced to stay here feeling like someone who keeps failing grade four. He once admitted that he didn't want to go to the polls in 2004 and that he wasn't in charge. I guess he just ran out of choices."

Why did he stay so long? For the simplest of reasons - his wife wanted him to stay. An extremely informed source insisted that Ralph Klein stayed almost three years longer than he wanted to stay. My source said that Klein wanted to leave before the 2004 election but his wife talked him out of it.

"Ralph called an election in 2004 that he didn't want to fight. While he won big, the story was the turnout. He knew people were unhappy with him," my source confided. "The day after the election, Ralph brought Rod Love back to prepare his graceful exit. Love agreed to put his lucrative consulting practice on hold for 10 months because he believed that he owed Ralph that much. The plan failed. After 10 months, Ralph said he was staying because his wife talked him into staying again. Rod finally gave up and returned to Calgary. After that, it was a disaster."

Media assessments of Ralph Klein's retirement all mentioned the debt retirement achievement. They also mentioned liquor and his bizarre behaviour in his last five years: his behaviour at the homeless shelter; throwing the Liberal health policy book at the Legislature intern; ranting at Liberal MLA Laurie Blakeman in a public meeting; walking out of a national health conference in Ottawa to gamble at a casino; his pathetic performance on national television on the night of the 2001 election; and others.

What was his public appeal? Plain and simple, a majority of Albertans trusted him more than they trusted the alternatives. His election was an act of faith, an expression of trust beyond reason or argument. Coming after the investment disasters of the Don Getty era, Klein was trusted not to repeat them. If Klein behaved stupidly, it would be against the left wingers in the special interest groups who always wanted more, or the unions, or the welfare types. Klein's enthusiasts believed he would never, ever do anything bad to hard-working Albertans like themselves. If his government screwed up, Klein, who seemed to behave like an ombudsman to his own government, could be trusted to make things right. He wasn't perfect but he was far better than the rest.

The record shows that Klein is a political lone wolf who functions better when he is in control and the agenda clear and simple.

His style of leadership defied conventional measurements of successful political leadership. Klein's leadership was about himself. He attracted few interesting people into politics. He didn't encourage citizens to participate in politics. He had little respect for his enemies or for people with different ideas. And he had no grand schemes to lead Alberta into a new era. Klein made countless speeches but none with vision, inspiration or hope. His spoke mostly of the economy, debt and taxes.

Klein eventually ran the Conservative Party into the ground and the Party membership got even by dumping him. The Conservative Party organization was a mere shadow of itself in 2007 compared to 1985 when Peter Lougheed retired. It was old, out of touch and leaderless.

Given his record as Premier after 1997, we now know that Klein had little vision of where Alberta should be in five or ten years. We know that he had little sense of how to build an economic infrastructure. He's good when he's tightly focused and directed but otherwise he drifts.

HE COULD HAVE BEEN A SUPERSTAR

In 2009, reflecting on the Ralph Klein era, I still don't have strong feelings about the man or his work. He did good work on the fiscal side - I believe to this day that most of it was Jim Dinning's work - but without Klein's leadership and popularity, it wouldn't have happened as quickly as it did.

When the deficit and debt work was done in the first term, Klein lost his focus. He tried the summit approach to get direction but the summits didn't provide the political solutions he needed. He tried numerous health reform strategies but didn't succeed in meaningful reform. He had numerous choices and alternatives and certainly the political power to make them happen but he didn't deliver.

He had won the lottery - the enormous political power granted to him by the voters - and he was well on the way to blowing it.

Alberta could have been a national leader in health reform. It could have been a national leader in environmental protection. It could have set up tax regimes to attract new industry and diversify the resource-dominated economy. Alberta, with government support, could have the best public schools and universities in the country. None of it happened.

The Athabasca Oil Sands development is a notable achievement - Alberta's recent economic boom is due almost entirely on oil sands investment - but it was the work of others. Klein's part was to reduce royalties and sit back and watch the rush to Fort McMurray.

In the end, the Klein era will be about deficits and debt. When historians analyze the legacy of a political leader, the ability to manage money doesn't rate highly. If it did, Tommy Douglas would be remembered more for consistent balanced budgets during the Great Depression than universal hospital care. Managing money is the stuff of accountants and administrators, not visionary leaders. Money has little value unless you know how to use it. You can't eat it, drink it, or smoke it and money can't keep you warm for long - you can only worship it.

Klein was unable to sell his policies outside the province. Not a single province followed retail liquor privatization or electricity deregulation. His attempts to privatize certain parts of the health care system, as in the notorious Bill 11 (Health Care Protection Act) controversy, were rejected by the western premiers. Bill 11, despite its innocuous title, would allow public hospitals to contract surgical procedures to for-profit hospitals. Klein's critics saw Bill 11 undermining the public system. Klein's attempt to sell the Mazankowski Council report package to the other premiers went nowhere, which may be the reason its impact in Alberta was minimal. While the other Premiers were intrigued by the radical, rapid deficit reduction plan in the 1993/97 term, not a single one copied any part of it either because it was deemed unnecessary or their citizens wouldn't tolerate it.

Klein was populist in perception but not in reality. He ran a closed political society inside the Legislature Building, sharing only what his own staff or professional communicators told him to share. The inside was closed to everyone but the elected, making the decision-making process vague and rambling, closeted at Government House or the upper floors of the Legislature Building.

When I asked one of the people who worked closely with Klein in the last years of his era about Klein's legacy, he shrugged and suggested that he was "one of Alberta's most colourful premiers."

The Klein era is a tragedy of political power gained but not used to make life better for the people in his province. One could argue that a vibrant economy makes life better, and it does, but so does an activist government that provides a progressive public education system from kindergarten through post-secondary, invests in research and development, promotes healthy lifestyles in arts and culture, and provides recreation and leisure facilities in all communities. People have to do something with their lives besides work and make money.

Great Premiers are builders, leaders who give more than they receive, who leave the condition of people and their communities better than they found them. Ralph Klein had almost everything to be a great Premier: money, political power, salesmanship and electoral support. However, he lacked a vital component: an ability to look ahead. As Professor Richard Hodgson of the University of Western Ontario said, "Some people see the edge of the rut and think they see the horizon."

Klein was in a rut for his last ten years. If he saw Alberta in the future as more than a massive oil sands plant, he didn't say.

He had no sense of history; he governed for the moment. Klein would have fit Woody Allen's theory that "80% of success is showing up."

Klein didn't abuse his awesome political power; he simply didn't use it. He did not understand the vast power of government when it is coupled with intelligence and foresight. He could have done so much more.

That, I believe, is a real tragedy.

PEOPLE I MET IN POLITICS

NANCY MACBETH (BETKOWSKI)

———————————————————————————————————

S he was Nancy Betkowski when we worked together in the Legislature
Building, both assistants to ministers in Don Getty's Conservative
Government. She remarried and became Nancy MacBeth. With either name
she was the same person.

Whether I was a minister's assistant or a newsletter publisher looking for
political information, I always had trouble reading her personality. She could be
friendly one minute and aloof the next. I never knew what to expect.

People are what they do, not what they say. Events between the first and second
ballots in the Conservative leadership race in 1992 may provide clues to her political
skills and personality.

She beat Ralph Klein by a single vote on the first ballot. Her lead was a surprise
because a large part of the Conservative caucus including the entire rural caucus
was with Klein. Somehow Betkowski and her campaign team got the silly notion
that the race was over and the final vote a formality. Her friends in Edmonton
insisted that the only question on the second ballot was her margin of victory.

Perhaps that notion was the reason she began to plan her cabinet rather than work the streets for votes. She even asked Reno Bosetti, a veteran deputy minister, to be her Chief Deputy.

Meanwhile in Calgary, Ralph Klein's campaign team was hustling to sell thousands of memberships. Rural Alberta was canvassed in a matter of days and teams organized to get the vote out. By mid-week, Ken Kowalski, a key Klein organizer, told me that the second ballot would be a slaughter. He was correct.

While Nancy Betkowski, with all her education and her connections with what was called the "white wine crowd", was in her office plotting the future of the province, Ralph Klein, with his modest education and street-smart politics, was stumping rural Alberta, having an occasional beer with the folks, and thinking only of winning the vote later that week.

He knew what it took to win; she didn't. She was beaten by a more personable and politically-astute candidate who knew how to win votes on the streets.

In the weeks following the leadership race, she did nothing to show she was a gracious loser. She and Klein bickered over her place in the new Conservative Government and when they didn't agree, she retired at the 1993 election. She later returned to politics as leader of the Liberal Party in 1998, which seemed to be purely an act of revenge.

What should have been a bright political career ended too quickly in disaster. In the end, I doubt that people had any idea who she was. I didn't.

2

MEDIA
A PREOCCUPATION WITH RALPH

Personal friendships with politicians are bad for the newsletter business. When reporters get too close to politicians, their inclination is to slant the story to maintain the relationship. When a story is too one-sided, readers are short-changed. A reporter can't win this battle. If politicians are able to use you, they don't respect you; if they can't use you, they don't like you and won't give good information. I learned that, to maintain the value and the integrity of **Insight into Government,** *politicians should be treated as business acquaintances rather than friends.*

Ralph Klein didn't become a popular politician by being a nice guy. He and his sidekick Rod Love worked hard and smart at making him popular, plotting ways to curb the natural inclination of the media to criticize.

All politicians have a media strategy and all are based on the simple premise that politicians can't be successful without the help of the media. Persistently negative reports in the media can destroy a political career. Strategies vary by politician and by organization. Some work, some don't. Klein and Love had one that worked for them.

They learned early in their political careers that the media could be exploited for their own political purposes. A successful media strategy was a vital part of winning the mayoralty in Calgary the first time and in every one of their successes afterwards.

The key to a successful media strategy, to positive reports on Premier Klein's performance, was to turn him into an entertainer who could regale reporters with information they could write without arduous research or interviews with people who might have a contrary view.

With Ralph explaining his version of government policy or launching a colourful attack on a real or imagined enemy, with Ralph as the top story on television and in the newspapers every day, with the opposition's criticisms of government policy buried deep in the stories because Ralph was more colourful and accessible, newspaper readers would learn to appreciate Ralph.

Political coverage became all about Ralph, Ralph and more Ralph. Reporters had to work overtime to keep up with him. That didn't stop him from complaining about the media, which he did almost nonstop after the 2001 election.

Love's media strategy worked wonderfully for more than a decade, an extraordinarily long period of grace for any politician. Media coverage of Premier Klein had a huge influence on his decisive election victories.

COLOURFUL POLITICAL RHETORIC IS SEXIER THAN POLICY ANALYSIS

Love's media strategy was not evil, illegal or sinister. Politicians always attempt to control the information available to reporters and if they can do it, good for them. After all, their careers are on the line. Their job is to get the government's side out; it's up to reporters to add balance and perspective.

After the secrecy and aloofness of Peter Lougheed and the reluctance and suspicions of Don Getty, Ralph Klein was an open book. Reporters loved the guy. He spent time with them, drank with them, laughed with them. He shared ribald stories with them. Some were invited into the Premier's office for a drink. He was a one-man news information outlet. Klein made every reporter's life easier with instant stories - not dull, boring policy stories but colourful interpretations of the political world and attacks on real or imagined enemies.

He used the media to keep his name in the headlines. They wrote about his agenda and as long as he entertained them and wrote their stories, reporters didn't have the time or space to cover the opposition parties, which is exactly what Klein and Love intended.

That left little time for reporters to pay attention to the relatively dull world of policy analysis or to pay attention to opposition parties. They didn't ask the Premier who was actually governing the province when Klein wasn't "under the Dome" (i.e. the Legislature Building) which, by his own admission, was as little as possible. There was minimal coverage of the opposition parties or how they reacted to government policy.

Alberta's four largest urban dailies - the *Edmonton Journal*, the *Edmonton Sun*, the *Calgary Herald* and the *Calgary Sun* - were skillfully neutralized by an entertaining Premier and a blizzard of paper and selective leaks, a strategy that Klein and his staff worked to perfection.

When Premier Ralph Klein constantly bragged about "getting out from under the Dome", who was writing policies for consideration in the Legislative Assembly? Certainly Klein wasn't and he wasn't afraid to admit it. In March 2009, Klein told *Alberta Views* magazine: "I appreciate the Fraser Institute and the Manning Centre (for Building Democracy) for doing their research and analysis, but a lot of it is beyond me, to tell you the truth. In politics, there's very little time to consider policy."

At an *Edmonton Journal* editorial board meeting in 2001, following passage of the law that restructured the electricity business and brought higher prices, Klein was asked to explain. He pulled cards out of his pocket and started to read from the cards, then stuffed them back in his pocket. He said he didn't know "what this means." In Question Period, when a Liberal MLA asked Klein if he said that, Klein changed the subject as he did so often when he didn't want to answer a question. He said the MLA wasn't at the meeting so how did he know what had happened – but Klein didn't deny that he said it.

Daily newspapers, radio and television outlets in Alberta would take an active interest in the Speech from the Throne, which lays out the government's annual agenda, and the annual budget, and in a pinch they reported on the opposition parties.

The relevant stuff in the Legislative Assembly - the political debate, the arguments, the controversies and diverging views over policy, the details of new law - got little attention. Even Question Period, once a prime source of media coverage, took a back seat to coverage of Ralph Klein.

Policy development may not be sexy but it matters because it institutes policies that frame our lives and govern our communities. Policy development is the real work of a government between elections; political rhetoric is merely the theatre. Policy development in Alberta occurs behind closed doors in the Legislature Building; political rhetoric is designed to divert media attention from policy.

Television is a natural forum for political debate. In the United States, the major stations carry a handful of vibrant programs talking politics. Alberta's television stations had little interest in political debate programs or political panels. They carried little regular political commentary and rarely provided editorial comment on issues related to the policies of the provincial government.

ACCESS Television, owned by the Government of Alberta, broke from the pack in 1993 with *Fair Comment*, a weekly panel on provincial politics. When ACCESS was sold and converted into an education channel, *Fair Comment* was cancelled. No television station would carry it until public television from Spokane, Washington, picked it up for a year. None of the Alberta-based stations - CBC, CFRN and CITV - would touch it even though it was cheap Canadian content. They assumed that political debate had no local audience.

Apparently, Alberta's mainstream media concurred. Media interest - or lack of it - in policy developed by the Government of Alberta may be the biggest and strangest political story of all. Television and newspapers didn't cover the government; they covered Ralph. And that's the way Klein and his Chief of Staff Rod Love wanted it. They wanted you to read about Ralph, not the opposition parties. Ralph had to be the essence of political coverage.

GET YOUR STORY FROM THE SOURCE, FROM THE PREMIER HIMSELF

Diverting media attention to Ralph and away from government policy that could create controversy and the opposition parties who criticized government policy wasn't an accident. Love designed the media strategy and while it wasn't subtle, it certainly was simple. He knew that most people get their political information from the mainstream media, primarily the print media. Love paid a lot of attention to reporters.

Political reporters in Alberta were taught to get their information straight from the source - Premier Ralph Klein. And Klein - being media savvy was a strength - was happy to oblige. He met with reporters every day the Legislative Assembly was in session and gave them a quick summary of his thoughts for the day, whether or not they were related to what was happening in the Legislative Assembly. When Klein had nothing to say, he whipped off a few quick one-liners, usually denigrating the federal government or an annoying interest group resisting his latest brainwave. He always gave reporters more than enough for the day's story. For reporters who could be counted on to cooperate, Klein invited them to his office for that extra bit of information that he didn't give during the scrum.

In time, almost every political story from the Legislature included comments from Klein. It got so bad that even Love complained. On a *Fair Comment* panel, he complained that "a story from the Legislature is not valid until the Premier comments on it". Ironically, dealing with the demands of a media hungry for access to the Premier had become a distraction.

Meanwhile, the Premier's office was bombarding reporters with an endless stream of media releases written by the Public Affairs Bureau. Love called this "feeding the beast". Its purpose: to keep reporters busy with information the government wanted them to report. If more detail was required, reporters were instructed to talk to Communications Directors in the departments.

Can you imagine a better situation? The Premier's office controls the information that goes out and heaven help any government employee who contradicts the official line as dictated by the Premier's office.

Intimidation? Occasionally it was direct. When *Calgary Herald* reporter Jim Cunningham, host of *Fair Comment*, got tough with the Klein Government, Love poked his finger at his chest and told Cunningham that he would be meeting with his publisher the next day. More often, a reporter who didn't follow the government's agenda found himself excluded.

Reporters loved to party with Ralph. To celebrate the 1994 budget in which many spending cuts occurred, Premier Ralph Klein and some of the Legislature media celebrated at Martini's, a pub on 109th Street within easy walking distance of the Legislature Building. According to Don Martin, in his book *King Ralph*: *The Political Life and Success of Ralph Klein*, they drank until 5 a.m., the extended drinking hours courtesy of a note signed by Klein that temporarily released the drinking establishment from provincial drinking law. It was one of the few celebrations in the province after the 1994 budget slashed another 10% off government spending, bringing the two-year total to 16%. Why were reporters celebrating a political accomplishment?

A handful of reporters were present at another beer-fest at Martini's when backbench Conservative MLA Jon Havelock and Love had a pushing match in the pub. Havelock was frustrated because he couldn't get a meeting with the Premier, and he blamed Love. None of the reporters at the pub reported the story, which, in a more competitive media environment, would have been a political story worthy of the front page.

ART OF THE STRATEGIC LEAK

Love didn't trust reporters. Nor should he; politicians and reporters are natural adversaries. They shouldn't trust each other. Covering politics is strictly business.

In December 1999, more than a year after Love had left the Premier's Office to open his own consulting company in Calgary, he described his media strategy at the annual Alberta School Boards' Association meeting in the Westin Hotel in Edmonton. The rapt audience of school board officials overflowed the large meeting room.

School district administrators rarely have direct contact with the Premier or his inside people.

Love was getting much of the credit for Klein's rise to the Premier's office and his widespread popularity. Although Premier Klein paid little attention to public education, they had heard and read much about Love and they wanted to see and hear him for themselves. Specifically, they wanted to know how he dealt with pesky reporters.

When Love walked into the crowded room, he saw me at a nearby table. "You going to write about this?" he asked. "If you have something to say," I replied. He did. It is one thing to witness a political process that works and quite another to hear its architect describe it.

Love talked of dumping numerous stories on reporters every day which kept them busy. Idle reporters go looking for information and when they find something, bad things can happen to the government. To prevent that, Love and his people at the Public Affairs Bureau kept them busy. He told the packed house of wide-eyed school board officials about strategic leaks to test government policy and to keep the government's agenda in the headlines.

A strategic leak works two ways, both of which benefit the government. Love explained the purpose in a column published in the *Calgary Herald* in 1999 under the headline "Leaks are an exercise in power." First, a leak can be used to test an idea the government is considering but is not sure of the reaction. He called it a "trial balloon". The vehicle: tell one reporter, who will be eternally grateful for getting a story not available to another reporter. Which brings us to the second advantage of a strategic leak: the grateful reporter owes the leaker - i.e. Klein or Love - a favour. The Sun chain was the favorite recipient of the leaks because Sun reporters could be trusted to handle the information the way the government wanted.

Then Love gave his attentive audience of school district people a taste of the stuff they came for: he talked about reporters, the bane of a public servant's existence. Unlike many political people, Love didn't fear reporters; he used them - and he was very good at it.

"Reporters are not your friends," he said bluntly. "If a reporter asks you to confirm a rumour, don't do it. A rumour is a rumour and nothing more. Never talk off-the-record to any reporter. If you do, expect to see it in the newspaper." He wrapped up with the old adage: "Tell reporters only what you want to see on the front page tomorrow."

Love was a hit. It may have been the first time they had listened to someone not intimidated by a mere reporter.

Public officials don't know how to deal with inquisitive reporters - fear was prevalent - and nobody before had offered free practical advice on how to do it. Some school districts hired a communications person to deal with the media and while this will work most of the time, eventually something will happen that will force public officials to face the media directly.

Love's presentation may have been the first time school district administrators heard a media strategist give them the straight goods in terms they could understand.

OPPOSITION PARTIES? WHAT OPPOSITION PARTIES?

Premier Klein's Communications office played one newspaper against the other and made no apologies for it. Reporters who treated the Premier well got little "extras" that reporters for the competing newspaper did not. Which meant that an editor would ask why his reporter didn't have that story. Heaven help the reporter who ignored one of Klein's rants only to see the competing newspaper run the story across the front page. In short time, reporters learned to behave themselves if they wanted to keep working the Legislature beat.

For example, after filming a *Fair Comment* segment in 1994, I noticed that a guest reporter from the *Edmonton Journal* was visibly distraught as we left the studio. *Fair Comment* moderator Jim Cunningham had invited her to the program to talk about the government's latest moves to overhaul welfare programs.

Sensing that she didn't like the way she handled herself on air, I said: "It was a good program. You did very well."

She turned to me, clearly upset. "Bob Scott won't like what I said. He won't talk to me on Monday," she said. Bob Scott was Family & Social Services Minister Mike Cardinal's communications guy.

"You must have other people you can talk to," I said. "He can't be your only source." Turns out, he was. The *Edmonton Journal* reporter was concerned that Scott would leak stories to the *Edmonton Sun* reporter and her editors at the *Journal* would demand to know why she didn't have the same stories. Which meant she had to cooperate. Love's media strategy was working better than he knew.

Opposition parties had difficulty attracting reporters scrambling to keep pace with the Premier. His every word was reported but overtures from the opposition were ignored. Policy alternatives written by the opposition parties rarely got attention. Even during the numerous health reform controversies, the Liberals and New Democrats wrote health reform papers that were often ignored. A speech from the Opposition leader might be buried deep in the back of the newspaper with the classified ads and obituaries. Opposition attacks in Question Period might be found buried deep in articles highlighting government policy.

Why? I can only believe the simplest of explanations: that most of the

Legislature Press Gallery liked Klein more than Decore who tended to be aloof to the point of appearing to be arrogant. Covering Klein was easier and more interesting. Liberal leader Laurence Decore didn't have Klein's political skills and didn't socialize or drink with reporters. Klein paid attention to reporters and drank with them. When reporters criticized them, Klein and Love reacted. Perhaps a call to a publisher, perhaps a nasty call to a reporter. Decore didn't do any of that. Opposition parties refrained from criticizing media coverage for fear they would be seen as whining.

Major bills before the Legislative Assembly were often ignored. The Throne Speech and budget make front-page news. But another 50 bills might go through the Legislative Assembly in the spring session and only the contents of a handful were reported. Many stories that Klein did not talk about were ignored.

Television and radio coverage? Surface coverage at best. The Legislative Assembly had to be in an uproar before television would pay attention. Unless you tuned in to Dave Rutherford's open line radio show on CHQR (Calgary) and CHED (Edmonton) where callers can rant about anything they like.

Until the internet explosion in recent years, the mainstream media were the prime source of political information. In Klein's first term as Premier starting late in 1992, newspapers and television set the tone and parameters of public awareness of political issues. When they read nothing except Ralph said this and Ralph said that, people assume that Ralph is in control and all is well. Your local media wasn't telling them anything different.

In this awkward media environment, two trends emerged:

First, reporters, tired of the deadlines, annoying editors, and mediocre pay, began showing up as Communications Officers in minister's offices and in the Public Affairs Bureau with better pay and a secure pension plan. One of Ed Stelmach's first moves after winning the Conservative leadership in 2006 was to hire Tom Olsen of the *Calgary Herald* and Paul Stanway of the *Edmonton Sun*. The pair worked themselves into jobs right in the Premier's Office, into jobs designed to manipulate the Legislature media that they had worked with for so many years.

Secondly, if mainstream media coverage was comprehensive, a political newsletter like my own *Insight into Government* would not have survived. Its growth in readership was greatest during the Klein era. In a way, Ralph Klein was a gift. While reporters were paying attention to what he said, *Insight into Government* was paying attention to what his government was doing. The difference between what Klein talked about and what the government did was often significant. Klein was very good for the newsletter business.

INSIGHT INTO GOVERNMENT: LIBERAL OPPOSITION?

Frank Dabbs' book *Ralph Klein: A Maverick Life* paid my newsletter *Insight into Government* a huge compliment. Published in 1995, nine years after *Insight* first issue, Dabbs' book discussed the Alberta media's treatment of Ralph Klein. He wrote: "The toughest Liberal assessments of Klein policy came from a cadre of academic writers and media commentators such as the University of Alberta's Allan Tupper and the University of Calgary's Roger Gibbins and from newsletter publishers such as Rich Vivone of *Insight into Government* ..."

My oh my. *Insight into Government* (a.k.a *Insight*), an obscure political newsletter, had hit the big time. While flattered at being noticed by someone of Dabbs' stature and put in the same heady company as Allan Tupper and Roger Gibbins, I wondered if Dabbs' assessment was different from conservative columnist Ted Byfield's claim that I was a "Red Tory", as he described me in one of his columns in the *Edmonton Sun*. Dabbs and Byfield were much more diplomatic than Love who, after a *Fair Comment* program, left a message laced with four-letter words on my office answering machine.

Insight was an independently-owned and independently-operated newsletter devoted to one purpose: to be a successful business. As a business, *Insight* adhered to basic principles of a viable small business: find the niche in the market place; develop a product to fill the niche; and work hard. *Insight's* business was politics and politics was its business. *Insight* covered only provincial politics except for the occasional foray into federal politics.

To be successful, *Insight* had to be different from the mainstream media, had to cover politics differently, and had to be accurate. If a subscriber paid $270 a year, the subscriber expected more than a condensed version of the front page of the *Edmonton Journal* or *Calgary Herald*. If *Insight* covered the same political material as the newspapers, a subscriber wouldn't need it, and *Insight into Government* would be out of business. Subscribers don't call to complain about errors or unfair articles; subscribers expressed themselves with their wallets - the dissatisfied don't renew. Over 19 years of steady growth, *Insight's* annual renewal rate always exceeded 95% and its subscriber list grew in 18 of those 19 years.

As a business, *Insight* didn't deal in partisan rants or irresponsible criticisms for the sake of criticizing. Subscribers expected the best possible information written fairly and with intelligence. *Insight* had to be useful to its readers. The focus was on what the Klein Government was doing rather than what the Premier said it was doing. Often there was a significant difference.

Independence from partisan political influence was *Insight's* soul. In 1996, John Zaozirny, a retired Conservative minister, proposed that he and I go into business together. His plan folded *Insight* into his consulting company. His offer was a surprise and flattering, but that combination had already been tried and deemed a bad match. As part of a company with clients lobbying politicians and government officials, *Insight* would become a harmless PR organ rather than a tool for political analyses.

In 2002, I was stunned to receive e-mail from Rod Love, now a political consultant in Calgary. Love asked about a partnership with *Insight into Government*, expanding it to include Don Martin's political column from Ottawa, and aggressively marketing it in Ontario "to make some real money." I wasn't certain Love was serious but nonetheless saw two problems with his inquiry: Ontario cares little about Alberta politics just as Alberta cares little about Ontario politics; and three editors working on the same newsletter isn't wise. This wouldn't be a good marriage either.

Insight into Government had its detractors in the Legislature. In 1994, rookie Conservative MLA Murray Smith of Calgary, angered by a comment I made on television claiming that few in Klein's cabinet had actual business experience while talking endlessly of running a government as a business, warned that he intended to write a note to the Conservative caucus urging that MLAs not subscribe. A businessman before politics, Smith took my comment personally.

If anyone should be interested in knowing what was going on in the Legislature Building, it is deputy ministers and their staff. Part of my marketing strategy was the simple phone call. Several times I was told directly that although *Insight into Government* was a useful tool, their minister might not think a subscription to be a good idea. Why? One deputy minister: "They think you're a Liberal." Ironically, some Liberals thought I was a Conservative.

In 1994, the Municipal Affairs department told me that all subscriptions to *Insight into Government* were cancelled as demanded by a memo from the minister's office. Dick Fowler of St. Albert was the minister.

In 2004, the Education department ceased distributing *Insight* after Deputy Minister Maria David-Evans and her senior staff sat stone-faced through my presentation to a school superintendents' meeting in southern Alberta. The cancellation, the department's librarian told me, "was a management decision".

In 2004, Steve West, Klein's new Chief of Staff, didn't appreciate a story about him in *Insight* and warned Ian Gray, my Legislature correspondent, that when it came time for another round of cost-cutting, *Insight* would be high on his list. West was fired before he could do the damage.

Finally, read the Stockwell Day profile on page 103. The symbolism is unmistakable.

A STRATEGY TO COUNTER A MEDIA STRATEGY

To be a successful business, *Insight into Government* had to counter Love's media strategy. I had to find a different way to get reliable political information without succumbing to the manipulations of the Premier's Office.

It became a game. To be different meant having credible sources outside the influence of the Premier's Communications Office; it meant being in places where reporters didn't go, and avoiding places reporters did go.

The Premier's scrum was the start. A year or so after Klein became Premier, I stopped attending the daily scrum. The reasons: a gaggle of reporters covered the scrum and all wrote basically the same story with modestly different slants. Everything Klein said was in the newspapers the next day. Better that I spend my time elsewhere because, in the beginning, I was a one-man business.

I read government reports religiously including annual reports and business plans. They are boring and sometimes dreadfully difficult to read but can be loaded with information of interest to people who need reliable policy information. Sometimes I got material I wasn't supposed to get. Waiting to talk to a Conservative MLA in the Legislature, I noticed a secretary throwing reports in the trash. She served several MLAs and trashed duplicate copies of everything. I suggested that rather than waste the reports, she could send them to me. She surprisingly agreed and I got some great material that was not meant for public consumption, including frank reports from private companies meant only for the eyes of Conservative MLAs. The source was eventually discovered and that game was over.

Because I was not seen to be a friend of the government, MLAs often refused to talk to me in the Legislature Building. Politicians like to talk, especially about themselves. In the controlled environment that the Legislature Building had become, I suspected that MLAs needed a more comfortable place to talk freely. I set up a table at the Forum Inn across from the hockey arena in northeast Edmonton. The restaurant, easily accessed from Wayne Gretzky Drive, was quiet and far from the prying eyes of Love and his Communications Directors, which made MLAs comfortable enough to talk more freely than they would at other places closer to the Legislature Building.

I discovered over time that MLAs were not particularly good sources of political information unless they gossiped about other MLAs, especially the ministers. On policy issues, MLAs relied on "Talking Points" supplied by a government researcher. Unless the MLA had a direct interest in the policy, the MLA usually had little to offer. They were approving laws they didn't understand.

Occasionally I got a gem. I asked one MLA about the numerous failed attempts at health reform and casually asked who was driving health policy: "Was the Health Minister making health policy decisions? Or was it Klein?" The questions were barely out of my mouth when he snapped: "Neither. It's Jack Davis." I reminded him that Jack is the CEO of the Calgary Health Authority. "But he can phone the Premier at any time and reach him," the MLA said. "Ralph will believe Jack before he believes Halvar [Health Minister Halvar Jonson]."

For those afraid to be seen with the publisher of an "antigovernment publication", as *Insight into Government* was widely viewed in the Legislature Building, I would purposely be seen in a place popular with the public service crowd, a place such as the Sidetrack Restaurant near Grant MacEwan College on 104th Avenue in downtown Edmonton. If Martini's, the pub on 109th Street near the Legislature Building, is where politicians went to drink, mingle with reporters and celebrate, the Sidetrack, a popular nightclub that opened for breakfast to expand its business, catered to a wider elite market: politicians, lobbyists, public service bureaucrats, judges, lawyers, business people and others who wanted to be seen with them.

An odd caste system evolved at the Sidetrack: Conservative MLAs often came to the restaurant for breakfast and usually sat on the raised floor at the back. When a group of Conservative MLAs occupied the raised floor, other customers, notably public servants, sat on the lower level closer to the front door.

I asked Chief Deputy Minister Jack Davis to breakfast at the Sidetrack so people would see that Jack thought I was OK to talk to. The same for Treasury Deputy Peter Kruselnicki. Breakfast in such a public place frequented by people like Davis and Kruselnicki validated my work. I also invited Liberal leader Kevin Taft for breakfast at the Sidetrack.

I found knowledgeable sources outside government. When an intriguing question was asked in Question Period, which was always followed by a minister's sanitized response, I would call people outside government and familiar with the issue for better information. Anonymity was always requested and when granted, they were willing to talk.

For an interpretation of a new law, talk to a lawyer with inside connections. For a perspective on the budget, talk to an accountant with a history in public finance. Municipal administrators, regional health authority officials and school superintendents were helpful. The leaders of interest groups always cooperated. They had their own agendas but they always balanced the story as seen from the Legislature. *Insight's* subscriber list was a long list of potential information sources since most of them dealt with politicians. They were a goldmine of information just waiting to talk. When readers learned that they could trust me, I would get calls that usually started with: "You didn't hear this from me but there is something you should know ..."

Leaders of interest groups want to balance information coming out the Legislature Building. They were more than willing to talk to a newsletter publisher who wasn't in the government's pocket. One tipped me off that he was meeting Family & Social Services Minister Lyle Oberg and asked whether I would be interested in what the minister had to say in a private meeting. How fast could I say yes?

Two hours after the meeting, he was in my office eight kilometers from the Legislature Building discussing details of the meeting, which I learned later were quite different from what Oberg was telling the media inside the Legislature.

In another case, I was told that many special interest groups were frustrated in dealing with Oberg because they thought he didn't listen, and had answers before questions were asked. My source said that because Oberg was a family doctor, he expected Oberg to approach interest groups the way a doctor approached a patient. As a doctor, Oberg is trained to listen and dictate a remedy; no other discussion is necessary. He said he framed his questions knowing that, and he got better results.

Over a casual lunch several days after the 2004 election, I got a rare exclusive. A deputy minister and I were having lunch to speculate about the new cabinet to be announced the next day. "There was a purge this morning," he said quietly. "The Chief Deputy, Julian Nowicki, has been let go. Ron Hicks is replacing him. Steve West has been fired. About a dozen deputies will be moved once they get the Premier's office sorted out."

I was stunned. "West is gone? Nowicki is gone? Are you certain?" Yes.

When I got independent confirmation of the moves, *Insight* carried the story of the wholesale restructuring in that week's edition. No other reporter had a clue. One reporter, after reading the story, called and insisted that my information was wrong and that I had flushed my business down the drain. He learned differently the next day when the Premier's Office hastily released its version of the unexpected purge.

In 1995, I started to accept invitations to talk to groups about government. I learned more from listening to these groups than I gave. They liked to talk and they liked to share, especially about the local MLA and the cabinet minister their group dealt with. I learned from these sessions which MLAs were respected and which were not, which were honest and which were not. All of it made *Insight's* political coverage better and good coverage was very good for business.

THOUGHTS ABOUT POLITICIANS

Finally, Rod Love had his thoughts about how to deal with reporters and I have my thoughts about how to deal with politicians:

First, personal friendships with politicians are bad for the newsletter business. When reporters get too close to politicians, their inclination is to slant the story to maintain the relationship. When a story is too one-sided, readers are short-changed. A reporter can't win this battle. If politicians are able to use you, they don't respect you; if they can't use you, they don't like you and won't give good information. I learned that to maintain the value and the integrity of *Insight into Government*, politicians should be treated as business acquaintances rather than friends. If I couldn't abide by my own rule, I'd find another line of work.

Secondly, I would not become drinking buddies with anyone I might write about. If there is an unwritten rule that certain topics are off-the-record which means the information can't be used, what's the point of pursuing the conversation? No possible good can come of such a relationship. I preferred that a source ask for anonymity, thus allowing me to use the information without identifying the source. Dealing with politicians is a serious business. As the *Godfather* said so convincingly, "It's business, not personal."

Third, never, never, never betray a confidence. If a politician - or anyone else for that matter - gives me a tip, I never reveal the source of the information, not even to my wife. Never. No exceptions. The great American author Ernest Hemingway said it best: "Integrity is like virginity; once lost, never regained."

These rules were good business and good for business.

PEOPLE I MET IN POLITICS

MIKE CARDINAL

N o one loved the prestige of being a cabinet minister more than Mike Cardinal. The power, the prestige and the attention were important to him, perhaps too important. He loved the personal status that politics gave him.

When cabinet was shuffled or a new cabinet appointed, Mike sat anxiously by his phone, waiting for the call. He strayed only to go to the bathroom.

He was fired from cabinet in May 1996 after his wife personally complained to the premier about her husband's affairs. It just about destroyed him.

Mike Cardinal isn't a complicated man. In some ways, he was not unlike Ralph Klein. Cardinal based his view of public policy on simple beliefs such as that children are best raised by a community, not by a government. He believed that welfare for individuals did more harm than good.

As the public service soon learned, Mike Cardinal wasn't a pen-and-paper guy. He was more comfortable talking about policy. He wanted policy briefings from his department to be verbal rather than be forced to plow through pages of notes and reports. When policy briefings had to be written, he wanted the essentials held to a single page.

As Minister of Family & Social Services, he viciously attacked the welfare rolls, and succeeded in reducing the number of people on welfare by more than half. It was easily his most successful term. Like Premier Klein, Mike Cardinal was at his best when he had a well-defined agenda.

If welfare reform was his best work, electricity deregulation was his worst. He had little to do with the deregulation policy except during the year it was in his portfolio. One of the most painful episodes I ever witnessed in politics was Mike Cardinal trying to explain the reasons retail electricity prices rose rather than declined after deregulation, as Premier Klein promised. Cardinal didn't have a clue. He simply read the prepared script and walked away.

He and I accidentally happened to be at a cigar night at Normand's Restaurant on Jasper Avenue in Edmonton. This was in the early 1990s when smoking was still acceptable in public places under certain conditions. Seated at a table with Don Hamilton, who would become Ethics Commissioner 10 years later, Mike talked all evening about the wonders of smaller government and less regulation.

"Too much regulation," he said emphatically, "is no good for anybody." He thought that with fewer regulations, some entrepreneur could open a drive-through liquor store.

Mike won the raffle for a box of expensive Cuban cigars that evening and shared the cigars with the entire restaurant.

I saw him angry just once. At the Sidetrack Restaurant one morning, he was at a back table with retired Conservative MLA Glen Clegg and several other members of the Electoral Boundaries Commission who were re-drawing riding boundaries for the 2004 election. It had recommended that Mike's riding be abolished.

As Mike was leaving the Sidetrack, he saw me sitting with another Conservative MLA and came over. Knowing about the Commission's recommendation, I asked him what he was saying to Glen Clegg. "He's not hearing my side," Mike stormed. "I should have brought a two-by-four with me to straighten him out."

67

3

DON GETTY'S LEGACY
A.K.A. Ralph Klein's inheritance

I arrived in Edmonton for the first time on a Sunday afternoon in the September of 1964, stepping off the train at the CPR station on the northwest corner of 109th Street and Jasper Avenue, a kid from small town Ontario hungry for the freedom of a strange city and excitement of university life far from the restrictions of family and relatives.

I had been warned not to expect too much, since Alberta was Canada's Bible Belt and if I didn't listen to the **Back To The Bible Hour** *on Sunday mornings, I would be doomed. I hoped it was a joke. I didn't listen and I survived but the warnings about the Bible Belt were correct.*

The Lord's Day Act ruled. The province shut down on Sunday. Jasper Avenue, the centre of the city, was dead quiet the day I arrived. No restaurant open for breakfast, no newspaper to find a place to live, no movie theatre to kill an afternoon.

Sunday sports were silver collection only. The junior Edmonton Oil Kings were the big draw and I could see them play on a Sunday afternoon by dropping a dime in the bucket at the front door of the Edmonton Gardens.

Bars were separated into two sections: Men's and Ladies & Escorts; a man travelling alone couldn't go into the women's side unless the bartender could be convinced that a lady was expecting him. Restaurants that served liquor were heavily regulated and provincial government inspectors prowled the bars at night to enforce severe liquor laws. Stores were closed by 6 p.m. on weekdays. Students at the University of Alberta behaved themselves. The activist 60s hadn't arrived.

The Bible Belt was alive and thriving.

Alberta, with its windswept open prairie grasslands dotted with oil rigs and cattle ranches and that magnificent horizon-to-horizon sky, was a beautiful place for the Conservative Party in the 1970s. A youthful, dynamic Peter Lougheed and his Conservative Party ended 36 years of Social Credit rule in 1971 with a promise to lead Alberta into the 20th century. The cloud of pervasive religious moralism that had been a core value of the Social Credit Government since 1935 finally began to lift.

The stagnant Bible Belt on the eastern side of the Rocky Mountains, the last whistle stop for the endless human trek heading for beautiful British Columbia, was in the hands of men and women with change on their minds.

The new Alberta began at the most elementary level, starting with the role of government in the affairs of people. Where Social Credit believed that while a certain amount of government was necessary, it should not unnecessarily intrude on the lives of its citizens. Lougheed's Conservatives believed in a big, active government with Lougheed as the all-knowing benevolent godfather.

The new enlightened government grew its bureaucracy and injected itself into the daily life of the province. Oil was $2 a barrel but within a few years the price would explode well into the double digits, giving the Conservatives money to spend. Government buildings began to appear in small communities. Parks were expanded; the Conservatives had ample money to build and operate culture and recreation programs in communities across the province. Horst Schmidt, the Culture, Youth & Recreation Minister, literally had money falling out of his pockets as he toured the province, looking for groups to hand it to.

Retail shops opened in the evenings and eventually on Sunday. Liquor laws were loosened - but ever so carefully to keep the moralists at bay.

Times had changed and would continue to change.

NO CONTROL LIKE TOTAL CONTROL

Lougheed made politics look easy. Tough, determined and loaded with ideas, he kept his thumb on every part of his administration. Careful preparation in all situations was mandatory; central control was absolute; nothing was left to chance.

Early in his reign when he was still a fresh face, Lougheed had time for journalists. Members of the new Conservative Government and Legislature reporters happily played softball together and jointly hosted an annual Christmas party in the Legislature Building's cafeteria - without booze. The coziness lasted until reporters began to ask tough questions. Lougheed respected the media's influence but didn't trust them. When Lougheed didn't appreciate newspaper reports about his administration, he'd personally call the publisher.

Lougheed was so careful of what he said and to whom he said it that he lectured the young people who worked for his ministers about talking politics in strange public places. "You never know who is listening at the table behind you," he warned a gathering at Government House. "They might be reporters, they might be the opposition. They are not your friends."

To construct a barrier between politicians and pesky reporters, the Public Affairs Bureau was set up to centralize and control communications and to put a protective barrier between politicians and the media. The operating principle was that a politician dealt with "good" news and a communications person employed by the Public Affairs Bureau dealt with "bad" news.

Opposition parties? Lougheed ignored the opposition. As opposition leader approaching the 1971 election, he demanded a televised debate. As Premier, he would not be seen in the same room as an opposition politician. He didn't consider the opposition to be part of the government. He instructed ministers not to write internal memos to the opposition because it would acknowledge that they were part of the government. Instead, ministers wrote letters to the opposition, as they would write letters to any citizen who made inquiries.

With larger majorities in 1975 and 1979, the political power of Lougheed's Conservative Government was absolute. The opposition had been decimated. And when Lougheed needed someone to blame, Pierre Trudeau's Liberal Government in Ottawa was handy.

If all this wasn't enough, Albertans were an inattentive lot when it came to politics, as they are today. Half the voting population showed up to vote in an election and quickly forgot politics until the next voting day about four years down the road. What more could a government want? The Conservatives couldn't screw it up if they tried.

Political life in Alberta was very good indeed - if you were a Conservative.

That was the secure, unchallenged Conservative Government Don Getty had been part of, remembered, and expected to find when he returned to politics in 1985.

Getty, a football hero with the Grey Cup champion Edmonton Eskimos in the mid-1950s, broke into politics with Lougheed in 1966 and was a prominent part of the group that won the 1971 election. After two terms in cabinet, Getty got out in 1979 for a life in the relative obscurity of the private sector. Nobody expected to see him in public life again. Everybody was wrong.

Getty was back in the Fall of 1985, a surprise candidate for the leadership when Lougheed announced his retirement. A shy, modest, soft-spoken man, Getty had shown little interest in the cut-and-thrust of competitive politics. The story still persists that Lougheed talked him into coming back because Lougheed didn't trust his legacy and the future of the province in the hands of the mediocre talents seeking the leadership.

Alberta's budget books were in good shape in 1985. Despite the Trudeau Government's National Energy Program, high interest rates and a world-wide recession, the province's energy revenues were still healthy, spending was under control and deficits were rare. Who could blame Getty for expecting that the 1980s would be a natural extension of the 1970s?

In a decade of fiscal luxury thanks to higher oil prices, Albertans had become accustomed to a government with plenty of money and a willingness to spend it. There was so much money flowing into the government's coffers that Lougheed had the money to subsidize every Albertan's mortgage when interest rates soared. Energy revenues were so huge in the 1970s that Lougheed established the Heritage Savings Trust Fund where 30% of energy revenues were parked "for a rainy day." The fund became a badge of honour, a tangible public asset that separated Alberta from the rest of the country. For the first time in a long time, Albertans had bragging rights for something other than the Rocky Mountains and the Edmonton Eskimos.

The oil-rich province was still floating in money in 1985.

GETTY'S CHOICES

Times were about to change again. Getty's return to political life was bad timing, or seen another way, Lougheed's decision to retire was perfect. Within six months of Getty's return, oil prices collapsed and Alberta's energy royalties plunged to $1.9 billion from $4.9 billion, or down 60%. The economy was a mess and getting even worse. Albertans looked for someone to blame: the Liberal Government in Ottawa was always an easy target and this time Albertans had just cause. Pierre Trudeau's National Energy Program was an unwanted intrusion into the energy industry and when the oil patch went bad, Trudeau was easy to blame. The fact is that regardless of any federal programs, the international price of oil collapsed in 1986, creating havoc in the energy industry. Alberta's unemployment rate soared and the real estate market crashed.

Getty faced unpleasant choices: blaming Ottawa was good politics but did nothing for growing unemployment and plunging oil royalties. To avoid a deficit, he had to choose between raising taxes or massive spending cuts, both of which would be unpopular. To balance the budget through spending cuts alone, health, education and infrastructure had to be cut massively, which would be pure political suicide in any province, even Conservative-loving Alberta. Getty reasoned that a balanced budget was desirable but only at a reasonable price. Substandard public services, Getty believed, was a price too high to pay. After a decade of the best in public programs, Albertans wouldn't tolerate anything less from their government. No matter which road he took, annual deficits would persist until oil and natural gas prices recovered. Price recovery took longer than he expected. Energy revenues wouldn't return to 1985 levels for 14 years, long after Getty was gone.

Getty's decision: do a bit of both. Personal taxes were increased modestly, the Heritage Savings Trust Fund was capped, but he refused to radically cut spending for essential public services such as health and education.

Insisting that spending be maintained, Getty made another extraordinary decision. With unemployment rising, the energy-dominated economy teetering, and two Alberta-based banks having collapsed, Getty instructed his cabinet to make money available to private companies in trouble. Executives heading private companies were trooping to his office in hordes, pleading for government money.

Getty couldn't say no. Peter Lougheed had used the government's fiscal power through the Heritage Savings Trust Fund to dabble in the private sector, so why shouldn't he? Getty's popularity and the province would pay dearly for his big, generous naive heart.

Smart politicians learn to handle bad news and the really smart ones learn to turn bad news into an opportunity. Not Getty. He could have taken his fiscal troubles public, explaining what had happened and the impact on the Government of Alberta's ability to pay for public services. Here's a speech he could have given but didn't:

"Oil prices have collapsed around the world. No state and no nation can do anything about that. The impact on our royalties from natural resources will be extreme. Our choice is either to cut our expenditures by almost one-third or accept annual deficits until energy prices recover. Neither will be easy. We are reluctant to cut education or infrastructure spending by anywhere close to that amount. If we cut education, we are jeopardizing the education of our children and their future. We can't do that. Nor can we reduce our spending on the public health system. We will contain spending but with reason and good judgment. Deficits go against my grain but it is the better choice of two difficult options. We ask all Albertans to be patient during these times. I assure you that they won't last.

"We are also concerned about the impact of these tough times on our private sector. Albertans expect their government to help in difficult times. This is one of those times. We can't afford widespread unemployment even if the downturn is temporary. We will make a limited amount of money available for extreme cases to help them through these times.

"These are difficult choices but we believe they are necessary. We ask you to be patient. We have persevered before and we will persevere again."

A plea for public sympathy wasn't in Don Getty. He might have exploited the media to bring Albertans into the game, as Ralph Klein would do in 1993. Had Getty done so, he might have survived politically. He did not try to explain, and he didn't survive.

TROUBLES DEALING WITH THE MEDIA

Don Getty wasn't at ease with the media; he wasn't comfortable around reporters. Although a popular athlete accustomed to media attention and despite a decade in provincial politics, he didn't trust the media any more than Lougheed. He wouldn't spend any more time with reporters than he absolutely had to. He refused to be coached to improve his media skills. Getty wanted nothing to do with manufactured politicians or the flummery of consultants.

He made statements to reporters that he would later regret. When explaining to reporters that wearing seat belts would become mandatory despite its unpopularity in rural Alberta, he said: "I maybe whack my kids, beat my wife, but I never abused a seat belt in my life." The comment lives in Alberta political folklore. He instructed his staff to inform the media that they should not take photographs of him from behind, presumably because he had a bald spot on the back of his head.

The killer was Premier Don Getty photographed on an Edmonton golf course while the Principal Affair was causing no end of public grief. When investors waited for relief from the Conservative Government, the Premier had gone golfing. The optics were terrible.

The affable Gordon Young, Getty's close friend and appointments' secretary, used an innovative software program that listed phone calls to his office and allowed him to input the reason for the call on a database. He scrolled through the list on the screen for me. It went on and on and on. "These are only the business people who want to see the Premier," he said. "It's ridiculous."

Young turned from the computer, rested his hands on his cluttered desk and leaned forward. He looked up at me. "You're a media guy now. You know what they're like. Maybe you can help me."

He was clearly frustrated as he talked about media attitudes towards the Premier. "He doesn't do well with the media," Young said. "They criticize all the time and they think he's not working. I guess they think he's lazy. You can see from this list that he's working hard. I'm thinking that we post his daily schedule in Jeff's office [Press Secretary Geoff Davey] so they can see how hard he works. What do you think?"

I replied, "If you post the schedule, you have to include some detail so reporters know it isn't fluff. You can't just say he's in a meeting and expect them to believe it. The meeting could be in Palm Springs for all they know. If you post the schedule, you will have to say whom he is meeting. It's a two-edged sword. If you do that, you are giving reporters information on the people he is talking to. Which means reporters will start calling people on the schedule asking why they are talking to the Premier and if their company is in trouble. If you do that, no one will come down here anymore. Then you really have trouble.

"Look Gordon," I continued. "If you want to do something to make the Premier more visible, you have to get him out of his office and into the communities. Set up all kinds of appearances. Have him speak to community groups and go to events. He doesn't have to make an announcement; he just has to show up and be seen. He's a politician; spending time with people is good for him. When he isn't out and about, reporters think he isn't working. When he is out, reporters will cover him because they will see him doing something.

"Remember the afternoon when those hordes of school kids were here last June?" I asked, referring to one of those days in the Legislature when school kids are on field trips late in the school year. He looked skeptical. I reminded him, "The rotunda was packed with 700 or 800 school kids. The Premier walked in the front door and those kids went wild, the boys especially. Obviously they knew who he was. What a great photo opportunity for the Premier and every one of those kids who gave him a high five and maybe had their class picture taken with him. They will go home and tell their parents that they met him and that he was a great guy because he spent time with them. Remember that day?"

He nodded, still skeptical.

"Remember what you did?" He didn't.

"You hustled him out of the rotunda before the kids had a chance to meet him. When I asked you later why you did that, you said that Treasury Board was waiting for him and he was already late for the meeting. You took the Premier away from more than 700 excited kids visiting the Legislature and plunked him down in a routine committee meeting somewhere up on the third floor. The rotunda was filled with votes because these kids would say good things to their parents about him. There are no votes in Treasury Board."

Young shrugged. "The Premier won't be manufactured. He doesn't want consultants to tell him what to do. We offered to get advice but he won't have any of it. Besides, there's too much to do here."

"You shouldn't be concerned about what reporters think," I said. "They will think what they will think and you can't do anything about that. I'm in the media now and I don't give a damn if the Premier is working hard. A Premier is supposed to work hard. You might spend more time thinking about the people out there and how you can influence what they think."

INVESTMENTS TURN INTO DISASTERS

Times were tough but Getty put his head down and ploughed ahead. Although energy revenues remained low, Getty still managed to cut the $4 billion deficit in 1986 by more than half in 1987 and held it at that level for four years. Then it all began to unravel.

Despite generous government money, private companies began to fail, one after another and their failures and lost government money were strung out across the front pages of the province's newspapers. As the budget deficit mounted, the bad news kept coming. And coming. And coming ...

NovAtel:

When the Government of Alberta privatized Alberta Government Telephones (AGT), a crown corporation, in 1989, the prospectus included inaccurate, overly-optimistic profit projections for AGT-owned NovAtel, a high-risk technology company in the cellular phone business in Canada and the United States. To save the privatization effort, the Getty Government promised to buy NovAtel if no other buyer could be found.

To make a long story short, the Getty Government bought NovAtel for $42.5 million and eventually took a $556 million hit. When Treasurer Dick Johnston stood up in the Legislative Assembly to announce the losses, the place was uncharacteristically silent. Ray Martin, then leader of the New Democrats, broke the silence with a soft whistle, the kind of whistle that describes an event well beyond expectations. In the silent chamber, Martin's whistle sounded like a tornado. No one would accept responsibility for the money, little of which was recovered.

Gainer's:

In the midst of a worsening provincial economy in 1986, the Getty Government intervened in the bitter strike at the Gainer's plant in northeast Edmonton. Peter

Pocklington, owner of the Edmonton Oilers hockey team, owned the plant. Pocklington was a smart but ruthless businessman. He was smart enough to know that if he held out long enough, the provincial government would move in and take over a plant that was losing money and expected to continue to lose money. The strike, so violent that newspapers from across the country sent reporters to cover it, went on for months. Alberta's labour laws took a national beating.

Unable to help negotiate a settlement, the Getty Government simply moved in and took it over. Gainer's employed about 1,200 people and was crucial to the hog farming business in northern Alberta. Treasurer Dick Johnston was so full of himself after the takeover that he mused that Gainer's would become profitable and might even be taken public and listed on the Toronto Stock Exchange. Eventually, the Getty Government paid Burns Foods to take over the plant and swallowed over $200 million in losses. Like NovAtel, no one accepted responsibility.

Later, in 1998 during a court case launched by Peter Pocklington, Johnston had finally admitted that the government-owned Alberta Treasury Branches were used to funnel government money to Pocklington so the money wouldn't show up in government accounts. Johnston continually denied it - until he was under oath in court. No apologies, no acknowledgment of mistakes or bad decisions, no regrets.

MPI:

Mortgage Properties Inc., a wholly-owned subsidiary of the government-owned Alberta Mortgage & Housing Corporation (AMHC), was set up in 1991 to sell its considerable real estate assets. At the peak of the energy boom in 1975, the Lougheed Government began to buy properties to increase rental units for the huge numbers of people flocking to the province where the vacancy rate was under 1%. MPI eventually paid over $5 billion for land and properties. When the boom went bust, land values plummeted and there were no tenants for the rental properties. The Government of Alberta got rid of everything and took losses of almost $900 million, but not before allegations that the independent Board of Directors appointed by the Getty Government was in a conflict of interest and padding the pockets of friends and relatives through exorbitant fees and contracts.

Other loan guarantees and investments:

After Don Getty retired in 1992, members of his cabinet who sought re-election in

1993 - including Ralph Klein - all pleaded ignorance at the extent of the billions in loan guarantees. How could they not know about: $1.14 million to Edmonton Space & Science Foundation; $900,000 to Integrated Technologies International Inc.; $103 million to Magnesium Company of Canada to build a plant in southern Alberta; $120 million to Millar Western Pulp of Whitecourt (government losses in this outfit eventually ran up to $272 million); a $25 million interest-free loan to Pratt & Whitney to set up a manufacturing plant in Lethbridge; a $726,000 loan guarantee to the North Saskatchewan Riverboat Company to build a tourist attraction on the North Saskatchewan River in Edmonton; $20 million for Fletcher's Fine Foods of Red Deer to expand its operations into the U.S.; almost $400 million in the Lloydminster Heavy Oil Upgrader; $205 million for Pacific Western Airlines; $226 million for Weldwood Plywood; and $205 million for Alberta Newsprint.

There were others. Once the government gave to one, others expected equal treatment. The line simply didn't end. In 1994, the single-line entries of loan guarantees and investments required two full pages in the budget. How much did it all cost in the end? Rough estimate: $5 billion. And Getty and Dick Johnston were the only members of cabinet to know?

Swan Hills Waste Treatment Plant:
The Klein Government, despite its high-faluting rhetoric of fiscal rectitude and ideological purity, was sucked in too.

Swan Hills opened in 1987 to burn hazardous waste. Year after year, it lost money. With their desire to get rid of all such investments, the Klein Government tried to sell it, but not before they spun that the plant could make money. In October 1994, Environment Minister Brian Evans, when asked whether the plant could become another sinkhole like NovAtel, said the end of losses was in sight. After $70 million in losses in three years, Evans insisted the plant could be profitable in six years under existing conditions but faster if out-of-province waste was allowed to be burned. His statement proved that the Klein Government was no better at assessing private business than the Getty Government. Swan Hills was a complex, tangled mess for 13 years. When the province finally got out of it in 2000, the losses were in the $700 million range.

Unfortunately, more was coming. The Principal Group went under in 1987 and took millions of investors' money with it. A public inquiry solved very little except to show that the Conservative Governments under both Lougheed and Getty were less than diligent in regulating it. By 1997, the Conservative Government paid out over $130 million for failing to protect investors.

As usual, no one was responsible - but Connie Osterman, a tough-talking Conservative MLA from Central Alberta who headed a department responsible for regulating financial companies, was fired in 1992. She claimed she quit but some of us know better. The lady took a hit for the boys and returned to the family farm, rarely to be heard from again. She teased that she would write a book about the Principal Affair one day, but after a few phone calls from her old political chums, she changed her mind.

BUDGET ESTIMATES THAT GO OFF THE RAILS

Tall, articulate and urbane, Dick Johnston had risen from a dreary accountant's desk in Lethbridge to Lougheed's cabinet by being elected in the right place at the right time. First, he got the Municipal Affairs portfolio, then the heady Federal & Intergovernmental Affairs portfolio after the 1979 election where he was in the inner circle of Alberta's constitutional battles with the federal Liberal Government led by Pierre Trudeau.

Although Lougheed did all the talking about constitutional issues, Johnston watched with starry eyes at how far he had risen and the power he had access to. So he couldn't hide his disappointment at being handed the Advanced Education portfolio after the 1982 election. It was a demotion. He tried to put on a happy face when his politically ambitious assistant in Federal & Intergovernmental Affairs, Nancy Betkowski, left her demoted position in Advanced Education to join Provincial Treasurer Lou Hyndman's staff. Nonetheless, Johnston loved the power of a minister's office. "You tell civil servants what to do," he told me. "And if they don't do what they're told, you throw it back at them and tell them to do it again and again until they do it right."

In one of those ironies of politics, Johnston was appointed as Provincial Treasurer when Lou Hyndman retired in 1985. Although engaging and gregarious personally, Johnston's arrogance as Provincial Treasurer would come to symbolize the public attitude towards the Getty Government. Where Getty was uncomfortable with the media, Johnston enjoyed toying with them. In the Legislative Assembly, he rarely answered the question asked, preferring to respond with whatever he wanted to say that day. When a New Democrat asked a detailed question about another of the Getty Government's investment failures, Johnston rose in the House and said condescendingly: "As usual, the honorable member has his facts wrong. Socialists usually do." And Johnston went on to talk about something completely different.

Dick Johnston, an accountant, had his own ideas on writing budgets. He told only partial stories - his budgets covered only the operating budget and not much of capital spending. The Heritage Savings Trust Fund was covered in a separate account and published in a separate book. The Auditor General criticized him for not following GAAP - Generally Accepted Accounting Principles. Johnston brushed him off, claiming that his books were perfectly acceptable.

The budget estimates further eroded Johnston's already shaky credibility. In a resource-based economy where about 20% of all revenues vary with the international price of crude oil and natural gas, variations in revenues are expected. In years when the price fluctuates wildly, resource revenues are impossible to predict with any reliability. Prices in the late 1980s did not swing wildly but Johnston's bottom line did. After all the bad investments, he didn't need other hits to his credibility. When he forecast a balanced budget in 1990 and ended up with a $2 billion deficit, the little credibility he had left was gone.

The good time Don Getty expected when he returned to political life in 1985 was anything but a good time. A public explanation from Getty would have been welcomed and Getty almost provided one. A book - *Don Getty: All Canadian* by Peter Tadman, one of Getty's communications staff - might have provided it. It wasn't published. Those who saw the rough drafts say Getty spent many pages blaming the media for his troubles.

At the end of the day, neither the media nor his government's spending did Getty in. Statistically, Getty and Johnston ran a conservative fiscal administration. In seven budgets, spending increased a total of 24%, or an average of about 3% a year, well under the inflation rate. The problem: revenues increased just 7% - over seven years, or an average of 1% a year. No matter what Jim Dinning claimed later, spending was not a problem, revenues were.

Getty and Johnston had been doomed by the seemingly endless failed investments that appeared in the newspapers week after week and Getty's inability to explain himself.

While voters may have trouble comprehending billions of dollars, they have no trouble understanding good money - taxpayers' money - thrown after bad money. Voters had no trouble comprehending the anguish of seeing investors' money lost because the provincial government didn't regulate the Principal Group. By the time the Code Inquiry into the Principal Group was settled, Getty's poll numbers were in the 20s.

SELECTIVE AMNESIA: NOBODY KNEW WHAT WAS GOING ON

Looking back at this sordid business, it is astonishing that Albertans would elect another Conservative Government with so many of the same people who were directly responsible for failed investments and the massive debt. By comparison, the sponsorship scandal that cost Paul Martin and the federal Liberal Party the election in 2006 was peanuts. Consider that seven of Ralph Klein's first cabinet - seven of 18 members - had sat in Getty's last cabinet for three years: Premier Klein as Environment Minister, Treasurer Jim Dinning as Education Minister, Municipal Affairs Minister Steve West as Recreation & Parks Minister, Economic Development Minister Ken Kowalski as Public Works Minister, Justice Minister Ken Rostad as Attorney General, Health Minister Shirley McClellan as Associate Minister of Agriculture, and Transportation Minister Peter Trynchy as Occupational Health & Safety Minister. Klein's organizer and advisor Peter Elzinga had been Economic Development Minister.

While all of these men and women denied involvement or responsibility for any part of the mess, common sense dictates that they knew but remained silent. How can anyone sit in cabinet week after week and not know what's happening?

Ignorance is no excuse - although Klein would use ignorance as an excuse again when his wife's investments in MultiCorp hit the media years later. A simple reading of annual budgets should have been enough for all these fiscal conservatives who talked so fervently of spending only what you earn and not a nickel more, who talk endlessly of ridding government of involvement in the private sector. No one in cabinet demanded answers. All sat back and meekly went along. Apparently, they didn't want to know.

Curiously, after Klein won the Conservative leadership and became the province's Premier, he and his cabinet began referring to the Getty Government as "the previous government", as if Getty had led a different political party defeated in the election.

Don Getty silently took the abuse from people who once sat in his cabinet but his Treasurer wasn't as reluctant. In March 1994, when Klein and Dinning were ranting about the mess that Getty and Johnston had left them with - bad investments in Millar Western and Gainer's - Dick Johnston told CBC radio in Calgary that he took notes on what and when he told cabinet about Gainer's and other loan guarantees. Klein and his front bench suddenly went silent.

In the 1993 provincial general election, voters decided that if these people made the mess, they should clean it up - and gave the Conservatives another term. And clean it up they did. But not until they dipped into public money twice more - $50 million for Canadian Airlines in 1993 and a $100 million loan extension for the company running the Swan Hills Waste Treatment Plant in 1994.

MEDIA AS VILLAIN - AGAIN

In April 1997, I was leaning against the wall near the bar at a hotel in Edmonton, watching politics as usual in a room filled with political people. This is what newsletter publishers do best: observe, make notes and report to readers.

The occasion: a farewell party for Oryssia Lennie, a well-known provincial government deputy minister who had taken a job with the federal government. Don Getty walked through the doors accompanied by Gordon Young, his close friend and assistant. Young, whom Getty appointed to Alberta's Hong Kong office, was one of the early victims of Klein's purge of trade offices.

Klein and his security man were already in the room. When Getty saw him, he purposefully strode over to him. Getty's face said he had something on his mind. They met about 10 feet from where I was standing. I held my breath. It all happened so fast that few in the room noticed.

The pair were a physical anomaly. Getty is imposing, broad and well over 6 feet. He played pro football and looked as if he could still play. As gentle as the man is off the field, he wasn't afraid to use his size to advantage. At a critical constitutional meeting in the 1980s, Prime Minister Brian Mulroney and the Premiers were trying to hammer out a new constitution. At one point, Newfoundland Premier Clyde Wells threw up his hands in frustration and said that as far as

Newfoundland was concerned, the meeting was over. Getty blocked Wells' exit. Wells reconsidered his situation, returned to his seat and the negotiations continued.

A man so imposing sees a lot of smaller men. Getty was looking down at Ralph Klein, the short, round popular former mayor of Calgary whom he had personally invited into the Conservative Party and into his cabinet.

The short, round popular former mayor of Calgary had not been saying nice things about his former boss. He told reporters how the "previous administration" was responsible for all those business losses including over $100 million for the Millar Western pulp mill in Whitecourt. Denying all responsibility despite being part of Getty's cabinet for three years, Klein dumped the business losses back into his former boss's lap as his ministers had been doing for months, and getting away with it. Everything was the fault of "the previous government." Of the hundreds of one-liners Klein used to entertain journalists, the one that still lives is "That was then, this is now." It is the classic "blame the other guy" routine.

Getty leaned down and asked Klein, face to face, why he was still blaming him. He was very serious. The instant response was classic Klein: he blamed the media for creating and perpetuating the story. Getty always had a tough time with the media. Media as villain once again struck home.

Surprisingly, Getty nodded his agreement. Both men reached for a drink. Klein asked for red wine.

PEOPLE I MET IN POLITICS

DICK JOHNSTON

D ick Johnston was two different people. In private, he was engaging, a gifted conversationalist, and an intellectual with a wonderful sense of humour. He was a man with whom you could have an intelligent conversation lasting for hours, covering topics ranging from the price of oil to the history of Fort McLeod to current hit movies.

But public politics brought out the demon in him and he often appeared arrogant and condescending. Worse, while he was tearing a strip off an opposition MLA in the Legislative Assembly, he often wore a maddening smirk on his face.

Dick was one of the best at deflecting difficult questions from the opposition. After an attack from an opposition MLA, his typical response went something like this: "As usual, the honorable member has his facts wrong, as socialists usually do. Now here's the story …" - and he would go on to talk about whatever he wanted, completely ignoring the question.

Unfortunately, I saw too little of the private side and too much of the political side. Either way, Dick Johnston was hardly the face of an accountant from

Lethbridge.

He was Don Getty's Provincial Treasurer at one of the worst times in Alberta's history. In 1985, he walked into a fiscal disaster brought about by the sudden collapse of oil prices. The government's share of royalties tumbled to $1.9 billion from $4.9 billion almost overnight. The $3 billion difference was 25% of total revenues.

Dick was told to handle the unfolding budget disaster. He did - he brought in a series of taxes, held the line on spending as he would for the next six years, and tried to make it all look better than it was. In his optimism, he once projected a balanced budget that turned out to be a deficit of a few billion. He ran eight straight deficits, earning himself the title "Deficit Dick" even though his birth name was Archibald.

He died in 2003 in the worst way - far from home, in a Paris hospital after collapsing on the street. He was 63, physically fit, and appeared to be in the best of health.

I saw him last in the Hub book store in Old Strathcona on Edmonton's south side. Back in the private sector, he was cordial, engaging Dick Johnston. We talked for almost an hour about life after politics and what we were doing with our lives. He said he was looking at setting up his own firm to counsel international investors.

I slipped in a political question on a matter that intrigued me: "Did you actually keep notes on every cabinet discussion?" I was referring to his comments to CBC radio in 1994 that he kept notes on what he told cabinet. He was angered by Klein claiming he didn't know that Getty was pouring money into private sector companies and the blame should go to Getty and Johnston. Dick warned that if the rhetoric continued, he would make his notes public.

He nodded affirmatively to my question. "I was ready to release them," he said.

4

APATHY
THE POLITICS OF KEEPING PEOPLE IGNORANT

The manifest from Ellis Island reports that my father, Alfredo Vivone, age 16, and his brother, Francesco, age 10, arrived in the Port of New York aboard the Pesaro on May 20, 1920.

They had come from war-torn Italy and they traveled alone. The boys would have passed the Statue of Liberty and when I watch **The Godfather** *movie, I imagine the rapturous look on their faces when they saw it for the first time and knew they were finally in the new world.*

The brothers settled in Northern Ontario. My father married and he and my mother, possessing only a driving ambition to be safe and financially secure, went into the restaurant business. Both were unschooled immigrants from Europe (they called it 'the old country') who could hardly believe their luck to be citizens of Canada. They opened their first restaurant in 1941 and named it the D-Day. Their second restaurant, much larger, was named the Liberty. Such was their love for their new home.

My father offered his name for town council when I was 10. On election day, he counted his friends and told me he would get 75 votes in our community of 2,000. He got 77 and finished dead last but it didn't bother him. My father spent weeks trying to find out who cast the other two votes for him.

He said that Canada was a great country because an unschooled immigrant like himself was able to run for public office. He insisted that the ballot was the most powerful weapon on earth. Voting, he said, is every person's right. Only fools don't vote. People should vote, he told me, because what kind of fool pays taxes but doesn't care who spends the money or how.

My father had never been to Alberta.

I f you believe in the reliability of public opinion polls, the 2008 election in Alberta promised to be the first competitive one in 15 years. The Conservatives, in power since 1971, had dumped the once revered Ralph Klein and replaced him with 57-year-old Ed Stelmach, a political unknown despite 15 years in the Legislative Assembly and three cabinet posts.

I covered the Legislature for 19 years as publisher of *Insight into Government* newsletter. I knew all the key political players. Ed Stelmach wasn't one of them. Nothing in his performance in three cabinet portfolios suggested a budding Premier. He wasn't noticed; he was only marginally interesting.

My newsletter readership, which covered the province, didn't know him either. In April 2005, *Insight into Government* asked its readers who they thought could win the coming Conservative leadership race. Jim Dinning, a Provincial Treasurer who retired in 1997, was the clear winner; Ed Stelmach was a distant seventh. Stelmach hadn't been discovered in his own province.

In his first months as Premier of Alberta, Stelmach showed little to indicate that he would end the unfocused, drifting regime inherited from Ralph Klein.

An election was looming. Conservative poll numbers weren't promising. One poll reported that the party's support had plunged to an unusually low 35%. Other polls suggested that a large percentage of voters were unhappy with the general state of public affairs in Alberta. Conservatives hadn't seen such poll numbers since the last days of Don Getty.

Maybe, just maybe, Albertans were paying attention. Economic growth since the explosion in oilsands investment began 10 years earlier brought thousands of new people to Alberta, perhaps people with different ideas and an interest in how they are governed. If the Liberals under leader Kevin Taft walked and talked like an alternative, the election might be that rarest of Alberta phenomenon: an election with serious choices, a competitive election generating widespread interest in politics.

The election outcome was, as they say, a shocker. The Conservatives, despite a leader who doused rather than inflamed passions, won 72 of 83 seats. That was the first shock. The second, just 41% of the eligible voters turned out to exercise their civic responsibility. Reversed, almost 60% did something else on election day, most likely shopping or working. Apathy plagued the Liberal vote as well. With a rare opportunity to cash in on apathy amongst Conservatives, the Liberals couldn't get their vote out either. The Liberal vote dropped for the fifth consecutive election.

The 2008 election turnout was one of the most blatant displays of voter irresponsibility in Canadian history. The shock reverberated right into the Legislature Building where Premier Stelmach with his first mandate mused that one day he might appoint a commission to examine why so few Albertans voted.

VOTER APATHY: THY NAME IS ALBERTA

If you were shocked too, you don't know Alberta's political history. Three years earlier, in 2004, 44.7% voted, the lowest turnout in Albert's history to that point. In the three previous elections, the average turnout was 50%. Political apathy had become so Albertan.

Considered in isolation, you might think those numbers are not so bad. When compared to Alberta's western neighbours, the numbers are pathetic. The comparisons tell a devastating story of consistent, widespread political apathy.

In Saskatchewan, five of the last nine elections saw turnouts over 80%. Saskatchewan's lowest voter turnout in that period rivaled Alberta's highest.

Manitoba? In three of the last four elections, the turnout was higher than Alberta's. In the two most recent elections, the spread was over 20 points.

British Columbia puts Alberta to shame. In all six elections since 1983, the lowest turnout in British Columbia was higher than the single highest turnout in Alberta in that period.

Here's the kicker. More Albertans vote in federal elections than in provincial elections. In three provincial elections since 2000, Alberta's average turnout is 46%. In federal elections in the same period, Alberta's average is 60%.

Albertans may be partial to federal politics but they still turn out in smaller numbers than the rest of Canada. In every one of the last five federal elections, the Alberta turnout has been lower than the average national turnout.

Even when a provincial election dealt with a significant issue of public concern, Albertans weren't interested. In 1982, Conservative Premier Peter Lougheed called a snap election, not entirely to take advantage of a weak opposition, but to demonstrate to Pierre Trudeau's Liberal Government that Albertans were solidly behind Lougheed's opposition to the National Energy Program (NEP). The NEP, Lougheed claimed, threatened Albertans' exclusive ownership of natural resources and would surely send the province into recession.

Were Albertans as angry as Lougheed? Nope. Albertans were so appalled by the NEP that just 66% showed up to voice their displeasure. In retrospect, Lougheed should have been pleased. It was Alberta's highest voter turnout in a provincial election since the 72% turnout in 1971 to elect the province's first Conservative Government.

If an economic recession brings out the anger in voters, Alberta was an exception. In 1989, the province was mired in a deep recession and unemployment was rampant. Did Albertans blame Don Getty's Conservative Government? No. Only 53% voted and gave the Conservatives yet another large majority. Albertans must have thought that the recession was an accident or caused by the federal government that, coincidentally, was led by Brian Mulroney's Conservatives.

ENERGY MAKES ALBERTA DIFFERENT

In many respects, Albertans are like people everywhere in Canada. They come in all sizes, shapes and attitudes. They want to work, live well, and raise their families in safe communities. Living in a participatory democracy, they should care about the people who make the rules under which they live.

Alberta has become an urban province. The majority live in rapidly-growing cities. They are becoming better educated and more global in their outlook. Farms and the rural way of life are declining. The stereotyped image of the ball cap and half-ton truck with a rifle hung across the back window applies only to a small minority in Alberta, as it does in all western provinces.

The energy industry makes Albertans different. With a ready-made economy that requires wealth exploitation rather than wealth creation, Albertans believe they are exceptional but it is the kind of exceptionalism that comes with money. They believe they are more successful entrepreneurs, more innovative in business and that if other provinces adopted the same conservative practices, they too would be successful. Calgary writer Aritha van Herk wrote a bestseller - *Mavericks: An Incorrigible History Of Alberta* - promoting the myth of a maverick people that some Albertans believe.

The kind of exceptionalism that exists in Alberta comes solely from the fact that Alberta is an energy province, heavily reliant on oil and natural gas. Without abundant energy resources, Alberta's economy is no better than any other province where wealth must be created. When Alberta's energy sector went into the tank in the late 1980s, entrepreneurial Albertans didn't create new businesses to fit changing circumstances. The economy recovered only when a huge royalty subsidy generated massive investment in the oil sands.

Myths and stereotypes aside, more than half of the province is united in one facet - they don't vote. Voters chose to abstain when the government was spendthrift, when it was thrifty, and when it was nonchalant. Even an examination of political party platforms doesn't tell us what Albertans are thinking. They voted Conservative no matter where the party stood, or whether it stood for anything at all. Klein promised "more of the same" in three straight elections, delivered a different agenda each time, and won big each time. The first time, in 1997, he had just slashed public programs by about 20%. The second time, in 2001, he had gone on a spending spree. The third time, the government he led was aimless. Did anyone know what "more of the same" meant? The more Klein promised nothing, the more people didn't vote. Make sense? Not to me.

Are times so good that people don't care about anything except themselves and greater personal wealth thanks to a booming economy and rising house prices? Are Albertans too preoccupied with themselves to think about politics?

VOTER INFORMATION IS SCARCE, EVEN WHEN YOU ARE LOOKING FOR IT

Public research into the voting characteristics of the citizens of Alberta is scarce. The Elections Alberta website offers a report of "Voters and non-voters" by Leger Marketing. It attempts to assess why so many Albertans didn't vote in the 2008 election. Among the reasons: 69% of non-voters said they were "distracted" or "dissociated". The report also said that of the 1200 respondents, 76% said they voted. The actual number was 41%.

Academics and political consultants produce little political analysis on voter attitudes. Finding the number of people who vote in each riding and their polling station is as sophisticated as it gets. We don't know who votes by sex, age, marital status, occupation or income. There is little valid research into why individual Albertans vote - or don't vote.

In the 2008 Presidential election in the United States, newspapers reported an astonishing range of voter information from the percentage of whites who voted Democrat to the number of young people who voted in advance polls.

Alberta has no independent research organization to analyze political policy or the budgets, research policy history and trends, or critically examine the current government's direction. Where can you get an independent analysis of the impact of various government policies including provincial tax policy, either personal income tax or corporate taxes? Where can you get an independent analysis of the impact of energy policy on the province's economy? Where can you get an independent analysis of handouts to the agriculture sector? Where can you get independent, accurate information on how the province's demographics are changing or how the government is reacting? Where can you get sensible information on the impact of a growing population on crime and welfare?

The provincial government gave up what little independent public research it had when it dropped the Alberta Bureau of Statistics early in Klein's first term.

Without adequate research, how can political parties - or anyone else for that matter - develop strategies to encourage people to vote?

WHY NOT CONSIDER AN ALTERNATIVE?

Albertans are terribly ignorant of the workings of their provincial government. What Albertans know about their provincial government is gleaned from television and the newspapers, and that isn't nearly enough. Alberta's mass media report a lot of what politicians say and little of what they do. Television ignores political activity - period. Television carries little editorial comment and few political panel debates. Telecasting of the Legislative Assembly is minimal. Newspapers are no better: they pay scant attention to the work of the Legislative Assembly and the policies that come out of it.

Since Albertans aren't aware of political issues as they develop and rarely hear the issues debated, how do they know what is happening?

Other trends are at work, none of which are any more sensible. Locked minds, for example. In recent elections, people have told me that they have always voted Conservative and they will always vote Conservative because, well, because they like the Conservative leader. And when they don't like a Conservative leader? Then they don't vote at all. That was the case with Ralph Klein in the 2004 election and Ed Stelmach in the 2008 election where thousands of Conservative supporters stayed home because they were ambivalent about the leader.

In 2004, Ralph Klein was a shadow of himself and had long exhausted his interest in governing. Rather than support an alternative, thousands of Albertans stayed home leaving the fate of their government to a minority that cared. Same in 2008: rather than vote for someone other than the uninspiring new Conservative leader, even more voters stayed home.

In seminars and speaking engagements around the province, I listened to voter after voter complain about the Conservative Government. They complained throughout the government's term. Yet inexplicably, on election day, they stayed home.

Why not vote for another party? Because a majority of Albertans don't like or trust the Liberal alternative, no matter who they are or what they stand for. The fact that Alberta hasn't elected a Liberal Government for 80 years doesn't matter; plain and simple, the majority of people in Alberta won't vote Liberal. Pierre Trudeau and the National Energy Program can't be blamed for everything; Albertans didn't elect Liberals long before Trudeau arrived in Ottawa. Ralph Klein understood that sentiment when he first considered provincial politics in the early 1980s. He flirted with the Liberals but joined the Conservatives not only because Don Getty asked him but because he knew that the National Energy Program cinched it. Liberals will never win in Alberta, either federally or provincially.

Rightly or wrongly, federal Liberals in Ottawa are seen to be connected to provincial Liberals in Edmonton. A Liberal in Alberta is like a Liberal in Ottawa, right? Then why isn't a Conservative in Alberta like a Conservative in Ottawa? The ethical mess that became Brian Mulroney's Conservative Government in Ottawa didn't automatically become a problem for Alberta's Conservative Government so why should the policies of Pierre Trudeau's Liberals be a problem for Alberta's Liberal Party?

DON'T WORRY, BE HAPPY. RALPH'S IN CHARGE

If Albertans have a natural disinclination towards politics, the Conservative Party did nothing to dispel it. Under Ralph Klein, the dumbing down of Alberta's politics accelerated.

As Premier, Klein took the public out of public policy. I believe that Klein's greatest political accomplishment was to convince Albertans that they didn't have to think about their government between elections, they didn't have to worry about deeds and misdeeds in the Legislature, and that he could be trusted to do the right thing. He mocked what he called "Dome disease", referring to politicians who spend more time in their Legislature offices than with voters. His remedy to "Dome disease" was to get out and stay out of the Legislature Building (a.k.a. the Dome) as much as possible.

What was going on under the Dome when Klein wasn't in the building, which was most of the time? Few asked. In the elections of 1997, 2001 and 2004, Klein didn't bother to offer a plan: just more of the same, as he promised not once but three times. Boredom is good. When something under the Dome went bad, Klein made it right. He acted as an ombudsman to his own administration. Who was watching Ralph? Has governing ever appeared to be so chaotic?

Meanwhile, under the Dome, the policy-making process was locked down, safe from the prying eyes of the opposition and from the public. Klein's administration did in public only what it absolutely had to, which is sit in the Legislative Assembly long enough to make its style of abbreviated governing appear to be legitimate. Legislation was always developed in the privacy of the Conservative caucus, either at Government House on the grounds of the Royal Alberta Museum or on the 5th floor of the Legislature Building. Caucus made the key decisions and never explained to anyone how or why the decisions were made, or the criteria or information they used.

The Legislative Assembly was an exercise in minimalism. Ministers in the Klein Government - they were the people on the government side who did most of the talking - treated the Assembly as a necessary legality that had to be honored. They wanted Legislative sessions to start as late as possible and end as early as possible. Sitting days were amongst the lowest number in the country. Right-wing ministers such as Stockwell Day and Steve West preferred the governing system in Montana where the State Legislature sits 90 days every second year.

Premier Klein sat in the Assembly only for the brief daily Question Period. He marched out when the real business of governing began. Watching him week after week, I thought about Chief Deputy Minister Jack Davis' comment. When I asked Davis whether Klein paid attention to the workings of government, Davis said Klein knew "only about 10% of what was going on in the Legislature but you have to believe that it is the most important 10%." In 2009, in an interview with *Alberta Views* magazine, Klein said, "in politics, there is very little time to consider policy."

When bills were introduced in the Assembly, their purpose and descriptions were brief. I remember one case where Stockwell Day, as Provincial Treasurer, introduced a bill for Second Reading with a single sentence - that the bill was ready for Second Reading - and promptly sat down. He didn't say a word about the bill's purpose or contents. When I asked him about it later, Day was surprised that anyone noticed. "I wanted to hear what the opposition said first," he told me. Day was proposing a bill that was written by his department supposedly under political direction and if anyone could accurately describe the bill, it should be him. The opposition can only react to what the minister offered and their own interpretation of the bill. It was another blatant disregard for the Legislative Assembly. I suspected that Day, not the most intellectual of ministers, didn't understand the bill, which dealt with a complex securities law, and didn't want to embarrass himself with lame attempts to explain it.

Government bills routinely whipped through the Assembly without a Conservative MLA - other than the minister proposing the bill - saying a word. How are voters supposed to know what their MLA contributed to the bill, or what the MLA thought about it? On those rare occasions where MLAs did talk, they read from notes written by researchers employed by the government.

Under the Dome, privacy reigned. The point was to minimize controversy and differences of opinion. No controversy meant no fodder for a media that feasts on controversy.

So provincial politics were all about Ralph, Ralph, Ralph. No others mattered, not his cabinet ministers who, like Ed Stelmach, worked in anonymity for years. Klein so dominated the public face of politics that opposition parties were marginalized to the point that no one paid attention to them.

Klein liked it that way. He believed his personal popularity was unassailable, that the public had enormous tolerance for his way of doing things. As long as he could keep the media spotlight on himself and away from his competitors and the work of the Legislative Assembly, he could govern as long as he could keep his own party happy. It is instructive that Klein's own party tired of him long before voters did.

No easy answers to public ignorance and apathy

Can voters be led to the trough and made to drink? Can they be encouraged to do nothing more than cast a ballot every four years? How do you get people to do something they don't want to do if there is no immediate reward?

There is no single, easy answer. No single, sudden change in anything done in Alberta will suddenly turn voters on to politics. Some commentators, such as conservative columnist Lorne Gunter of the *Edmonton Journal*, argue that citizens have the right not to vote. That's classic Conservatism, which can be defined by three words: me, me, me. Loosely translated, individual freedom means I have a right to do, or not to do, as I please. In other words, who cares who writes laws? Taken to its logical extreme, no one has to vote. Ignorance rules.

If Klein with his anti-Dome attitude isn't writing laws as he was paid to do, who is? Perhaps these anonymous lawmakers could use help because the populist Premier with his finger on the public pulse isn't around. The Legislature's doors can be opened and the air can be cleared. Public business must be done in public.

Political change too often arrives last in Alberta. Politically the province is a virtual banana republic when it comes to change. Resisting change until it can no longer be avoided is very Albertan. The province was the last to make seat belts mandatory, the last to bring in an access to information law, and one of the last to write a law governing conflict of interest for politicians and public servants. The access to information and conflict of interest laws are among the weakest in the country.

Alberta ignores current political thought. Its laws governing political finances haven't been looked at in decades. The mechanism to elect governments has been studied in other provinces but Alberta has paid little attention and certainly won't put its own mechanism under a public microscope.

The Conservative Government with its dominating rural caucus likes things they way they are.

Television

Throughout the rest of Canada and in the United States, national, provincial and state governments televise legislative proceedings. The degree of broadcast time varies but most televise not only debates on new laws but committee meetings as well. Some have separate television channels specifically to carry Legislature debate so citizens can watch whenever they want.

Not so in Alberta. At its height, one local station televised Question Period and rebroadcast it late in the evening. The annual budget speech and throne speech were also telecast. Nothing else. The excuses: telecasting costs money, no one watches anyway, and when cameras are rolling in the Assembly, politicians might grandstand. A better reason to limit television: the opposition gets public exposure. If citizens see that their government can be legitimately challenged in the Legislative Assembly, they might get the novel idea that it's okay for them to do the same.

In their cost-cutting frenzy in 1993 and 1994, the Klein Government threw out the baby with the bath water. The nightly television re-broadcast of Question Period was cancelled. Citizens wanting to watch Question Period must take the time from work in the afternoon four days a week. How many are able to do that?

Citizens have the right to watch what their government does. Minimum, television coverage should be increased to include a Question Period re-broadcast in the evenings. Committee meetings and debate on prominent bills should also be televised. What's the harm in an educated electorate?

Thankfully, in recent years, the Legislative Assembly Office has made Legislative Assembly proceedings and some committee meetings available online.

Citizen participation

Under Premier Klein, voters views weren't taken seriously until election day.

Public consultations were a common feature under Klein but when the hearings were over and the reports were taken back to the Legislature Building, they promptly disappeared in a maze of public service committees. In time, something might change - maybe. More often, the reports were shelved and MLAs congratulated themselves on connecting with their communities.

Citizen participation was thought to be good at the beginning of the Klein Revolution in 1993, but disappeared quickly when the government lost control. Regional health authorities are a prime example. At the beginning, the Klein Government talked of the wisdom of locally-elected boards to manage local public health services. It works in education, why not in health?

Regional health authorities (RHAs) based on the Saskatchewan model were set up. As a first step, the Klein Government appointed members to each of their boards. When RHAs were operational, they would be set free with their own locally-elected boards.

A plan that appeared to be so promising in theory turned out to be not so promising in practice. People were elected whom the government didn't like to see get public attention: people with a legitimate platform who publicly challenged the government's health policies. Elections were soon cancelled and every RHA board member was a government appointment again.

Community lottery boards were set up to distribute money from the rapidly-growing provincial Lottery Fund to local organizations. The idea for community lottery boards originated in a report written by Conservative MLA Judy Gordon, arguably the Klein Government's foremost expert on gaming policy. Following her report, community lottery board members were appointed. Board members also announced the good news when a local organization was given a provincial government grant. It worked well - until Conservative MLAs started to complain that they had no cheques to hand out and they weren't getting their pictures in the local newspaper. The less exposure, the tougher their re-election chances. Community lottery boards were scrapped.

Referenda are a common feature of democratic governments. Except in Alberta. Under Conservative rule since 1971, you can count the number of referenda on one hand and have three or four fingers left over. Under Klein, the only referenda - two, I believe - were local and involved whether VLTs were allowed in communities.

Finally, four attempts to allow citizens to propose legislation that might be debated in the Legislative Assembly were defeated by the Conservative majority even though all four were proposed by Conservative backbench MLAs looking for ways to involve citizens in the political process.

The Citizens Initiatives Act, proposed by Conservative Jon Havelock in 1994, Conservative Lorne Taylor in 1996, Conservative Denis Ducharme in 1998 and Conservative Tony Abbott in 2001, didn't threaten anyone's authority or relinquish any measure of political control. The essence of all four bills was an onerous public process to obtain widespread public participation in writing a bill. If the public participation process was successful, the Legislature's responsibility was to debate the bill. If MLAs scrapped it in 10 minutes, that was fine.

Four times up, four times down.

Going forward, two measures might be helpful to get citizens involved. First, the oft-defeated Citizens Initiatives Act might be enacted on a trial basis.

Second, major legislation with significant public service implications should be subject to public scrutiny before being debated by the Legislative Assembly. The proposed law should go out for public hearings. Then the Assembly can do with the bill what it wishes, either going along or rejecting what citizens say. An explanation would be in order at the next election.

In the end, the Klein Government trusted only itself. Lyle Oberg said it for all Conservative MLAs when he told his department officials that consultations would not be held until he decided on the outcome. In other words, government consulted, and did what it wanted.

Reforming political finance

Alberta still allows corporations to directly finance political parties. The federal system has limited corporate contributions to $1000 annually since Prime Minister Jean Chrétien's Liberal Government changed the law effective January 1, 2004. Manitoba and Quebec have banned corporate contributions and limit individual contributions. Alberta hasn't even thought about reviewing its corporate and individual contributions.

Money to support political parties comes too easy in Alberta. Corporations such as the big energy companies give lavishly to the Conservative Party and throw a few crumbs to the Liberals to make it appear that they are spreading it around.

In 2006, the ratio of corporate to individual contributions to the Conservative Party was 8:1; for the Liberals 3:1. In both cases, contributions from individuals totalled just over $200,000.

Banning corporate money will force political parties to seek greater contributions from individuals, which means getting individuals involved in the political process. We have already seen the success of the federal Conservative Party to raise money from individuals. The Barack Obama campaign in the United States used the Internet brilliantly to raise vast amounts of money, $5 at a time.

To get people to donate, a political party must tell them why they need it and why you should give. It means communicating with individuals, something that political parties in Alberta do not do in any meaningful way.

With easy corporate money coming in year after year, political parties in Alberta don't aggressively recruit members or solicit money from individuals. Building province-wide networks to increase support and raise money is expensive and time-consuming and, under the current setup, not essential. The New Democrats, who refuse corporate money, are the exception.

With no need for money from individuals, political parties have little interest in political events to encourage interest in public issues other than the elitist leadership dinners in which companies and organizations buy tables costing in the thousands of dollars to listen to a leader talk about how good things are. Political conferences to debate current issues are rare in Alberta.

Alberta hasn't even considered changes to political institutions such as political party financing and the electoral process. As long as the Conservatives get the lion's share of corporate money, they won't think of changing the process. Change will come only when citizens demand it.

A united opposition

Alternatives are essential for an effective public dialogue. Alberta has political alternatives, scattered and weak as they are, but citizens either don't see them or don't listen to them.

In other words, the opposition parties aren't getting their message out. If the opposition parties recognize the public's disinterest in their work, they aren't admitting it.

The behaviour of the Liberals and the New Democrats is odd. Alone, neither is going anywhere. Election results over the last 25 years should tell them that. The Liberals had one chance to defeat the Conservatives - in 1993 under Laurence Decore. In 2008, the Liberals believed they had a chance to make significant inroads into Conservative support in Edmonton and Calgary when Ed Stelmach was almost nobody's idea of a viable leader. They failed miserably both times.

The New Democrats have never been going anywhere and won't go anywhere in Alberta. They do offer a dissenting voice but the message either isn't loud or one that Albertans generally listen to or accept.

Sometimes it seems that the Liberals and New Democrats take greater delight in pounding each other than the Conservative Government.

If neither party can defeat the government, they might do better together. Radical thought? Federally, the right-wing Alliance and moderate Conservatives merged when they understood that they had a better chance of becoming the government together rather than separately. Say what you will about Stephen Harper's politics, the man wasn't too big to prostitute his right-wing views to get the Liberals out of office. As Prime Minister, Harper is as moderate in policy-making as any Liberal Prime Minister.

The late Conservative leader John Diefenbaker had a message about the purpose of an opposition: "Our job is to change places with the fellows on the other side." Alberta's Liberals and New Democrats haven't figured that out yet. Looking at the New Democrat strategy in recent years, I have to believe that the New Democrats hate the Liberals more than the Conservatives.

It's time for both parties to grow up. Neither has been building a membership that will stick with them. The Liberals had more votes in the 1993 and 1997 elections than they have now, even though the province's population is growing. The New Democrats reached their voting peak 20 years ago and are reduced to the bare margins of public interest, and all of their support is in Edmonton. They have to build a membership - plain and simple.

Liberals and New Democrats should unite. Combined, they have a better chance to make an impact on voters, to get around the province and speak on issues before the Legislative Assembly. Together they can provide a solid alternative. They might not form the government any time soon but they will have more people capable of traveling around the province talking politics. The more people see and hear them, the more people will begin to think. Isn't that what politics is all about?

If the Liberals and New Democrats don't come to their senses and emerge from the little worlds they live in, they face certain extinction. Alberta's political history says a new party will emerge, as Social Credit did in 1934 and the Conservatives did in 1966, and become the dominating alternative.

A new political party will not relate to either of the existing parties but will be promise a different agenda and be politically moderate. Former Reform Party leader Preston Manning said that such a party would have an agenda based on concern for the environment. "Green conservatism", he calls it.

A new political party will emerge when the Conservatives appear to be too comfortable, too complacent and consistently out-of-touch with mainstreet Alberta. It will happen when a group of politically ambitious Albertans sees no future with the existing political parties, and when they tire of seeing the same old, uninspiring faces running the province year after year.

Depending on who I talk to, that's either next year, or sometime in the next decade.

Reforming the voting mechanism

The first-past-the-post system has come under serious scrutiny in other provinces. Two - British Columbia and Ontario - set up citizen panels to study the system and propose alternatives. Both arrived at MMP (Mixed Member Proportional), a voting mechanism practiced in other places, notably New Zealand, Germany and Israel. Basically, MMP delivers an elected governing body that mirrors the vote won by each party. The buzzword is that MMP reflects the vote.

In Ontario and British Columbia, those committee recommendations were on the ballot at the following provincial election. British Columbia did not get the required 60% majority but MMP did get more than 50%. MMP was soundly beaten in Ontario.

Some groups - Public Interest Alberta, for example - are pushing for a citizens' panel to examine Alberta's voting mechanism. The Stelmach Government might relent. If they do, it will surprise anyone who pays attention to the practices of the Conservative Government. They won't do it unless there is a widespread demand for change. Don't count on it. Besides, the Stelmach Government has too much to lose by any change, including their majority.

CHANGE IS NOT IN THE WORKS

Will these measures help to make the citizens of Alberta more interested in the way they are governed? Perhaps. The greatest barrier to change, however, is the group that has to support change for change to happen, and that's the Stelmach Government. They just won a huge majority and, given the state of the opposition, Stelmach is assured of at least two terms. Why, then, would he and his caucus have the slightest interest in changing anything when any change will only make re-election more difficult?

Proportional representation means the Stelmach Government would lose at least one-third of their seats; a more open Legislature means they have to explain themselves; revamping the financial system means they lose millions in easy, reliable money so vital for re-election. If Stelmach and his people do nothing, the only people who care are the opposition parties - who have just been decimated - and a few vocal interest groups who have a limited following anyway. Besides, Stelmach was not a reformer as a minister and most of his cabinet have done nothing to suggest they see the need for fundamental change. They like things as they are, thank you.

Had my father lived in Alberta today, he would be appalled. He would have said that people who don't vote live too well, have never struggled, that they never had to understand the importance of the vote. He would have said that people who don't vote have no respect for democracy or freedom.

Sounds about right. Former Prime Minister John Turner put it in equally simple terms: "Democracy doesn't happen by accident, you've got to work at it."

PEOPLE I MET IN POLITICS

STOCKWELL DAY

How Stockwell Day got as far as he has in politics - he is a federal cabinet minister touted as a contender when Conservative leader Stephen Harper leaves - baffles me. Like many hard-line conservatives, Stockwell Day knows what he knows and nothing will change his mind.

According to people who worked with him, he has a modest intellect. His life experience before politics is modest. His education is modest.

So how did Day get so far in politics? He picks ridings safe for a Conservative. He still sports a youthful look and is an aggressive self-promoter. Appearances and showmanship can go a long way in politics. It's rewarded him with 23 years in elected office so far.

Day was elected to the Alberta Legislative Assembly as a Conservative in Red Deer North in 1986 and almost made it into cabinet immediately. A story that made the rounds for years is that in 1986, Premier Don Getty told his staff that he wanted "that young guy from Red Deer" in his cabinet. His staff thought he was referring to John Oldring, a rookie MLA with a much more impressive background from Red Deer South. Oldring ended up in cabinet and Day on the backbench until appointed to cabinet as Labour Minister by Ralph Klein six years later. I couldn't get an answer to this question: If Getty wanted Day in his cabinet in 1986, why was Day overlooked in the new cabinet appointed after the 1989 election?

Day was so excited about his first cabinet post that he moved into the minister's office before Elaine McCoy, the departing minister, had moved out. On McCoy's desk, Day discovered a copy of my newsletter, *Insight into Government*. He picked it up by a corner with his thumb and forefinger, as one would pick up a smelly diaper, and dumped it in a wastebasket. He told his staff that he didn't want to see it in his office again. Having watched his performance on the backbench for six years, it didn't surprise me.

I believe the story that when Day sought the leadership of the Canadian Alliance Party, Ralph Klein and his caucus were happy to see him leave, and even got Rod Love to work with him to improve his chances. Day had not endeared himself to Ralph Klein's inner circle with his ardent public stands against homosexuality and abortion, two issues that Klein preferred to ignore. His intemperate statements about convict Clifford Olson showed little confidence in the justice system. Day said that Olson could be dealt with more appropriately in the prison yard by "moral" prisoners. The out-of-court settlement over a letter Day wrote to the *Red Deer Advocate* defaming a school trustee didn't help. It cost the Government of Alberta some $800,000. Besides, Day always appeared to be a tad too ambitious.

Day's political achievements as a Conservative in Alberta are modest. As Provincial Treasurer, he promised frugality but raised spending substantially. He introduced a single-rate tax, an achievement somewhat muted given that the Klein Government loved to distance itself from federal legislation. A different tax regime fit the bill nicely. Rarely mentioned is that when the Conservative caucus unanimously approved the single-rate tax, every one of them got a tax cut. Other than the single-rate tax, Day's record is sparse.

5

FEAR

THE SILENCE IN ALBERTA WAS DEAFENING

Who makes the Government of Alberta accountable? As I see it, the answer is no one. Not the officers of the Legislative Assembly, not the special interest organizations, and most of all, not the citizens of Alberta who will privately complain about the conduct of their provincial government day after day and dutifully re-elect it every four years.

Special interest groups represent specific sectors in their relationships with the province, be they health, public and private education, municipal administrations, lawyers, dentists, doctors, or disabled peoples. They fight for their own interests, which are often contrary to the interests and agenda of the provincial government. You would expect the relationship between these groups and the Klein Government to be adversarial some of the time. Surely, everyone didn't agree all the time. Or did they? Or were they afraid to disagree in public?

Organizations in Alberta that depend on the provincial government for policy and money feared what the Klein Government would do to them. That is a statement of fact. These organizations, from trustees of the public education system to some of the unions, learned quickly that criticism did not endear them to the Klein Government. They learned to mute their criticism for fear that the Conservatives would come down hard on them.

Midway through Ralph Klein's first term, as Conservative popularity began to rise and the Liberals started to self-destruct again, it became clear that there would be no other immediate alternative to the Klein Government. The more popular a government becomes, the more it believes that it is doing everything right. The more it believes it is right, the less tolerant it becomes to criticism. The Conservatives saw enemies everywhere, including the media. "Cooperative" reporters got the leaks and the best stories; "uncooperative" reporters had to explain to their editors why the competition got the stories first.

When organizations subjected to government decisions recognized that the province lacked a political alternative, when there was little indication of political change, they started to knuckle under to a government that might last many more years. You were either "with us" or "against us".

I saw the fear and intimidation factors first-hand in 1998. Intimidation began with MLAs such as Mary O'Neill, a Conservative from St. Albert in the first and second terms and a former teacher and public school trustee. I was Chair of a political affairs panel sponsored by the Alberta Teachers' Association. In front of MLAs representing the other political parties and a room full of teachers, O'Neill warned that people who criticize the Conservative Government shouldn't expect to get a sympathetic hearing from Conservative MLAs. "Whom do you think I will listen to?" she said sternly. "People who complain all the time or people who are positive and show respect?" She wasn't smiling. Her message was clear.

In 2000, I started to hear about intimidation from others. A municipal commissioner in a small city told me that Conservative MLAs from the region warned municipal administrators about criticizing the government in public, especially in the newspapers. "We were told very clearly that Conservative MLAs don't appreciate critics," he said. "If we persisted, our grants will take longer, and we might not get as much as we need. Our MLA wasn't joking."

In 2002, a trustee representing a public school district in Northern Alberta told me that everything she said for publication in *Insight into Government* had to be anonymous. Her request was not unusual but I usually ask the reason. "The province controls everything we do - how much money we get, the programs we teach, whether and where we build schools, who we hire as superintendent. If we complain in public, everything we ask from government is harder to get and takes longer. A few months ago, our MLA warned us that if we complained about money at a meeting, he would walk out. It wasn't a public meeting. Money was our main concern and because government controls all the money we get, why else would we want to talk to him? So we insisted on talking about money. He got up and walked out. We haven't seen him since."

ROUGH LANGUAGE SENT A MESSAGE

Fear and intimidation was communicated through action and language. The Conservative Government's combative tone against criticism was set early in the 1993/97 term. Having won an election in which their own "massive cuts" were pitted against the Liberals' "brutal cuts", the Klein Government believed that its way was the only way. Organizations were either with it or against it; there was no middle ground.

Ralph Klein set the combative tone himself. In 1995, when Liberal Grant Mitchell persistently questioned Klein about his position on abortion clinics, Klein asked Mitchell if he was calling him a liar, then he called Mitchell "spineless." Klein later used the word "stupid" in referring to a letter Mitchell wrote.

In another instance, Klein responded to a Liberal question about a health issue: "The answer to the silly dumb question is quite simple. It is hard to provide intelligent answers to stupid questions." And again: "Could I pose a question to the Honorable Member: Is he deaf or just stupid?"

In 1997, Premier Klein, sensitive to criticisms from Kevin Taft, then a private citizen, called him a "communist" for his popular book, *Shredding The Public Interest: Ralph Klein and 25 Years Of One-Party Government*. Later, Klein took on the Parkland Institute at the University of Alberta for its "anti-Alberta" rhetoric.

In his book *The Klein Revolution*, journalist Mark Lisac said that Klein called him "an asshole." In 1994, with polls showing his popularity rising as he slashed spending, Klein taunted the premiers of other provinces who raised taxes rather than cut spending as "brainless" and "cowardly".

In a well-publicized confrontation at a Legislature committee meeting in 2004, Klein bullied Liberal Laurie Blakeman who asked for copies of his expense accounts, a legitimate request by Legislature rules. He taunted her, asking whether she was calling him a liar.

Just normal partisan bickering? That's not how it was interpreted. Organizations heard the tone and recognized the implications of playing around with a government that tolerates no criticism.

How could Klein and his caucus get away with bullying behaviour? By having the power to punish offenders.

THE STEVE WEST FACTOR

Some called it the Steve West factor. West, a veterinarian from the Vermilion area in central east Alberta, didn't believe in an intrusive government. With his first appointment to a ministry, to Recreation & Parks in 1989, he began to dismantle it. Staff were laid off, staff were sent to district offices, services were privatized, and spending was reduced - classic right-wing stuff. Bureaucrats who didn't like it were fired. In 1996, West bragged to an eastern group that when he took over the Economic Development department, it had 1,000 employees. When he was finished, it had 113. He described it as "nakedizing" the department.

To politicians like West, government was too big, provided more services than it should, and spent too much. He believed the private sector could do much of government's work more efficiently. West left a trail of destruction in every department he headed; he was feared wherever he went.

West's tone soon permeated a provincial government hell bent on eliminating the deficit. Throughout the public service, staff were cut, services privatized, salaries were reduced and those who resisted were soon gone. And heaven help those who dared to criticize, even in the Legislative Assembly where one group's constitutional duty is to oppose government policy.

Others watched and learned.

In 2004, paranoid about the Kyoto Protocol being imposed by the Liberal Government, Environment Minister Lorne Taylor wrote to a number of oil companies he suspected of dealing privately with the federal government. Taylor wrote: "In recent weeks, the federal government has signed certain Memoranda of

Understanding with some industry sectors and specific companies. We strongly urge you to carefully consider any suggested new federal/industry agreements. We think it is only fair to advise you that costs related to any federal-only system will not be tax deductible for provincial royalty or corporate income tax purposes."

Energy Minister Murray Smith, who knew nothing about the letter when it was sent, tried to calm the industry. He said that nothing will happen to royalties without proper consultation. Taylor, however, had made his point.

YOU ARE EITHER WITH US, OR AGAINST US

Criticism of government policy comes primarily from the Official Opposition in the Legislative Assembly. Criticizing government policy is their constitutional responsibility. Criticism also comes from special interest groups including labour unions and the news media. In the stilted political environment that was Alberta, the rest of the province paid scant attention to the provincial government unless something dramatic occurred or they were hit hard in the wallet.

Special interest groups represented specific sectors in their relationships with the province, be it health, public and private education, municipal administrations, lawyers, dentists, doctors, or disabled peoples. They fought for their own interests, which often was contrary to the interests and agenda of the provincial government.

You would expect the relationship between these groups and the Klein Government to be adversarial at least some of the time. Surely, everyone can't agree all the time. Or can they? Or is it that they won't disagree in public?

As evidence, how often did you read or hear any group speak forcefully in public against a provincial government policy when Ralph Klein was Premier? If you can't remember, your memory isn't failing. The fact is that duelling in public with Alberta's provincial government was rare.

Curiously, the most silent were the largest public organizations in the province: school districts and municipal governments. No organizations had more cause to speak out. In the last decade, the fiscal autonomy of municipalities and the public education system including the colleges and universities had been usurped by the Klein Government.

Fear permeated the public education system where locally-elected school trustees lost their ability to tax locally - about 30% of their total revenues. Instead, the provincial government collected all taxes for education and redistributed them based on a formula that they wrote. With the province providing 100% of every school district's revenues, you had to believe that they who provided the money also influenced the agenda. When school districts complained about provincial policies, the Klein Government simply yanked the chain.

Municipal grants from the province were cut and tightly controlled. When municipalities didn't cooperate, grants were manipulated until they did cooperate. Grants were smaller and some came with instructions on where to spend it. If municipalities complained about their loss of authority or money, they didn't do it in public.

It is one thing to discourage criticism; it is another to be in a position to do something about it. Money has always been the Klein Government's ace in the hole. The energy industry was threatened with higher royalties when it didn't do what it was told. Money would work just as well with municipal governments and the education system.

Rather than fight back, school trustees whined and whimpered and celebrated when the Klein Government didn't inflict as much damage as trustees expected. In one budget, the Learning Minister gave school districts a fraction of the amount the Learning Commission recommended - and school trustees gave him a standing ovation at the Alberta School Boards' Association convention. Even student groups from the universities, who should have no fear of government, were reluctant to go public in a big way to curb the growth of tuition fees.

The message was clear: you are either with us, or against us. That was the tone the Klein Government set out early after its election in 1993. They were on a mission to save the province from the ravages of what they considered to be excessive spending. They believed that if the spending problem was resolved, many of the province's political and economic problems would be resolved as well. Whether they came to that dubious conclusion honestly by themselves or whether they picked up on the political mood of the day is uncertain. The point is that they believed that the future of the province depended on a balanced budget and anyone who criticized the Klein Government was an enemy. They had the power to make critics pay, and they used it. Examples:

In 1996, Guy Smith, a social worker employed by the Government of Alberta's Department of Family & Social Services, spoke in public twice about the impact of cuts to welfare programs. Then he claimed that department officials tried to silence him through intimidation. The case went to an arbitration hearing, where he received a short suspension and a letter of warning. The implication to civil servants was clear: speak in public at your peril. The rumoured "gag order" was no longer a rumour.

The Provincial Health Council was set up by Health Minister Shirley McClellan in 1995 to monitor and assess the progress of the Conservative Government's health system reform program. After a handful of critical reports, some based on extensive public surveys, the Council was quietly disbanded.

Deputy ministers who resisted the rapid pace of government restructuring disappeared. Robin Ford, a veteran in the Labour Department and a pioneer of department business plans, was given an hour to clean out his desk. No reason was given. In 1995, Harvey Alton in Transportation & Utilities, an experienced deputy minister, cautioned his new minister Steve West about the implications of rapid privatization. Alton was gone in days. In 2000, Lynne Duncan, a top-rated Deputy Minister of Health, was fired along with her entire senior executive team when the government, under heavy criticism for legislation that would have allowed for-profit hospitals, felt Duncan and her staff weren't doing enough to help the government.

In 2002, David Swann, Chief Medical Officer at the Palliser Health Authority in southeastern Alberta, spoke his mind on the Kyoto Protocol. The chair of the health authority was Conservative MLA Lorne Taylor's riding president. Swann was fired. When the story got national attention, the board changed its mind. Swann knew better; later he was elected as a Liberal in Calgary. Today he is leader of the Alberta Liberal Party.

In 2004, Premier Klein, taking a correspondence course in communications from Athabasca University, was accused of plagiarism on a term paper. Media played the story big. Learning Minister Lyle Oberg personally called the presidents of the universities of Alberta, Calgary, Lethbridge and Athabasca to defend the Premier. Although the Premier had compromised generally-accepted academic rules governing plagiarism, three of the university presidents heard the call of the Learning Minister and wrote public letters defending the Premier's "commitment to learning".

In 2004, Ian Gray, a reporter working for my newsletter, *Insight into Government*, attended a Christmas Party hosted by the Legislature Press Gallery. Many MLAs on both sides of the Assembly attend. A slightly inebriated cabinet minister, who had rated poorly in several *Insight into Government* surveys measuring reader opinions on the performance of ministers, asked Gray where *Insight into Government's* publisher was. When Gray said he didn't know, the minister said: "That's OK. I know where his wife works." My wife was a senior government administrator at the time. Gray was so concerned about the threat that he offered to write an affidavit in case something happened to her.

In his 2007 book, *Democracy Derailed*, Liberal leader Kevin Taft wrote that a Conservative MLA, disenchanted with the Klein Government, urged him "to have our offices swept for electronic listening devices." Liberal offices are in the Legislature Annex where Legislative Assembly staff, backbench Conservatives and their research staff also have offices. Taft wrote that while he appreciated the warning, "we hadn't gone that far yet." Perhaps he should have. Opposition MLAs are always too trusting of a Conservative Government that is ruthless when it feels threatened. When senior management in the Department of Family & Social Services were concerned that information was being leaked from within the bureaucracy to the news media, they hired a private detective to sweep management offices for electronic bugs. Department staff didn't know if they were looking for bugs, or planting them.

THE FEAR WAS PALPABLE, THE SILENCE PERVASIVE

I didn't only hear about fear and intimidation, I saw it in the eyes of people who had legitimate reason to criticize the government but were afraid to do it.

In the spring of 2000, a group of parents of disabled children in the Hinton-Grande Cache area asked me to come to their community to talk to them about the manners and operation of the Klein Government. The group - about 25 parents, teachers and school trustees - said that money from the provincial government for schools was not sufficient to provide adequate programs for disabled children.

To help them understand who they had to deal with, I described the mechanics of how the provincial government functioned and its current attitude towards the public education system. I said that the Klein Government was convinced that the public education system had enough money to do its job.

This group just as adamantly believed they did not receive sufficient money. After several hours of complaining about the Klein Government, I told them that they had a choice: do something or do nothing. Since doing nothing wasn't working, they had to do something, such as talk more vigourously to their MLA and to the minister. I proposed traditional lobbying techniques including letter-writing, phone campaigns and interviews with local reporters. "Turn up the heat," I suggested. "Let them know you are serious. Let them know that people really care."

The silence was deafening. People were looking at each other, wondering what to say. Finally one spoke. "We can't do what you are suggesting," one parent said. "Ivan [Conservative MLA Ivan Strang] won't like that." Another parent stood and said that Ivan was a friend of everyone in the room and they couldn't say anything negative in public about him. A school trustee got to the real story: "If we go public with our case against government funding, they will ignore us for a long time. We won't get meetings, we won't get money, we won't get help. That's how these people do things."

"I understand that this government likes to spread fear," I said. "Other groups like this around the province say exactly the same things about dealing with this government. I also understand that you aren't getting anywhere doing things the way you do now. The situation is very odd: if you don't fight, your community thinks everything is fine. If you fight, the province puts you on its hit list. It seems to me that you should think of your children first and then decide how to proceed. This is about children, not about Ivan Strang's hurt feelings or the Conservative Government's resentment of criticism."

At the end of the evening, the group decided against a public statement and chose to write a private letter to the minister responsible for education with a copy to the local MLA.

In another example, a group of rural doctors was frustrated because all the Conservative MLAs in central Alberta - Stockwell Day of Red Deer, Victor Doerksen of Red Deer, Ty Lund of Rocky Mountain House, Gary Severtson of

Innisfail - were ignoring them. They said that no matter how much they complained to the MLAs about the difficulty in getting more doctors into the area and asked for the province's help, the MLAs didn't respond. "How," they asked in obvious frustration, "do we get these guys to listen?"

At the end of the meeting in which various strategies were discussed, the doctors promised to be more persistent with Conservative MLAs. But one, clearly frustrated, wouldn't let it go at that. "They think we're afraid of them," he hissed. "I know some who are not. If these guys won't listen, I'll find someone to challenge one or two of them for the nominations. If that's what it takes to get attention, that's what we'll do." Nothing happened.

I participated in many such meetings and the outcome was always the same. Although frustrated to the point of anger, groups looking for action from their own government were afraid to react when Conservatives MLAs either didn't respond or ignored them. Always, the fear was palpable and the silence pervasive.

This reaction is puzzling. Is criticizing provincial policy "un-Albertan?" When the question was raised with school trustees, the answer was downcast eyes and a shrug. When the question was raised with municipal councillors, the answer was more expressive - fear that the provincial government will "get even" with organizations that dare criticize it in public. How will they get even? Meetings with MLAs are tougher to get, letters get lost, requests aren't heard, grant money takes longer to arrive, grant money is gone, and information channels break down.

Conservative MLAs weren't shy about it; groups that complain in public won't get a sympathetic ear. MLAs will lecture organizations that speak their minds. Over time, the message sinks in: suck up or else.

This is the same provincial government that does exactly the opposite when it deals with the federal government. While demanding that organizations in the province be silent and cooperative, Premier Klein ran to the nearest newspaper reporter with another of his many complaints about the federal government. If talking tough and loud to the feds through the media is the preferred approach of the Klein Government, why aren't Albertans entitled to the same practice when dealing with their provincial government?

With a big majority and no political alternative in sight, the Klein Government could do just about anything it wanted. Groups were conditioned to beg quietly - in private. Conventional wisdom says that by begging quietly in private, government will be grateful and generous. If only it were true.

Silence rarely worked. School districts still got minimal increases in funding. Without local taxation, they were completely controlled by the province. To meet expenses, municipal governments raised their own taxes and suffered the wrath of local taxpayers.

The province decided all by itself who got lottery money - and who didn't. As elections approached, the payoffs began.

This was a frightening way to run a province. Only the foolish think that politicians have a monopoly on wisdom. Only the irresponsible give up their voice on public affairs between elections. But, in Alberta, that's exactly what happened. It was tough to stand up when everyone else was lying down.

Some might call it classic bullying behaviour. Ironically, the provincial government that practiced bullying saw fit in 2004 to set up a Roundtable on Family Violence and Bullying. Two months later, an individual in the Department of Children's Services was appointed as "Executive Director for the prevention of family violence and bullying".

Oddly, the bullies were against bullying.

WHO KEEPS AN EYE ON THE GOVERNMENT?

More curious is the behaviour of the people hired by the Legislative Assembly and charged by law to keep an eye on the government of the day: the Auditor General and the Ethics Commissioner.

Both positions are hired by the Legislative Assembly for five-year terms and they report directly to the Legislative Assembly. When a secure majority runs the Assembly, the future of the Ethics Commissioner and the Auditor General is tied directly to the wishes of the seemingly endlessly secure Conservative majority. I don't have to explain what that means to job security. Nor do I have to explain the kind of personality the Legislative Assembly would appreciate in these positions. Certainly not aggressive muckrakers determined to keep the government in line.

The federal government and the other provinces also operate under the same system - their governing bodies select their Auditors General and their Ethics Commissioners - but the difference is that they work in competitive political systems.

Governments change regularly everywhere except in Alberta where competitive politics died almost 40 years ago. People hired by Alberta's Legislative Assembly know that.

The Auditor General has a huge responsibility to monitor how the government bureaucracy spends public money, to report on it annually, and to comment on it. No Auditor General has been more effective than Sheila Fraser with the federal government. Tough, uncompromising and fearless, she is primarily responsible for uncovering evidence that led to the unveiling of the sponsorship scandal. Media-savvy and tough, she follows the money relentlessly. Politicians in Ottawa feared Sheila Fraser's investigators.

Comparatively, Auditors General in Alberta have become sheep. No Conservative politician feared the Auditor General's office. His staff even briefed each government department in advance of his annual report so officials wouldn't be totally shocked when it became a public document. In 2004, the Premier's Office, not happy that the Auditor General still had a smidgen of influence, hired Nick Shandro, one of the Auditor General's key people, to act as an "internal" auditor. His job: find trouble and deal with it before the Auditor General found it. In other words, deal with matters before they become public.

Rather than follow the money and take tough positions on the conduct of politicians, the Auditors General slid past the controversial issues and talked about bureaucratic performance measures, "inputs" and "outputs" and other such nonsense of little value to anyone other than senior public servants. Nor did the Auditors General offer their perspectives on the adequacy or inadequacy of financial policies and political practices. Alberta's Auditors General rarely reprimanded politicians for misdeeds, even when they found them.

Take the case of Health Minister Gary Mar's former executive assistant Kelly Charlebois. Over a three-year period after the 2001 election, after Charlebois left Mar's staff, Charlebois received $389,000 from the Health & Wellness department for consulting services. That kind of money will buy you a very nice home. There was no competitive bidding for his services, no written contract, no terms of reference, and no written reports given to the Minister or the department. Basically, Charlebois was paid handsomely for talking to his former boss. Conduct like this in Ottawa would have seen someone fired. Mar has no excuse. He is a lawyer and knows all about contracts.

The Auditor General noticed the irregularity. Liberal leader Kevin Taft, in his book *Democracy Derailed* in 2007, translated the Auditor General's findings: "The Auditor General said that he couldn't find out what the contracts were for. He didn't know why Charlebois was chosen for the job. And there was no tangible evidence that Charlebois actually did any work for the Department of Health & Wellness."

What did the Auditor General conclude? "If the policies are not complied with, there is risk that the department may enter into inappropriate contracts. Also, if payments are made without adequate support, the expenditures may not be correct."

That's it! No one was responsible, accountable or reprimanded.

Even venerable Bob Clark, Alberta's first Ethics Commissioner, walked softly. He is one of the most personable people I have ever met and a delight to talk with. When I reflect on his personality and on his description of his job as "90% priest and 10% policeman", his performance in the MultiCorp case becomes easier to understand.

When faced with a probe into Premier Klein's wife's involvement in MultiCorp, a financial investment that should have been reported in detail to the Ethics Commissioner, Clark showed mercy. More detail is provided in the chapter on Scandals but for our immediate purpose, the issue is shares in a public company that Colleen Klein received but did not pay for upon receipt. The Ethics Commissioner was not told that the shares, purchased at less than the price available to the public, were not paid for upon receipt. Curiously, Clark accepted partial responsibility, saying that he couldn't fault the Kleins because he didn't ask the question. In the report on his investigation, Clark writes that he assumed the shares were paid for. Further, he reports that because payment was promised, he did not see the shares as a gift.

In Clark's defence, Alberta's Conflicts of Interest Act wasn't the toughest in the country, as would be shown a year later when a review recommended that "apparent" conflict of interest be added. Like the Freedom of Information & Protection of Privacy Act (FOIP), its language was written to pacify the public and protect politicians, not expose them. FOIP was intended to make information available to the public but its exemptions clauses make certain that the public will obtain only what the government wants them to have.

The Klein Government rejected the recommendation to include "apparent conflict of interest" in the Conflicts of Interest Act.

To indict a new Premier at the height of his popularity and working with weak legislation, Clark needed nothing less than a smoking gun. He needed indisputable evidence.

Let's be clear. Only Ralph Klein and his wife know what they did and what they talked about regarding her investment in MultiCorp. It was the Ethics Commissioner's duty to get to the bottom of the allegations.

Was Clark as thorough as he should have been, as thorough as he had been in investigating Peter Trynchy's involvement with a paving company that did work on Trynchy's driveway and did work for a government department that Trynchy headed? (More information in the chapter on Scandals starting on page 165).

The answer depends on whether you think the Ethics Commissioner is at fault for failing to ask all the questions, or the Premier is at fault for failing to provide all the information. The answer depends upon whether you think ignorance of the law is an excuse.

Another factor is at play. In 1994, when Clark did his first investigation into the MultiCorp case, Premier Klein's popularity was rising. Ask yourself under what conditions would a new Ethics Commissioner come down hard on a new Premier?

Alberta's business community is small and tightly woven into the province's political culture. It loved a Premier who supported business, as Klein did. It would have little sympathy for anyone who brought the Premier down.

I believe that if Clark had come down hard on a Premier as popular as Ralph Klein at the time, he would be eviscerating himself only 30 months after his appointment. In my view, the Conservative majority in the Legislative Assembly would not reappoint him for another term if he was too tough on Klein. Conservatives across the province would disown him and in Alberta's small political community, that would be Clark's personal hell.

In giving Klein the benefit of a doubt on the MultiCorp investigations, I say, Clark saved the Premier's career and his own.

Contrast that with the investigations of Premiers in British Columbia, first Bill Vander Zalm and then Glen Clark. Serious, thorough investigations based on a tough law led to resignations.

Bob Clark's work caught the attention of two political scientists in Ontario who were writing a book on ethics in Canadian politics. The book - *Honest Politics: Seeking Integrity in Canadian Political Life* by university professors David Sugarman and Ian Green - was published in 1997. Essentially, the authors wrote that they understood why Clark absolved Premier Klein and his wife, but not because they were clean. They wrote: "Bob Clark's failure to be as strict with the Kleins as, for example, Ted Hughes [a retired judge who served as British Columbia's Ethics Commissioner] was with the Vander Zalms, may be the result of his background as a politician rather than a judge. If the political culture in Alberta condones the 'nest egg syndrome', then this culture is just as likely to have affected Clark and the Kleins. Since the Kleins did not reveal to Clark the shares were received without payment at a below-market value, it was impossible for Clark to give adequate advice. Clark was generous to accept the blame for this omission - from our perspective, overly generous. Even those convinced that Clark's judgment was correct would find it hard to deny that the Kleins were in an apparent conflict-of-interest situation."

Seen another way, it would take incredible political courage for one man in Alberta to make a popular Premier accountable for his actions.

When Clark retired, the Legislative Assembly hired Don Hamilton, an Edmonton businessman who had worked in Social Credit Premier Harry Strom's office in the dying days of the Social Credit Government and a member of the group of young men around Strom referred to as the "Young Turks". Clark was the Education Minister in Strom's Government. Years later, when Clark was the Ethics Commissioner, he occasionally sought advice from Hamilton.

Like Clark, Hamilton had no legal background and no investigative experience. He would however have an appreciation for the plight of Alberta's politicians.

All this raised an obvious question: who made the Government of Alberta accountable? As I see it, the answer is no one. Not the officers of the Legislative Assembly, not the special interest groups, and most of all, not the citizens of Alberta who privately complained about the conduct of their provincial government day after day and then dutifully re-elected it every four years. When citizens didn't appreciate the conduct of their government, they stayed home silently on election day as they did in big numbers in 2004 and 2008 rather than choose an alternative. Meanwhile the cycle of fear and intimidation repeated itself.

PEOPLE I MET IN POLITICS

ROD LOVE

For a guy who worked in the Premier's Office for about five years, Rod Love left quite a legacy. When Premier Klein was doing well in the first term, Rod got much of the credit; when Klein was adrift in the second and third terms, Rod's absence was considered a factor. His reputation did well both ways.

Rod was smart and when combined with Ralph Klein's teflon-like qualities, the duo was formidable. They won six elections plus a leadership race. Rod was smart enough to get out of the Legislature at the right time. He returned to Calgary to set up his own business before the end of Klein's first term, when the deficit had been eliminated and balanced budgets were written into law. He got out at the right time because there was no agenda for the second term and even if there was a new agenda, it couldn't be as clear, as manageable, or as successful as deficit reduction in the first term.

Rod Love had a simple agenda and he pursued it ruthlessly and aggressively - to re-elect Klein. It meant getting reporters to write articles that made Klein look good. How? Love has talked about manipulating reporters working the Legislature beat and he has written about using strategically-placed leaks to the newspapers to assess the impact of policy. He knew what he was doing.

From my experience with him, he didn't hold grudges, certainly not for long. While he was working in the Legislature, he left a few nasty messages on my answering machine after the *Fair Comment* television program in which something was said that he didn't like. Then he'd invite me to the Legislature for a beer. In private business, he subscribed to *Insight into Government*. When he was angry at a story, he'd cancel. Later, when he cooled off, he subscribed again. That happened twice.

When the *Fair Comment* show was filmed on Friday evenings in the early 1990s, the panel sometimes met at Martini's on 109th Street in Edmonton for a beer before heading home. Rod often held court in the bar. He presided over a large, round table in the middle of the room and regaled reporters with political stories.

He was tough and feisty with a steely glare over that handle-bar mustache. I always knew where I stood with him. He always told me what he thought about my work straight out. I never heard second-hand anything he hadn't told me himself.

In politics where gossiping, conniving and backstabbing are a way of life, Love was different. He may not have been universally liked - in some cases, he was feared because of the power he held over the Premier - but he was respected.

6

HEALTH

A POTENT MIX: CONFUSION, CHAOS, PERSONALITIES AND POLITICS

If Premier Klein insisted on cutting health care costs, he could eliminate a cadre of services not required by the Canada Health Act the next morning – more than $2 billion worth in Alberta. He did not have to plead for changes to the Canada Health Act or ask the federal government's permission but he would have to face the wrath of the citizens in Alberta when they saw some of their health services eliminated. Klein needed only the courage to commit a politically unpopular act. He didn't have it.

"Who runs the health system?" I asked the Conservative MLA. A smile crossed his face. "You know who it is - Jack Davis, of course." Jack Davis, formerly Premier Klein's Chief Deputy Minister, was the CEO of the Calgary Health Authority.

T o fully appreciate Canada's national health plan, you have to spend time in an Americxan hospital and be responsible for the costs. I knew someone who did. Six hours cost him $19,600 and he didn't have a life-threatening problem.

Canada's health plan was designed to help Canadians afford the kind of life they want to live without worrying about poor health driving them into bankruptcy. To say it succeeded is an understatement. Canadians are so spoiled by their "free" health plan that they complain vociferously when asked to pay a larger part of the costs.

Canadians have come to believe that they have the right to the best in health services at no direct cost to themselves. They believe they have the right to use the system when and where they want, and if money is a problem … well, that's what governments are for.

Governments, however, aren't dealing with rising health costs very well. The federal and provincial governments, all of whom agree that the health plan is necessary, have turned health into a political football. Faced with high citizen expectations and rising costs, provincial governments persistently complained that the federal government should pay a larger portion of the costs of the provincially-run programs. The complaints started shortly after the national health plan became law more than 40 years ago and continue to this day.

No government can complain about the federal government like the Government of Alberta. If provincial governments were rated according to time spent complaining about the federal government, the Government of Alberta would rank at or near the top. Face it: despite being the wealthiest province in the country, Alberta governments under Peter Lougheed, Don Getty and Ralph Klein regularly used the federal government for target practice. Alberta's participation in nation-building under Ralph Klein was dominated by complaints about the federal government's approach to health care. Klein's complaints masked the real story of health care in Alberta that has nothing to do with the federal government.

Health reform in Alberta is a fascinating story of simplistic ideas, political ego, jealousies, incompetence, mistrust of the public service, and an inability and unwillingness to use political power for the public good. Health reform was another classic case of a group of people who, because they were elected, believed that wisdom in all endeavours automatically came with the job. Winning sizable majorities for three decades can do that to politicians - make them believe they and their political beliefs are right and those who criticize or believe differently are wrong. They begin to believe that they are smarter than they are. In reality, these people who served in the Conservative caucus between 1993 and 2005 - a doctor, a few lawyers, many farmers, some with small business experience, a number of career politicians - had little organizational experience and knew virtually nothing about organizational behaviour. Yet they believed they could overhaul the health system themselves.

The story deserves to be told fully.

STUDIES, STUDIES AND MORE STUDIES

The story starts in the mid 1980s when Health Minister Marvin Moore, a farm boy from the Grande Prairie area and a staunch fiscal conservative, repeatedly warned Premier Getty that health services will become unaffordable if their costs escalated as they had in the previous decade. Moore set off a near political panic in recession-stricken Alberta as the Getty Government struggled to get a handle on its persistent deficits.

Alberta's provincial governments sometimes study issues fully before considering action. In the next 20 years, health services would become the most studied public service in the province's history, far exceeding attention given to the energy industry. The politics of health would become a preoccupation of the Klein Government and health reform would be its most blatant failure.

After Moore sounded the alarm, Premier Getty asked for ideas. Accordingly, his next Health Minister, Nancy Betkowski, hired her former boss, retired Provincial Treasurer Lou Hyndman, to chair a Premier's Commission On Future Health Care For Albertans. Hyndman delivered a smart, sensible report that was soon dubbed the "Rainbow Report" for the colours of its final report.

Before the Getty Government could act on the Rainbow Report, Premier Getty retired, a leadership race ensued, and Ralph Klein became Premier.

Klein's immediate mission was not to reform the health system but to cut its costs to balance the budget as soon as possible. Health would have to suffer its share of the pain.

Klein started quickly. He cut health spending by $200 million in each of his first two budgets, he attacked the feds for not paying enough while demanding too much of the provinces, and he launched his own review of the health system while ignoring the Rainbow Report.

"Starting Points", Premier Klein's first attempt at health reform, was chaired by rookie Conservative MLA Lyle Oberg, a medical doctor from Brooks in southeastern Alberta. It would be the first of many Klein-appointed health reform strategies. The report identified a redefinition of basic or essential services defined by the Canada Health Act as critical to system-wide reform.

No matter how often Klein asked the federal government, usually through the media, the answer was always the same: the Canada Health Act will remain as is until Canadians demand change. Klein's frustrations with the federal government's resistance to his ideas reached a peak in the Fall of 2004 when he stomped out of a federal-provincial meeting on health in Ottawa and hopped on a taxi to play blackjack in a casino across the river in Hull.

Health reform frustrated Klein throughout his 14 years as Premier of Alberta. He launched study after study but didn't deliver on any of them. After Starting Points, he had a seven-point plan, a 90-day plan, a six-point action plan, the Health Summit, the Premier's Advisory Council on Health (a.k.a Mazankowski Council), the Third Way and a smattering of mini-plans in between - each touted to be the elusive answer.

These reform plans brought numerous ideas for the government's consideration. For one reason or another, the Conservative caucus rejected most of the ideas, rarely giving a reason. Each study disappeared, one by one, and was soon replaced by yet another study.

PLAYING POLITICAL GAMES WITH MAZANKOWSKI'S COUNCIL

On a rare warm sunny November day in Edmonton in 2001, Premier Klein was regaling reporters working the Legislature beat with another of his frequent attacks on the federal government over health care. The attacks had been part of his political showmanship since 1993 when he determined that what the health care system really needed was a heavy dose of his brand of fiscal discipline. His public attacks served a second political purpose: it diverted attention from his own successive failures to reform the system.

Klein always demanded more money for health care, of course, but he also demanded that the Liberal Government in Ottawa redefine in more liberal detail the "essential services" terminology in the Canada Health Act. If Klein convinced Ottawa to redefine the term, he could do what he believed was necessary to lower government spending: terminate many "non-essential" health services now paid by the Government of Alberta. In his mind, the private sector would step in and offer the services. He would kill two birds with one stone: cut government spending on health and allow the private sector to grow.

To a political schemer like Klein, it was a no-brainer. He could get what he wanted and he could blame the despised Liberal Government in Ottawa if there was a strong public reaction.

So there he was, outside his office on the third floor of the Legislature Building, gathering reporters around him and telling them that he was continuing the fight for affordable health care if only the federal government would allow him to do it. His inability to get what he wanted was always the fault of others. Reporters were scribbling feverishly, as if they hadn't heard any of this before.

What was different on that November day in 2001 was an article that appeared in the morning edition of the *Edmonton Journal*. The newspaper article, based on anonymous sources, outlined proposals that the much-touted Premier's Advisory Council On Health, set up in August 2000 and chaired by retired Deputy Prime Minister Don Mazankowski, was said to be considering.

Frustrated at the lack of progress from his previous half dozen or so health reform strategies between 1994 and 2000, Klein asked Mazankowski, a retired federal Conservative politician making big bucks in the private sector by sitting on the boards of big corporations, including Great West Life that was big in private health insurance, to form a committee to write another health reform plan for him. Mazankowski carried considerable weight in Alberta's political circles and the expectation was that Klein had to promise action on the report before Maz, as he was known, would lend his good name to it.

No one knew for certain who leaked the interim report to the *Edmonton Journal* but suspicious minds looked directly at the person who would benefit from early speculation - Premier Klein. Leaks to favoured reporters from the Premier and his staff had become a staple in the government's communications strategy and there was no reason to think that this leak came from a different source. In essence, the Premier or one of his staff leaked the story to the newspaper so the Premier could use it for another public attack on the federal government.

While Premier Klein was entertaining the Legislature media horde with his rant against the Liberal Government, Mazankowski, incensed at the careful work of his committee being abused for political purposes, issued a curt one-page statement expressing his "disappointment over the leak of a document summarizing preliminary ideas under consideration by our Council." He said the Council was considering various ideas and the media should wait for the final report before speculating on the final proposals.

After listening to so much rhetoric for so many years, I had little interest in Klein's rants for the benefit of the Legislature media. Oddly, while Klein was talking to reporters, I noticed that Health Minister Gary Mar wasn't present, mentioned, or missed. Where was he?

I found Mar in his office one floor down. He was in the outer office talking to his staff when I walked through the open doorway. Always welcoming, he waved me into his inner office.

SILLY GAMES IMPEDE SERIOUS BUSINESS

Gary Mar, a lawyer of Chinese descent, was elected in 1993 in Calgary. In my eyes, Mar was one of the few forthright ministers in Klein's Conservative caucus. When I asked a straight question, I got a straight answer. He didn't scramble for his notes when answering questions. He admitted to me several years earlier that he would not have been elected in 1993 if the Conservative Party leader had been anyone but Ralph Klein. "I owe him," Mar told me. "Without Ralph Klein, I'm practicing law in Calgary and bored out of my mind."

Five years after his first election, Mar was being talked about in leadership terms. There was something about the man and the politician that people liked. In every *Insight into Government* survey on reader attitudes towards ministers, Gary Mar always rated highly. People liked him: he was smart, politically moderate, and thoroughly engaging. And he was moving up in cabinet - from the junior Community Development portfolio to Education, Environment and finally Health - a sure sign that his work was being recognized.

Mar and Premier Klein seemed to get along until a lengthy two-page feature story appeared in the *Edmonton Journal* in January 2002 entitled "The Man Who Would Be King." The article appeared about six weeks after Klein had gone public with warnings about so-called 'tire-kickers' looking for his job. Gary Mar was one of them.

For months, the political rumour mill worked overtime on speculation that Mar had raised a ton of money in Calgary for an eventual run at the leadership. It was rumour - until sometime around Christmas of 2001 when Mar admitted to an interest in the leadership when Ralph Klein retired.

Not surprisingly, the *Journal* feature did not go over well in the Premier's office or in certain parts of the Conservative caucus. I was talking to a Conservative backbencher who I knew well and casually mentioned the Mar article. Her demeanor abruptly changed, her face turned cold and she said icily, "No chink ever becomes Premier of Alberta."

In November 2002, 10 months after the *Journal* feature touting Mar's ambitions, *Insight into Government's* cover story was entitled "The Undressing Of Gary Mar - In Public." In part, it read: "This is a story of power, succession and a majority too large to control. It starts with the Premier and the Health Minister. Try the morning that Mar read in the newspapers that the Premier had talked to the media about the interim report from the Mazankowski Council. Mar hadn't seen the report. How about the Premier's last-minute decision to put his friend Marvin Moore on the Expert Panel reviewing health's drug policies but didn't tell Mar? Perhaps it was the day that the Premier ridiculed Mar's anti-tobacco strategy in cabinet even though health and wellness promotion is a key element of the Mazankowski report. Perhaps it was the day Ernie Isley, a key player in Klein's leadership campaign in 1992 and now chair of the Lakeland Health Authority, called Mar a liar - in public ... in every case, the story ended up in the newspapers."

Insight into Government continued: "Cabinet put the boots to Mar again this week. He was told to take his health authority reduction strategy and talk to every Conservative MLA - individually. As usual, the story was leaked to the media. Not one of Mar's colleagues came to his defense. The Premier behaves like an innocent bystander."

"I only have a minute," Mar said to me as I followed him into his office. "I have to be at a meeting downtown in 20 minutes. What's on your mind?"

As I started to talk, he was pulling his sweater off and reaching for a shirt hung over the chair behind his desk. He smiled and patted his slightly protruding stomach. "I'm biking a lot."

"The Premier is talking about health care again," I said. "Do you agree with what he's saying?"

Mar stopped buttoning his shirt and looked directly at me. "What's he saying?"

"You don't know?"

"No."

"Did you see the *Journal* this morning?" I asked.

"Yes."

"Do you know how the story got in the newspaper?"

"No."

"Did you know this morning that it was going to be in the *Journal*?"

"No."

"Have you seen any report from the Mazankowski council?"

"As far as I know at this point, there is no report."

"The Premier must have a copy of something because he's attacking the feds and he mentioned user fees and nobody has mentioned user fees for months," I said. I couldn't tell at this point whether Mar was thrown off by my questions or by that morning's newspaper story.

"We haven't made a decision on user fees," he said.

"Are you looking at radical change because of Mazankowski, whatever he reports?"

"Don't expect anything to happen quickly," he said. "Change must be discussed carefully."

I looked up from my notepad. "You have no idea what's happening here, do you?"

The knot on his tie was giving him trouble; it was clear that he was frustrated. "Not this morning for certain. If you want to talk more, set up something before you leave."

When he was satisfied with his tie, Gary Mar, the man who would be King, was gone.

If Premier Klein was unhappy with his Health Minister in 2001, what could he have been thinking in 2004 when, after rudely excusing himself from a national meeting on health to gamble at a casino in Hull, Mar drew raves for his performance in Klein's curious absence.

Insight into Government reported in October 2004: "What new delights now await Health Minister Gary Mar? He substituted for Premier Klein for most of the health meetings in September, but according to reports, they were constantly in touch. But Mar got all the positive coverage - the *Globe & Mail* ran a large picture of Mar with Ontario Premier Dalton McGuinty over a headline that read: 'While Klein skips talks, Mar makes his mark.' One columnist noted that Mar praised the Prime Minister for 'listening'. He wrote that Mar 'showed himself to be much more low-key and collegial than his Premier.' Another columnist chastised Klein for going to the Hull casino. A third said Klein went home after the first day because he is "bone lazy". *Edmonton Journal* columnist Graham Thomson had nothing but positives for Mar during the health meetings; his column was entitled 'Sitting in for Klein, Gary Mar already looks like a leader'. This is the same Graham Thomson who wrote the lengthy piece on Mar that appeared in the *Journal* on January 20, 2002 entitled 'The Man Who Would Be king?'"

What could Premier Klein have been thinking while reading those newspaper reports? I don't know what he thought but what he did is on the public record. Within two months, Mar was back in Community Development, the same portfolio he had as a rookie minister in 1993.

$2 BILLION COULD BE CUT WITHOUT ASKING THE FEDS

In Prince George, British Columbia, in January 2008, in a speech to a health organization, Ralph Klein admitted that he failed miserably in revamping the health care system. The fault never lies with himself. A direct quote: "The strict interpretation of the Canada Health Act is the single greatest impediment to meaningful health-care reforms that we face." His line hadn't changed: to lower government's costs, he wanted fewer government-insured services and more for-profit services offered by the private sector.

What Klein didn't say is that the Government of Alberta's Health Care Insurance Plan pays for many services not required under the Canada Health Act. These services are covered because the Government of Alberta wants to pay for them. It isn't required to pay for them - it is doing so by choice.

The financial implications were laid out by Health Minister Gary Mar in May of 2004, when he explained his budget to a group of MLAs on one of the upper floors of the Legislature Building, far from the eyes and ears of the public. Mar cited the usual litany: the costs of health are killing the budget; by 2020, health will consume more than half the entire budget, etc., etc. Then he said that of the $8 billion provincial health budget, "almost one-third pays for non-Canada Health Act related services."

Mar paused, looked at the opposition MLAs around the table and when none of them showed an interest in the point he was making, he continued.

The implications of Mar's admission were clear to me: if Premier Klein insisted on cutting health care costs, he could eliminate a cadre of services not required by the Canada Health Act the next morning - more than $2 billion worth in Alberta. Klein did not have to plead for changes to the Canada Health Act or ask the federal government's permission but he would have to face the wrath of the citizens in Alberta when they saw some of their health services eliminated. Klein needed only the courage to commit a politically unpopular act. He didn't have it.

Or maybe Klein's sharp political instincts kicked in. In April 2004, two years after the Mazankowski Council report was dispatched to a shelf in a backroom, *Insight into Government* offered a reason for consistent inaction on health reform: "Most of the ideas to reform health care kicked around in the last 10 years survived only until Conservative MLAs came crawling back to the Legislature Building bloodied and beaten by their constituents who saw their health system threatened."

Without the federal government to blame for reduced services, Klein would have to absorb the blame himself. He knew better.

REGIONAL AUTHORITIES: CONVOLUTED THINKING AND UTTER FAILURE

Public service administration was amongst Klein's favorite targets. He believed that the public service was too large and too expensive, that there was far too much administration in the provincial government.

He had accepted the view of the "Rainbow Report" and of his own "Starting Points" report that health care governance could be more efficient by reducing the role of the Health department in administering the entire health system, including hospitals, and turning governance over to yet-to-be formed regional health authorities. Regional authorities were working in Saskatchewan and British Columbia so, the reasoning went, regional authorities should work in Alberta too.

Restructuring a massive, expensive public service is never easy. When Alberta's public education system was downsized several years later, the outcome was much tidier because regional school boards had been operating for decades. It was a relatively minor matter of shuffling a number of smaller boards into larger existing boards.

The health system had no regional structure; it consisted of numerous health districts and hospital boards scattered around the province and overseen by the Health department. Everything in the proposed regional structure would be new: the existence of regional health authorities was new, their administrations were new, the laws and regulations governing them were new, and the relationship between the new health authority administrations and existing hospitals would be new. Not discussed in public was the relationship between the authorities and the provincial government; specifically, who would run the health system. Time would show that neither did nor could.

The first sign that the Conservative caucus was moving too quickly on organizational matters it didn't understand was the Regional Health Authorities Act setting up 17 regional health authorities. The bill introduced in the Legislative Assembly was 19 pages long. Before the legislation became law in 1994, it had 21 pages of amendments.

The role of the public service is to advise politicians. Administrative restructuring on such a massive scale demanded a healthy, effective public service. Unwittingly, Klein's massive downsizing of the public service in 1993 was coming back to haunt them. Middle managers and policy advisors had been reduced significantly, compromising the public service's ability to research and write sensible policy and to provide sound advice. Without a public service, the Conservative caucus was flying on its own - flying blind as it were.

Like other departments in the public service, Health itself was undergoing organizational change. A revolving door of deputy ministers meant that the Health department averaged almost a deputy minister a year for a dozen years, rendering the department intellectually impotent.

The revolving door began when Deputy Minister Rheal Leblanc resigned in March 1993, two months before the provincial general election. Don Philippon, already on the department staff, got the job seven months later. Skip forward another 14 months: Philippon joined the Capital Health Authority for more money and less stress. In September, eight months after Philippon resigned, Jane Fulton was hired out of Ontario to be Deputy Minister. She was fired a year later, replaced by Jack

Davis who had been Deputy Minister in Economic Development for all of five days. Just over a year later, Davis was promoted to Chief Deputy Minister and Don Ford replaced him in Health. You get the picture. Over 14 years with Klein as Premier, Alberta Health had a dozen deputy ministers, two of whom were fired, and two massive organizational overhauls.

With the Health department lacking leadership, the formation of regional health authorities was left to a group of politicians with no administrative, organizational or health-related experience. They were trying to restructure a system of essential public services of which they had no knowledge and no experience.

Fourteen years after the Klein Government set up 17 regional health authorities, the Stelmach Government disbanded what was left of them. The most visible and comprehensive instrument of health reform, the regional health authorities were an expensive failure.

EFFICIENCY IS BEST SERVED BY IGNORING VOTERS

In February 1996, one year before a provincial election, Health Minister Shirley McClellan said that as far as she was concerned, the 17 regional health authorities would be governed by boards with two-thirds of its members elected and the remaining one-third appointed by the Conservative caucus. The elections, the first in 1998, would be tied in with municipal elections.

For a government that considered itself to be of a populist nature and responsive to political wishes of voters, electing a portion of regional health authorities made sense. After all, provincial governments are elected as are municipal governments and the boards of trustees that run school districts. Why should an important public service such as health be different?

Eighteen months later, Bud McCaig, a prominent Calgary businessman and the government-appointed chair of the Calgary Health Authority and Dr. Lorne Tyrrell, Dean of Medicine at the University of Alberta, met in public with a government committee. They spoke plainly. McCaig said that if elections were held in 1998, he would not be a candidate and, should the government consider reappointing him, he had little interest in working with elected people.

Dr. Tyrrell was equally clear. He was concerned that special interest groups might organize and, through elections, take over the board in Edmonton and perhaps in Calgary, thus impeding reform initiatives.

For the two gentlemen, the bottom line was obvious: elected boards under political pressure from communities could compromise, if not derail, changes taking place at the regional health authorities. They agreed that elected boards are susceptible to takeovers by single-minded, single-issue interest groups. They said that quality people, perhaps themselves, will not be involved if health boards are elected. Finally, internal conflict could ensue with both elected and appointed people on boards of the health authorities.

The voices of McCaig and Tyrrell were heard. Another consultative committee of Conservative MLAs toured the province to talk about electing health authority boards. When it reported that some people were indeed worried about elected boards, the Conservative caucus delayed elections until 2001. Health Minister Halvar Jonson said that elected boards could lead to political instability.

That was the last the Klein Government spoke of electing members to the boards of regional health authorities. An elected government didn't trust the people who elected them to make a second wise decision and elect good people to regional health authorities.

INCOMPETENCE IS NOT TOO STRONG A WORD

Regional health authorities, designed to bring local control to the health system, turned out to be more than Premier Klein and his caucus bargained for. Reflecting on the experience, I can describe reasons for the failure of the regional health authority structure.

First, the health authorities naturally attracted provincial government staff that wanted more money, less stress and more distance from politicians who neither respected nor trusted them. Deputy Minister Don Philippon was only the first to go. Even Chief Deputy Jack Davis defected to a health authority. Meanwhile, the government was busy flipping deputies and trimming middle management staff.

To compete with an agency it created itself, the Government of Alberta was forced to increase its own salaries. Staff who were downsized in the public service restructuring found work with the health authorities. Some became consultants who hired themselves out to the authorities at far better money than they were earning in the public service.

Contemplate the lunacy: an organization attempting to cut costs sets up 17 alternative organizations that compete with itself for staff, thereby increasing staff costs and the complexity of administration.

Second, the health authorities, with their board members appointed directly by the Klein Government, became more politically powerful than the government anticipated. Board loyalties were divided between their communities and the provincial government that appointed them and expected them to follow the government's tight fiscal agenda. Boards governing the regional health authorities soon learned that it was easier to ignore a Health Minister in Edmonton than be confronted by a local citizen angry at the health system.

While Klein and whomever his Health Minister was at the moment expected the health authorities to respect the provincial budget, the health authorities spent everything they could coerce out of the province. Boards learned the political value of subtle threats. Unlike so many other groups, regional health authorities had no reason to fear the provincial government. If the province refused money beyond the allocation in the provincial budget, an authority could threaten to close the emergency room when money ran out, and blame the province. The Health Minister buckled every time.

Hence, one deputy minister of Alberta Health told me: "My prime job is to write cheques to the regional health authorities."

The Auditor General annually reported that the health authorities thumbed their noses at the province, rarely completing their business plans on time or sticking to the province's budget.

Third, Conservative MLAs didn't know how to deal with voter complaints about the work of the authorities. The authorities were under the management of government-appointed boards, including some very political appointments such as former Treasurer Jim Dinning in Calgary and defeated cabinet minister Ernie Isley in Lakeland. The Boards of Authorities didn't have to listen to an MLA's complaints, which frustrated Conservative MLAs who wanted to satisfy their constituents. Some, like Conservative Stan Woloshyn in Stony Plain, complained that his local health authority in Stony Plain was closing a hospital and offered to mediate between frustrated constituents and the authority. The authority Woloshyn helped set up had become his problem. He too had divided loyalties - did he support the authority or his constituents?

Fourth, the Klein Government struggled between appointing boards and allowing communities to elect them. Klein's caucus didn't know its own mind. First, boards were appointed. Then they were elected. Then the elections were overturned and the boards appointed again.

WHO WAS RUNNING THE HEALTH SYSTEM? JACK DAVIS, OF COURSE

The obvious question must be asked. If the politicians are not competent to run the health system and the Health department wasn't being heard, who was running the system?

"Who runs the health system?" I asked the Conservative MLA sitting across the table from me at the Sidetrack. A smile crossed his face. "What took you so long to ask? I thought you would know who it is - Jack Davis, of course." Jack Davis, formerly Premier Klein's Chief Deputy Minister, was the CEO of the Calgary Health Authority.

Strange business. The Chief Executive Officer of the Calgary Health Authority, one of the largest health authorities in the province, is actually running the provincial health system. Not directly of course, but through his political pipeline directly into the Premier's office. Nowhere in the democratic world could such an obvious conflict be tolerated, except in Alberta.

"Why should I know that?" I asked.

"If you know who fired Lynne Duncan, then you know who runs the health system," he continued. Lynne Duncan, acknowledged throughout the public service as a superb administrator, was Alberta Health's Deputy Minister, hired by Jack Davis when he was Chief Deputy Minister. She was accused of not sufficiently supporting the government's health agenda.

"Jack fired Lynne? Not possible. I don't believe it," I argued. "He doesn't have the authority. She works for the Premier through the Health Minister and the Chief Deputy Minister. Davis has nothing to do with this."

"Things here aren't always the way they appear. Davis fired her. I know that for a fact," the Conservative MLA insisted. "He talks to the Premier all the time. The Premier trusts him more than anyone in the Health department."

I later asked Lynne Duncan if that was the case but she refused to answer, which is an answer by itself. Another Legislature veteran independently confirmed the story.

Early in his public service career, Jack Davis tied his professional future to Steve West, one of Klein's early drinking buddies and the toughest, most right wing minister in cabinet. Together they ran three departments from 1993 through 1996: Municipal Affairs, Transportation and Economic Development.

West didn't ask deputy ministers for advice. He told them what to do and if they resisted as Harvey Alton did in Transportation, they soon found themselves working somewhere else, usually in the private sector.

A tough minister like West requires a deputy minister with the same toughness to run the department. Under West and Davis, departments were run from the top down. Davis soon became known throughout the public service as "Steve's boy". Davis also caught the attention of the Premier's office who liked deputy ministers who did what they were told without too many questions and who were willing to play the government's right wing game of cutting costs and privatizing where possible.

West and Davis played the same ruthless game in each assignment. The minister's authority was established quickly through his choice of a new deputy. Management reductions followed to reduce costs and to remind staff who was calling the shots. Then they picked through the programs and services in the department and targeted the ones that might be privatized. When the damage was done, they moved on and left others to clean up the mess.

The song-and-dance team of West & Davis ended when Halvar Jonson, assigned to straighten out the Health department in June 1996, asked for a strong deputy minister to end the revolving door at the top of the department. Jonson, a calm, quiet, competent politician who had been a high school principal in Ponoka in central Alberta, knew that successful organizations had strong people at the top. Jonson asked for, and got, Jack Davis who just five days earlier had followed Steve West to the Economic Development department. It would be the beginning of Davis' huge influence in health policy that lasted until Ralph Klein retired in 2006.

In September 1997, Premier Klein needed a new Chief Deputy Minister to replace the retiring Vance MacNichol. Davis moved again, his fifth new assignment in four years, this time into the big leagues - the Premier's Office to be the boss of all deputy ministers and the only deputy with regular access to the Premier.

Jack Davis, an obscure Assistant Deputy Minister in the Solicitor General's department until he met Steve West, had risen to the top of his profession in Alberta's public service in just over four years. His salary rose from around $100,000 as a deputy minister of a department in the provincial government to a starting salary of some $400,000 as CEO of the Calgary Health Authority. His rapid rise demonstrated in spades that it pays to know the right people.

Portly and bearded, Jack Davis was a willing interview. I found him smart, articulate, cunning, and always careful. Intrigued by a deputy minister so clearly on the rise, I asked him why he stayed in the public service with its meager salaries. "An administrator like you could do much better in the private sector, or setting up a consulting practice," I told him. "You could hire yourself back to government at twice the price, be your own boss and pick your own jobs."

"I am committed to public service," he intoned. "I enjoy the work and I like developing programs to serve people. A guy can do good things in the public service to help people. The money is secondary," he said. I believed him.

Meanwhile, trouble was brewing at the Calgary Health Authority. Retired Treasurer Jim Dinning had been sent in to clean up the mess and institute the same fiscal discipline he had shown in eliminating the provincial debt. Klein's view was that there was no public agency that wasn't too fat and too expensive. They all needed tough medicine, the sooner the better. The newly organized health authorities were no different. If Dinning needed help, he would get it.

Dinning needed a new CEO he could work with. A national advertising program had shown that Calgary couldn't attract a CEO to serve for less than $400,000, far more than Dinning expected to pay. Dinning brought the matter to Premier Klein in his office on the third floor of the Legislature Building.

Here's the way the meeting went, according to people who knew the situation: when Dinning outlined to Klein the salary expectations for a new CEO, Klein balked at so much money for someone he didn't know. He looked at his Chief Deputy Minister Jack Davis who was watching all this and said that Jack could do the job. Yes, Jack could do the job, but at the same money others were asking. Which was more than double his salary as Chief Deputy Minister. Davis accepted the job.

I was surprised at the news. I called Davis on his cell phone. He was in his car traveling to Calgary.

"Why did you take the job?" I asked. "You told me that public service was more important than the money."

"It is," he said. "The Calgary Health Authority is still serving people."

"Tell me you aren't doing it for the money," I said.

"I'm not. The money is important but it isn't everything." There was a long pause. "I want to be in Calgary because it's closer to my condo in Fernie."

Jack Davis' career in Alberta's public service was masterful personal politics. He rose from a second tier manager in a peripheral government department to the impressive salary and stature as CEO of the Calgary Health Authority.

Having worked as Chief Deputy and trusted by the Klein/West/Love triumvirate, Davis could call Premier Klein and talk to him directly. Because Klein didn't trust Gary Mar, his Health Minister, Jack Davis became the default choice as his health policy confidant.

The relationship lasted as long as Klein was in office. When Klein was gone and Davis went public with loud demands for more money for the Calgary Health Authority - he didn't have the same relationship with the new Premier - Premier Stelmach dissolved the health authorities and Davis walked away with an estimated $1.5 million in severance pay.

THE FAILURE OF HEALTH REFORM

Ralph Klein was correct when he said in Prince George that he failed miserably in revamping Alberta's health care system. How could a political leader with a mythical attachment to a large base of voters, with immense political tolerance and power, fail so miserably? There are clear reasons.

The Premier Klein/Jack Davis relationship

Davis advised Klein on health reform but when Klein tried Davis' ideas on the Conservative caucus, it wanted nothing to do with ideas from outsiders like Davis. Though Davis was with the Calgary Health Authority, he still influenced Premier Klein on political matters relating to health reform. Rural MLAs especially, always suspicious of bureaucrats, resented Davis's continued influence.

The Conservative caucus was more concerned about the views of its constituents than the views of Davis who was accountable to nobody. With its extensive veto powers, the caucus could derail any policy that might anger voters. Health reform had the potential to anger voters.

Peter Elzinga's Bomb Squad

Peter Elzinga, a veteran of federal and provincial politics and a cabinet minister in the Lougheed and Getty governments, was a key Klein insider in Edmonton. Looking for a friend to replace his long-time assistant and advisor Rod Love as Chief of Staff of the Premier's Office, Klein turned to Elzinga, one of the few people he felt he could trust. Klein and Elzinga were drinking buddies.

Elzinga valued control. To keep tabs on what ministers were doing, Elzinga appointed a committee that was soon dubbed the Bomb Squad. This insider committee, chaired by Elzinga to prevent this disorganized, undisciplined government from embarrassing itself, vetted policy proposals before they were put before cabinet or the caucus. The Bomb Squad was not part of any organizational chart and not part of the formal political decision-making process. Its purpose was to defuse potential political bombs - period.

With a moderate political thinker such as Elzinga as Chair, the Bomb Squad rejected everything moderately controversial. Health reform proposals, whether from the Mazankowski Council or elsewhere, were always too controversial.

Other Premiers tuned out

If Premier Klein truly believed that the federal government should revise its definition of essential services, Klein would need the help of other provincial premiers. He played his cards badly from the start. Insults are not a way to win friends. In 1995 with his government's massive spending cuts well underway and his poll numbers rising, Klein told the Vancouver-based Fraser Institute, the right wing think tank that continues to honour him, that Premiers who raise taxes to balance their budgets are "brainless" and "cowardly". One premier who raised taxes was New Democrat Roy Romanow in Saskatchewan. Is it any surprise that when Klein took his various health reform strategies to Western Premiers' meetings, Romanow opposed them. Treasurer Jim Dinning didn't help Alberta's relationship with Ontario when, in the dying days of Bob Rae's New Democratic Government, he referred to it as the "People's Republic of Ontario." Over the years, not a single Alberta Government health reform strategy found favour with other premiers - not a single one. Klein's bullying behaviour worked in his own province but not elsewhere.

Klein expected too much too quickly
Some institutions can change quickly; health is not one of them. It is far too large and organizationally complex to be altered as quickly as Klein expected. By seeking the next quick "solution" that would bring him the desired results, he found none. Alberta's system did change under Klein in some areas, but he was not able to control costs as he wished. Costs kept going up and up. In 1992, health took 25% of the province's budget; in 2010, it is expected to take almost 40%. Raw costs rose from $4.1 billion in 1992 to an estimated $14.5 billon in 2010.

An unpredictable system without brakes
The nature of Canada's health care system defies the ability of any government to predict and control costs. The system, because it is open, has no natural brakes. A citizen can go anywhere in the country, visit a doctor as often as the citizen wishes, expect first class service every time, and expect to get it all at no direct personal cost.

Medical technology is advancing day by day, helping to extend life. The longer people live, the more they use the health care system. The system has few safeguards to prevent abuse. Doctors can prescribe tests, remedies and visits to specialists without limit.

A public system without brakes is a system that defies strict budgetary controls.

WHY DIDN'T HE USE THE POWER THE PEOPLE GAVE HIM?
Through all the political turmoil covering 14 years, Alberta's health care system did see change. Among them: advances in the use of technology, extensive organizational restructuring through regional health authorities, and changes in primary medicine are important. Some were more successful than others but they were changes and they did make a difference.

But what Ralph Klein wanted most - an ability to control and predict costs in the public system and a greater role for the private system - didn't happen.

I think he could have done better by using the very formidable political capital the voters had given him. If Klein really believed his brand of health reform was right and important, he could have exercised political muscle to get it done. He didn't have to plead with the federal government to change its own legislation that would allow him to do things in Alberta. By working with what he had, by eliminating some of the health services provided in Alberta but not required under the Canada Health Act, he could have cut a billion or so from the health budget immediately. But he had to be willing to face the public flak that would inevitably follow.

He was the consummate salesman. In the early years, he sold bad news unlike any politician in the country. He sold bad news better than some Premiers sold good news. How could a politician cut spending by 20%, inflict considerable pain with cuts to social programs, and see his poll numbers rise? In his first decade as Premier, Klein was at the height of his political power and easily the most popular premier in the country. His poll numbers were consistently high. He could have done anything he really wanted to.

Why, then, at the peak of his political power between 1997 and 2002, did he shy away from health reform? The Mazankowski Council in 2002 gave him all the ideas and rationale he needed. Having just won another large majority in 2001 and at least four years from another election, Klein could have implemented the key elements of the Mazankowski Council report and survived. He didn't and by walking away from a comprehensive report written by a prestigious man, widely respected in the province, Klein had blown the last of his political capital.

Within two years, the Mazankowski Council was shelved and Klein set up yet another new reform consultation called the Third Way. The province yawned. By 2005, Klein's popularity had waned and his own party drew a bead on him. It was too late for health reform.

Klein often said that Albertans trusted him. If he believed what he said, they would have trusted him to reform the health system. A superstar believes in himself and his work. Klein could have been the superstar of health reform.

Could have been ...

People I Met in Politics

Ron Liepert

If you followed Alberta's provincial politics in 2009, you know the name Ron Liepert. If not, I can fill you in. He is Premier Ed Stelmach's Health Minister who undid more than a decade of organizational restructuring in an hour by abolishing the regional health authorities and setting up his own superboard to govern the health system. He did it because he could. The regional health authorities had been set up a decade earlier by Health Minister Shirley McClellan to make the health system more manageable and accountable. Seems that, like so many of the Klein Government's other health reform measures, regional authorities were the wrong move.

The Ron Liepert I know is friendly, personable and smiles easily: traits that might surprise Albertans watching his tough act as Health Minister. We worked together in the Legislature Building for five years, from 1980 through Lougheed's retirement in 1985. Out of politics, he remembered people. When he saw me in a crowd, he always came over to talk. He wanted to know what was happening in the Legislature and whether the newsletter business was treating me well.

I discovered that he sometimes read Hansard, the verbatim transcript of proceedings in Alberta's Legislative Assembly. How many people read Hansard? Ron did as a businessman in Calgary. He called one afternoon to talk about comments made by Murray Smith in the Assembly and he wanted to know what I thought about him. It was the only time in 19 years of publishing *Insight into Government* that someone called to discuss the contents of Hansard. Clearly Ron was paying attention.

He was part of Nancy Betkowski's inner circle in her 1992 leadership bid and he was on Jim Dinning's 2006 leadership team.

Ron is a rarity in politics. Most budding politicians talk tough before an election and back off when put in a position to make a decision. Ron talked softly before his election and then became much tougher than I imagined he could be after his election. His top-down approach to health reform certainly surprised me, and I thought I knew him. Apparently I was wrong. Time will tell whether dismantling the health authorities was the right decision. So far, it's his legacy.

7

CHILDREN
THEY ARE THE FUTURE – AREN'T THEY?

"One has to ask where is the Alberta Advantage for the almost one-fifth of our population who are not sharing in the general prosperity, and whose after-tax incomes fell in the last ten years ... Alberta has strange priorities. As one of the wealthiest provinces, we spend $102 per child while financially-challenged Nova Scotia spends $104 and Quebec spends $225 per child! A cynic has commented that it appears Alberta's priorities are skewed towards those who vote."
- *Bob Stollery, former president of PCL Construction whose name adorns the children's ward at the W. C. Mackenzie Hospital in Edmonton, speaking on child poverty, in 2001*

"We are debt-free but our government does nothing about hungry children. We, the people, have to start, operate and fund programs to provide lunch to students who otherwise would do without. We, the people, have to because, we, the government, do not. All children deserve an opportunity to compete equally for their future. Putting an end to homelessness, feeding the hungry, providing all

our children with equal opportunities: are these revolutionary ideas or common decency? Who will stand up and say no to these ideas?"

    - Bruce Saville, self-made millionaire, philanthropist and part owner, Edmonton Oilers, 2004

"One of the most compelling issues we face is access for all Albertans to education. We've got to break down the barriers to education and give all our people access and opportunity to create a good quality of life for themselves. Education is the only tool I can think of for a high quality of life and creating the best business environment."

    - Eric Newell, CEO, Syncrude, 1996

T hose are passionate statements by men of respect who no longer could be silent about what they saw around them. Eric Newell, Bob Stollery and Bruce Saville are men of progress not given to negative thinking or mindless public thrashings. When such men talk, I listen.

Can you sense Bruce Saville's anger, Bob Stollery's frustration and Eric Newell's impassioned plea? To go public took courage, the kind of courage not often seen in Alberta, not when politicians who breed fear govern the province. These men question whether Alberta's Conservative Government cares for children.

It is said that the purpose of our generation is to prepare young people for the next generation, and we are failing. Life is that simple: our children are the future - both their future and our future. Children must be given a strong start to enjoy a full life. We should raise them with all the love we possess, with affection, respect and do everything possible so their young years properly prepare them for adulthood. We should raise them well so they will raise their own children well.

Everyone cares about children, whether the children are their own or of other families. Everyone wants children to be happy, to have a full stomach, to get a proper education in a safe school building, to get adequate medical care, and to fully participate in the life of their community. We all believe that, don't we? Aren't children, beautiful in their innocence and helplessness and unspoiled by the rigours of responsibility and accountability, the real future of the province?

The Heritage Savings Trust Fund isn't the future; the Heritage Fund is merely money. The future isn't a balanced budget, zero debt or the oil sands. People are the future and today's children are tomorrow's adults. Or are they comfortable clichés to be trotted out at election time to pacify parents?

The astute, caring gentlemen quoted above certainly believed that Alberta's children weren't getting what they needed.

THEY HAD THE WORDS BUT NOT THE DEEDS

Did Ralph Klein's Conservative Government care for children? Absolutely. They care as much as anyone whose heart is gladdened by the sight of a happy child and saddened by the sight of an unhappy child.

A government that cares for children will demonstrate that care through investments in education, in social programs dedicated to helping young people through difficult times, in safe, comfortable school buildings with competent teachers, and in the recognition that all children have basic rights.

Did the Ralph Klein Government do the best it could, use all its power and resources wisely to do its part to provide the best possible public programs for our children? Did the Ralph Klein Government provide the best possible education system? Did the Ralph Klein Government do its best to protect children unable to protect themselves? Did the Ralph Klein Government do its best to help children from dysfunctional families? The answers to these questions do not come quickly or easily.

After watching the Klein Government deal with children's issues for 14 years, it became apparent to me that while Premier Klein and his Conservative caucus said they cared for children, they didn't know what to do beyond words to prove they cared.

They talked a good game. At his most eloquent, Premier Klein said in 1998 that "our ultimate goal must always be to preserve the quality of life that we cherish for our children and grandchildren". A month later, he said it again: "Our greatest obligation is to leave our children and our grandchildren a province that is even better than the one left to us."

They spoke all the proper words, likely written by professional communicators employed by the government, but couldn't develop programs that fit their agenda: affordable programs consistent with conservative ideology in which families are primarily responsible for children, not the government.

150

The Klein Government was inconsistent at best, or confused at worst, in its efforts to work with children. An inconsistent or confused person doesn't know who he is, what he wants, or who he wants to be. Remember, this was the province that initially opposed the federal government's National Child Benefit.

KINDERGARTEN NIGHTMARE

First impressions last a long time. It was bad enough to treat public education as a business rather than a vital public service and operate it as a business. The Klein Government talked about public education as a commodity, not about children and the future of the province. They went, however, a bit too far.

Cuts to kindergarten programs would hurt this government's public image more than they ever suspected in their worst nightmare. A strong public backlash against spending cuts to health and education was expected in 1993 and 1994, but even Conservative MLAs were shocked at the vociferous public reaction to kindergarten cuts. A group unable to fight back had been unfairly targeted.

To reduce the annual deficit inherited from the Don Getty Government, Provincial Treasurer Jim Dinning shocked a province when, through his budget decisions, he implied that five-year-olds had to pay their share to balance the budget. It was heartless and politically dumb. When neither the Education Minister nor the Premier could adequately explain the reason five-year-olds had to pay the price for a government's extravagance five years earlier, the image of a cold, thoughtless government was planted firmly in the minds of people who cared for children.

Education Minister Halvar Jonson had been a high school teacher, a high school principal, and a president of the Alberta Teachers' Association. If anyone in the Conservative caucus knew about public education and children, Jonson was the one. Astonishingly, he determined that there wasn't sufficient evidence to prove that 400 hours of preschool kindergarten would have a beneficial influence on children. The savings: $35 million in a $12 billion budget.

When Premier Klein and Jonson tried to justify the cut, Klein told the Legislative Assembly that fewer hours will not affect the quality of education offered to those young children because 200 hours "was sufficient to prepare children for grade one." He said he knows that because his Education Minister told him so.

When the Education Minister was asked the same question the next day, he admitted that the evidence is inconclusive. He said there were many studies on both sides of the issue. Later, adjusting his argument, Jonson insisted that studies showed that by grade 3, the impact of preschool education was negligible. Unable to prove conclusively that 400 hours was beneficial, he cut the program to 200 hours.

Targeting young children to save a paltry $35 million wasn't a smart political move. It was only the beginning of allegations that the Klein Government wasn't deterred by the impact of its budget cuts on the young and the helpless. When the Premier and his Education Minister couldn't adequately explain their decision to reduce kindergarten hours, the criticisms appeared to have substance. The 14 former public school trustees and 10 teachers in the Conservative caucus couldn't explain it either.

By any political or educational measure, cutting kindergarten hours was dumb. Within three years, on the eve of the 1997 election, full funding for kindergarten was restored. Too late - the political damage had been done. Despite the high-sounding rhetoric, the Klein Government had demonstrated that it didn't care about children.

RIGHTS OF CHILDREN

In the early 1990s, the Government of Alberta was asked by the Chretien Government in Ottawa to ratify the United Nations Convention on the Rights of the Child. Shiraz Shariff, a Conservative backbencher from Calgary and a social worker, explained to the Legislature that the Convention"sets out special protection for children based on the universal declaration of the Rights of the Child." He said the Convention gives children the right to survive, the right to be protected, to develop the right to have a name and a nationality, and the right to live with their parents where possible.

Realistically, the Convention was another high-minded United Nations document that carried more symbolism than authority. Alberta was the only province to reject the charter, its resistance based on two clauses. The Premier said that one clause pertains to parental control over whom children can associate with - he said parents don't want their children associating with criminals and people who would have influence on them to do bad things. The second clause deals with free and unlimited access to media, which could mean pornography. No way would Alberta sign such a Convention, Klein said. He didn't say that he would never agree to

152

anything a Liberal Government proposed.

In December 1998, Archbishop Desmond Tutu of South Africa, on a visit to Alberta, personally appealed to Premier Klein to sign the Convention. Suddenly, what had been a domestic political dispute between the federal government and a provincial government had international implications. Archbishop Tutu had a sterling reputation in fighting for human rights. If he trained his eyes on Alberta, he could do the province considerable harm around the world.

Within months, Alberta quietly ratified the Convention.

Klein's resistance, however short, didn't help the growing public perception that his government didn't care about children. Not mentioning children in a Throne Speech until 1996, three years after he was elected, was a serious mistake. Nothing will turn citizens against a government faster than its inability - or its unwillingness - to do everything within its authority to make life better for those unable to protect themselves - namely, children.

If the strength of the Klein Government was its fiscal record, its weakness was its inability to help improve children's lives.

OF BACK-PEDALLING AND BULLYING
The back-pedalling began in earnest.

In 1999, six years after becoming Premier and now loaded with money, Premier Klein started to talk sensibly about children and the role the provincial government could play in making their lives better. Some good things happened.

To battle the perception that it ignored children, a much-publicized Children's Forum was organized to consider issues involving children for no other apparent reason than the government was trying to do better. Add a new Children's Services department led by Iris Evans, MLA for Sherwood Park and the strongest advocate for children in the Conservative caucus. A government that had just slashed the number and size of government departments because the public service was too large and too expensive had reversed itself and was now adding departments.

The first report of the Children's Forum was released in February 2000. *Insight into Government's* report: "The final report on the Children's Forum arrived this week. If you are looking for a report that drives the Klein Government to action, then you have to look elsewhere. It is exactly the kind of report on the emotional, often explosive world of children that a government - any government - wants to see. It is the kind of report expected from a public meeting chaired by the Premier's wife.

Colleen Klein was the Chair of the Children's Forum because she is the wife of the Premier. Be assured that she would do nothing to embarrass her husband. Accordingly, the Children's Forum report has no specifics. It sets no priorities. It makes no demands and puts no pressure on the provincial government or any other organization responsible for the welfare of children. The report makes no recommendations. It's just a compilation of a lot of nice words conveying nice thoughts about what ideally should be done for children in Alberta. It doesn't contain even one, new interesting idea." But Albertans will get a Children's Week every year and another meeting of the Children's Forum in that week.

The end result of the Children's Forum was $48 million over three years for five programs including the protection of children involved in prostitution, children affected by fetal alcohol syndrome, assistance for new-born children, and help for children leaving the child welfare program.

Later in the spring of 2000 came another report called *Start Young, Start Now! Report Of The Task Force On Children At Risk*, the government's response to the shooting at Taber in 1999 in which a young teenaged boy shot three students and killed one in the Taber high school. Chaired by the new Children's Services Minister Iris Evans, the Task Force recommended a plethora of new services ranging from help for new parents to improvements in low-cost housing to expanded programs for pre-schoolers to crisis response plans in schools.

In 2004, the province hosted a *Roundtable on Family Violence & Bullying*. I remember the conference well, not for its content or conclusions but because just days before the conference opened, Premier Klein exhibited the bullying traits the conference tried to combat.

In a Public Accounts committee in the Legislative Assembly, Premier Klein's behaviour towards Liberal MLA Laurie Blakeman, when asked to account for his spending, was classic bullying. How do you explain to children that bullying is wrong when the province's political leader does it?

Children would get more attention. The Premier's Council on Alberta's Promise Act led off the 2003 session of the Legislative Assembly. Premier Klein got the idea from his friend, Mike Harris, Premier of Ontario. It was a feel-good effort to link good corporate citizens to community resources to help children.

The government's attention to children went over well. While specific action was slow to come, the perception that the government cared was welcomed.

Preparing for a provincial general election in 2001, the Conservative Party knew it was on to a good thing that could be exploited. This time, a grade 6 class from Jean Vanier School in Sherwood Park, the constituency a few miles east of Edmonton, represented by the Children's Services Minister, was invited to participate in the writing and reading of the Speech from the Throne in February.

It was unlike any Throne Speech in decades. Rather than the usual bland, boring, hazy version, this one came with special theatrical effects. Those grade 6 students saw their thoughts reflected in the Throne Speech. They had been asked to describe the future of Alberta, and they responded.

On a day when the Premier decided to call a provincial general election, when the media was thirsting for news, these children were exploited to make a partisan political point. Children, who make great television images when they are on their best behaviour, were used to advance the government's political agenda. This was not a celebration of children. If children were required to brighten up Assembly proceedings, it could have been done any number of times when the Assembly is sitting. Nope. The Conservative Government chose the same day they decided to call an election.

Cynical as it was, the strategy worked. The Conservatives won another dozen seats, raising their total to 74 in the 83-seat Legislative Assembly. Since Klein's first election in 1993, he raised his seat count by 23 in two elections.

Life in the political lane was very, very good. But the children who played a role in the pre-election Throne Speech were not invited back after the election. They were no longer of use.

TEACHERS FIGHT BACK

2002 would be a difficult year in public education. A government that had made significant efforts to change public perception of its attitude towards children couldn't help itself. Conservative MLAs didn't appreciate teachers, especially public school teachers backed by a union. Time after time, I listened to Conservative MLAs, notably MLAs representing rural communities, complain about how well teachers are paid, how little they work and how comfortable the schools are where they work. Teachers had to be put in their place, they insisted.

The Alberta Teachers' Association, with Edmonton high school teacher and political activist Larry Booi as president, was gearing up. Teachers had played ball with the provincial government through the cost-cutting in the 1990s and now teachers wanted their reward. With Booi encouraging teachers to finally take a stand and hold to it when times got tough, strike votes were being taken across the province. The votes were consistently one-sided suggesting that teachers had had enough and would fight back.

Having seen this type of political environment before, I could smell trouble. The confrontation between an intransigent government and frustrated teachers would turn mean and ugly.

Earlier in the year, the Education department's annual report included a poll reporting that public satisfaction with the public education system was slipping badly. From 1997 through 2000, public opinion polls reported that public support for public education hovered around 70%. In 2001, support dipped to 63%. Turned around, 37% of people surveyed said they were not pleased with Alberta's public education system. The same percentage - 37% - told the pollsters that public education was no longer within their financial means. Coincidentally, a report surfaced showing that Alberta's elementary and high school classes had the largest average class loads amongst all provinces.

Teachers wanted better salaries, fewer students in their classes, and more money for the system as a whole. Teachers had watched the government spend lavishly since the 1997 election and heard Premier Klein say that teachers would be rewarded for their cooperation in holding salary demands down. Now teachers expected the reward Klein had promised. The Conservatives had opened the vault to get re-elected. Safely re-elected, they wanted to shut the door again.

Lyle Oberg, a medical doctor from Brooks, was the new Learning minister. A determined fiscal conservative and a stubborn man always insisting that his way was the right way, Oberg had no intention to give teachers more than he thought they deserved, no matter what Premier Klein had promised. Dr. Oberg was behaving like a doctor: a doctor diagnoses the problem, writes a prescription to resolve the patient's problem, and no further discussion is needed.

An impasse led to teacher strikes in 22 school districts and provincial legislation to break the strike in 2002.

The hastily written Education Services Settlement Act denied teachers the right to strike and imposed an arbitration process on them. Teachers had to return to work immediately and an arbitration tribunal would settle all unresolved issues. On salaries, the legislation said that whatever the number, it cannot drive a school district into debt. When the arbitration panel defied the government and wrote larger settlements, the government refused to provide money to keep school districts out of debt.

I was at a school trustee zone meeting in Lethbridge, waiting to speak to the group representing school districts across the southern region of the province, when Michelle Mulder, President of the Alberta School Boards' Association, described the Education Services Settlement Act to school trustees and superintendents. Reaction was immediate. One superintendent was on his feet and he was angry. Sensing a moment I should note, I took my pad and pen from my briefcase. School district officials rarely spoke angrily with a stranger in the room. If they noticed me at all, it's because I was the first speaker in the afternoon session, not as the publisher of a political newsletter.

"How can we accept this?" he roared. "This is the most draconian piece of legislation I have ever seen. If we agree to this, how can we go back into our schools and face our teachers? The relationship we have worked so hard to build for years will be destroyed in a minute. The morale in our schools will be damaged beyond repair. And what about the students? Doesn't anyone care about teachers and students anymore? I'm sick of all this!"

Few in the room disagreed. I hadn't heard such anger from school district people for years.

Cooler heads prevailed in Edmonton. Three weeks later, a deal was negotiated in strict secrecy at the Alberta Justice Staff College in southwest Edmonton and teachers went back to work. The most startling part of the secret meetings is that the animosity between Learning Minister Lyle Oberg and the Alberta Teachers' Association was so strong that they didn't meet face-to-face during the entire process. Lawyers for the two sides met with Tim Christian, an arbitrator and former Dean of Law at the University of Alberta, to hammer out a deal.

In time, the politics of public education returned to near normal conditions. The Learning Commission reviewing public education issued its report, the government responded and the arguments began over whether the government was honoring the Commission's recommendations. Are Alberta's teachers the best paid in the country? Where do Alberta's class sizes rank amongst the provinces? Is government money for public education in Alberta the highest in the country, second highest, or fifth highest? In all cases, it depends on what numbers are chosen and who does the counting.

Meanwhile, the struggle in the classroom defies easy solution. When 30% of all students in Alberta high schools take more than six years to complete a four-year program, something is terribly wrong. Despite the political games played in education, the classroom experience is the most important element in the education of children and the least-mentioned element when the big boys are arguing.

In this technological age, the struggle is to make the school experience relevant to every student who walks through the doorway. Competition for the student's mind and attention is fierce. Young people get more information from the music channels on television, from the internet, and from the street than they get in the classroom. Can a formal education be encouraged when astonishingly successful people like Steve Jobs of Apple Computer and iPod fame, and Bill Gates, founder of Microsoft and one of the world's richest men, admit that they found the classroom experience lacking and dropped out of university to find fame and fortune. Young people admire Jobs and Gates and see them as evidence that formal education isn't everything.

Better work must be done by the people responsible for public education. Good young people must be attracted into the teaching profession by paying teachers the money they deserve for dealing with two dozen or more students all day, by improving teacher education, by renovating Alberta's 1,000 school buildings built back when Social Credit governed the province, and by constructing new schools in rapidly-growing cities. Mostly, the provincial government must develop a greater respect for public education and the people in it.

Public education in the Klein era lacked vision. The Conservatives made an effort to change the system but they lurched from idea to idea, always with a political agenda built around control and money, always uncoordinated and unfocused.

From the beginning in 1993, the Klein Government made a critical strategic error: it didn't try to make friends to smoothen the road to change. There was no reason to make enemies of teachers and school districts. It believed change could be forced by demanding it from their perch in the Legislature Building. Compromise was a word they wouldn't speak. Pity.

CHILDREN AT RISK AND THE CHILDREN'S ADVOCATE

Having modest success in improving the public education system, would it be a surprise to think that the Klein Government wasn't doing any better with children at risk?

The office of the Children's Advocate brought no comfort to those concerned about the safety and the future of young people from dysfunctional homes. These are the troubled young people who fall between the cracks of the government's social programs. These young people looked to the Children's Advocate for support and protection, often from their own families.

The Children's Advocate is an agency of the provincial government that is advertised as an independent voice for young people up to age 18 who receive services under the provincial government's Child Welfare Act. In essence, the Children's Advocate's job is to support young people who aren't getting proper attention from the provincial government.

"Independent voice" is a matter of interpretation. The Children's Advocate is hired by the Minister of Children's Services and reports directly to that minister. Clashes between the Advocate and the provincial government, which doesn't appreciate criticism, are inevitable. The Children's Advocate ended up criticizing the minister who hired him.

A pattern began to emerge. Tough annual reports from the Children's Advocates were leading to either their retirement or their resignation. Bernd Walter unleashed a very tough report in 1993 and soon ended up working in British Columbia. In 1997, John LaFrance wrote a tough report and ended up at the University of Calgary. In 2001, Rob Rechner wrote another tough report. And what happened?

Insight into Government reports: "Rob Rechner, the Children's Advocate, who speaks for children in the province's child welfare system, released a scathing report on what's happening with some children in the government's care. Too much of the report is bad news: the number of children served by the Advocate is up 23%; 122 cases of sickening abuse are reported; he is concerned that there may be attempts to keep the Advocate quiet. To be fair, some of the news is good: 3,190 children received services from the Advocate and 83% were satisfied with services received. One case of child abuse is too many; 122 suggest serious problems."

Rechner recommended that the Advocate report to the Legislative Assembly and no one else, suggesting that the report will get more attention if the Assembly deals with it. Rechner soon retired.

The 2002/03 annual report from the Children's Advocate was released in 2005, two years after it was written.

This uncomfortable employee/employer relationship can be alleviated with the Children's Advocate reporting to the Legislative Assembly, as do the Auditor General, the Provincial Ombudsman and the Ethics Commissioner. A fearless Children's Advocate will be more effective if reporting directly to the Legislative Assembly.

In 2002, Harvey Cenaiko, a former police officer and Conservative MLA from Calgary, reviewed the Child Welfare Act. Eighteen months later, Cenaiko reported to the Children's Services Minister. When a politician writes a report, he naturally favours his political side. His report did little for the Children's Advocate, suggesting that the role be expanded and that it report quarterly to the Children's Services Minister. Cenaiko saw no merit in the Children's Advocate reporting to the Legislative Assembly.

In short, little had changed. The Children's Advocate wanted a stronger forum to get help for the young people he was expected to serve. If he feared to speak his mind, or if no one was listening, what happens to these kids?

WHAT HAS CHANGED?

The Klein era was rampant with political rhetoric, organizational change and public attention primarily through high-profile initiatives such as the Children's Forum and Alberta's Promise. There was no shortage of rhetoric on the performance of Alberta students in national and international tests or on the performance measures published in annual reports produced by the Government of Alberta describing all the good things your government is doing.

That's barely half the story. In 19 years of covering politics in Alberta, I listen to politicians but try always to make assessments based on a balance between what politicians tell me and what I hear from people impacted by government programs. I prefer to make assessments based on a healthy dose of reality. If I want to know what's happening in the schools, I talk to children and parents in the neighbourhood and ask them what's happening at school. Want to know the school experience of children from low-income families? Drop in at an inner city school and talk to students. Ask whether they had breakfast and what they brought for lunch and where they are going after school. Ask what they enjoyed about their day at school. Ask how many days of school they missed and ask why. Ask often enough and you can detect a trend.

Sometimes forgotten, when I think about the Klein Government and their attitudes towards children, are the children of families affected by cuts to welfare programs. Considering how low welfare benefits were before the cuts, the meagre benefits after the cuts caused havoc especially with single mothers. Forgotten are the children of single mothers on welfare. Their children suffered more than any others. Some went to school hungry and most likely didn't have money for lunch either. There was no money for organized sports or community cultural programs.

Conversations with these children will tell you much more than a book of debatable statistics and well-meaning rhetoric. Only then can these questions be answered. What has changed in Alberta's classrooms under the Klein Government? What changed for children in care? Are fewer children going to school hungry? Has access to decent child care improved for low income families? Have government-sponsored social programs helped the plight of families on the poverty borderline? Can disposable income be increased through higher tax credits, making essential services more affordable? Is affordable housing sufficient in the cities?

I would argue that the impact of the Klein Government's programs on individual children has been minimal.

In 2004, a 20-year strategic plan to guide the Conservatives didn't mention child poverty, affordable housing or support for disadvantaged peoples. I know of no serious government-wide efforts to make sure kids always have food to eat through programs in schools, or to create affordable child care programs for low-income families, or to encourage after-school programs to keep children off the streets. I know of no appreciable decline in the number of children in poverty in Alberta since 1992. In 2008, the number is still around 10% despite a roaring economic boom and a government with the financial means and political power to act meaningfully. The most recent numbers show that child poverty in Alberta is the second lowest amongst the provinces, which is still far too high. Imagine - one in 10 children in Alberta still live in family conditions considered to be too low to provide the essentials for a healthy life.

I believe Bob Stollery when he spoke of child poverty in 2001. I believe Bruce Saville when he spoke of hungry children in 2004. I believe them before I would believe a member of the Conservative Government who would argue differently.

The statistics game may be perilous but statistics are one way to track trends over time. In public education, the high school dropout rate is a key indicator in determining whether school is relevant to students. Tracking the dropout rate over a decade tells us how those responsible for public education respond.

Statistics Canada says the rate of high school dropouts - students who leave secondary education before graduating with a degree - in Alberta was sixth among the provinces early in the 1990s and second 12 years later. Statistics Canada reports that Alberta's high school dropout rate was the highest in the country in 2006. The dropout rate in small towns and rural areas was double the rate in urban areas.

The high school dropout rate is the outcome of various factors. A strong economy seduces young people to enter the workforce and earn money quickly and perhaps return to school later. A school environment that isn't relevant to young people is another. Not to be discounted is the number of young people who fall into the poverty class and can't afford to be in school.

Bob Stollery knew that in 2001 and spoke out. Bruce Saville knew that in 2004 and spoke out. Eric Newell was concerned about access to public education 13 years ago. Did anyone listen to these men?

I argue that the Klein Government did listen, but with one ear. When faced with arguments to improve social programs, they were always concerned about angering the party's vocal right wing. They have always been concerned about adventuring into the private sector whether to increase the minimum wage or improve workers' conditions. They hesitate to commit themselves too strongly to social programs because the programs might be too costly in the long run and encourage recipients to become too attached to the programs.

The Klein Government, from the beginning in 1992, had always believed that parents are responsible for the welfare of their children. Government's role, if it has one, is secondary. The level of their involvement with children is consistent with what they believe. With that philosophy under Klein and then Ed Stelmach, the Conservatives continually won large majorities. Why change?

PEOPLE I MET IN POLITICS

ELAINE McCOY

E laine McCoy - she called herself McCoy - was a smart lady who never got the political respect she deserved. She got no respect from the Conservative caucus although she was years ahead of them on matters that became government practice: running a government on business principles, downsizing public service departments, user-pay principles, and privatizing selected government services. She talked of economic diversification before they knew the term. She respected human rights and gender issues when a majority in the caucus thought them to be the work of lefties.

McCoy ran for the leadership of the Conservative Party in 1992 against the likes of Ralph Klein and Nancy Betkowski. I never saw a campaign go down so quickly. I was never so surprised at a campaign's sudden demise. How could a politician as smart as McCoy fail so miserably?

Actually, it was easy. At the first public forum, when called to speak, McCoy mumbled something about fulfilling a childhood dream to be "a fairy princess" and help people. A Premier as fairy princess? Her excuse: she told me she wasn't prepared to speak.

McCoy's campaign didn't end that evening though. It had ended several weeks earlier at City Lumber's east Edmonton mill site. McCoy chose the site to announce her candidacy, expecting it to highlight her solidarity with the working man. Dressed in an expensive designer coat and sporting a classy new hairstyle, she looked as if she was heading to the opera. Tom Korski, the *Edmonton Sun's* political reporter and a fellow panelist on *Fair Comment*, was amused by it all. He poked me in the ribs and said: "Watch this." Korski reminded McCoy of her promise to campaign full-time for the leadership. "Does that mean you are giving up your $40,000 cabinet salary?" he asked casually.

The question should have been easy for the lawyer-turned-politician. All she had to say is that the law does not allow her to decline the salary unless she resigns and she doesn't intend to resign. If, however, she could have declined the salary, she would.

Instead, McCoy was unable to answer Korski's question.

After a brief, embarrassing silence, another reporter asked a question. Korski turned to me and shrugged his shoulders. "One candidate down."

"How did you know she couldn't answer?" I asked.

"She can't think on her feet," he replied.

When I asked McCoy about it later, she said she didn't anticipate the question. I thought she was smarter than that.

165

8

SCANDAL
SCANDALS, SCANDALOUS BEHAVIOUR AND BAD GOVERNMENT

It must be the Alberta air. While other governments frequently suffer from scandal, Alberta's politicians are either too smart to be caught or too honest to be involved. The Mulroney Government's antics earned an entire book. Quebec sees resignations regularly. Ontario Premier Bob Rae fired five ministers in three years. Who can forget Bill Vander Zalm in British Columbia? You have to wrack your brain, or have a great memory, to find four cabinet resignations in Alberta in 50 years.

Alberta hasn't been inflicted with the kind of political behaviour that led to resignations of three premiers in British Columbia and part of Grant Devine's cabinet in Saskatchewan. Alberta has had no serious scandals that drove the media to distraction, but there was plenty of evidence of scandalous behaviour. The difference is that a scandal is wrong and illegal, but scandalous behaviour is wrong and stupid.

P rovincial politics in Alberta was my professional life for 24 consecutive years until my retirement in 2005. As publisher of *Insight into Government* political newsletter, I covered the Alberta Legislature for 19 years beginning with Don Getty's first election in 1986. I worked in a minister's office for five years before that. Politics, whether I was involved from the inside or observing from the outside, was a fascinating experience and I loved every minute of it.

I saw enough politics up close to last a lifetime. I saw not enough good government and too much bad government. I saw smart politicians and dumb politicians, astute politicians and foolish politicians, heartless politicians and generous politicians. Some made good decisions based on their perceptions of the public interest and others made decisions based on blind ideology. Some politicians were so quiet and so innocuous that I wondered why they were in politics. Infrequently, I would see a politician who exhibited class and grace.

In all those years, however, I didn't see or hear of a single act that could be described as a heavy-duty political scandal in a league with the federal sponsorship scandal or compared remotely to the scandals that occurred in the provinces surrounding Alberta. By scandal, I mean a case where a law is clearly broken and a politician personally benefits.

In Saskatchewan, some ministers in Grant Devine's government in Saskatchewan got jail time. Scandals in British Columbia led to the resignations of three premiers: Bill Vander Zalm in 1991, Mike Harcourt in 1996 and Glen Clark in 1999.

Bad stuff was happening in Ottawa at the time. Books by Toronto journalist Stevie Cameron nailed the Conservative Government under Brian Mulroney from 1984-92. The first - *Ottawa Inside Out* in 1989 - devoted a dozen pages to money scandals. In 1994, *On The Take: Crime, Corruption And Greed In The Mulroney Years* was everything its title implied, from cover to cover. Cameron concluded her trilogy with *The Last Amigo* in 2001 that described the Airbus affair. Although her books were tough and accusatory, and although I heard numerous Conservatives claim that Cameron got it all wrong, there wasn't a single libel suit over the contents.

Nasty business, all of it. Certainly the kind of business that drives public cynicism and leads to changes in government.

Until the 1990s, allegations of improper conduct, whether involving money or sex, were rare in Alberta. Alberta's MLAs appeared to be so clean for so long that one questioned whether they were normal.

Alberta in the 1970s had the classic environment for political scandal. The economy was booming with big money rolling into the Provincial Treasury. The government bureaucracy was in a constant state of evolution after so many dormant years under Social Credit. A growing bureaucracy meant evolving tracking systems and opportunity to manipulate it for personal gain.

Easy money might have tempted MLAs earning ridiculously low wages in the early 1970s. An MLA elected in 1971 earned around $7,200, although the salary was almost doubled within two years. My salary as a lowly communications staffer at Edmonton's Catholic School District was equal to that of an MLA after the wage increase.

Could politicians and public servants, with modest salaries in the 1970s while others were thriving in a buoyant economy, avoid the temptation?

We'll never know whether Alberta's elected members were more purely motivated than in other provinces, or the informal rules of conduct were too loose to be meaningful, or politicians and public servants were not caught because no one cared enough to look. We'll never know whether the Conservative Governments under Peter Lougheed, Don Getty and Ralph Klein were just better at burying the embarrassments before the media caught on. What we do know is that the public record is comparatively clean.

Loose guidelines helped MLAs earn extra income to supplement their salary. As Deputy Premier Jim Horsman rationalized to the Legislative Assembly in 1990: "MLAs are entitled to carry out their ordinary business. They are not deprived of being in business whilst they are members of this Assembly unless they are members of Executive Council." He said nothing about MLAs putting themselves in conflict of interest situations by doing business with organizations funded and regulated by the government.

If an MLA did violate whatever rules were in effect at the time, who would catch them? Until the 1990s, the Government of Alberta had no law and no person designated specifically to monitor MLA conduct. The only person who could call an MLA to account would be the Premier.

A Premier is immensely powerful in Alberta. With the odd, short-lived exception, large majority governments have governed Alberta since 1935. With modest opposition in the Legislative Assembly and no political alternative, a Premier can do what he wants as long as it is legal without worrying about defeat.

Until Premier Don Getty relented in 1991 and accepted that the time had come for written public rules to guide MLA behaviour in the province, the Government of Alberta had only guidelines written by former Premier Peter Lougheed in 1973. Lougheed's "Statement on Public Disclosure of Interest" read into the record of the Legislative Assembly demands that ministers, and only ministers, filed statements of personal and family holdings with the Clerk of the Legislative Assembly. The Legislative Assembly Act guided MLAs in their dealings with the Crown but was silent on other dealings.

Reading Lougheed's statement, it appears he asked for the statements of holdings merely as a precaution. He told the Assembly that the Social Credit had no requirements on personal holdings but he cited a situation in Ontario that saw an apparent conflict of interest. He said the Premier of Ontario then required public statements of holdings. "Although there was no particular reason to call for similar action in Alberta, I nevertheless felt the approach had merit because it would assure the public that there would be full knowledge of a Minister making or participating in a government decision which might conflict with his personal interests."

Lougheed's statement and the rules run four pages.

Several years later, when the Lougheed Government set up Alberta Energy Company, it contradicted its own requirements. Alberta Energy was made into a public company, expecting that Albertans would buy shares. To make sure that MLAs would participate in the public offering, the Alberta Energy Company Act allowed MLAs holding shares to participate in political decisions involving the company.

Statements of holdings are admirable. Statements of holdings that do not apply to all members of the Legislative Assembly are not so admirable. Because all discussions and decisions made by ministers are kept confidential, who beyond the cabinet table knew whether a minister was violating Lougheed's statement of holdings?

Secrecy was a feature of the Lougheed and Getty governments for 22 years, as it would be with Ralph Klein as Premier for 14 years. They made the Legislative Assembly irrelevant by doing all their work in private and bringing only the final version into the Assembly. Despite the secrecy, they were re-elected handily - so why change?

The prevailing political attitude of the time: if voters didn't make a fuss about such behaviour, why change? The Conservatives pretty much had everything their own way since 1971 and liked it that way.

To his credit, when Lougheed had to act publicly, he did. Cabinet Minister Gordon Miniely was fired in 1979 when he absolved a physician from repaying over $100,000 in contentious health insurance claims. Solicitor General Graham Harle resigned in 1983 after he was discovered with a prostitute in a government vehicle. He claimed to be doing research.

Where the federal government and other provinces had laws to guide political behaviour, the Government of Alberta waited until they couldn't procrastinate any longer before introducing the province's first Conflicts of Interest Act, 86 years after the province was created and 20 years after Peter Lougheed's Conservatives came to power.

With the new Conflicts of Interest Act became law in 1993 and an Ethics Commissioner was appointed to enforce it, things started to happen in public that hadn't happened before. It took some time, but things did change.

A LAW CAN'T BE BROKEN UNLESS A LAW EXISTS

The Conservative Government escaped with this behaviour until 1989 when a series of events created public demands that MLA conduct be subject to tougher rules and regulations. Under calm political conditions, the sequence of events I will describe might have passed quickly without repercussions. But the Getty Government was already under heavy attack for its multitude of failed investments in private businesses and the mounting annual deficit. The combination of these events forced Getty to act.

Had Getty's poll numbers not fallen to unusual lows for a Conservative in Alberta, he might have ignored the public furor.

First, the right wing Reform Party, formed in 1987 and catching on quickly with conservative-minded Alberta, instituted a means test for its candidates, insisting that personal honesty and integrity be prerequisites for Reform candidacy. Albertans believed the Reform Party was on to something that was lacking in their provincial government. If ethical conduct was important to the Reform Party, why wouldn't it be important to the Conservatives?

Secondly, the so-called Zarusky Affair, a.k.a. "Chickengate". Steve Zarusky, the Conservative MLA for Redwater-Andrew during the Getty regime, was alleged to have improperly encouraged a municipal government to purchase land in which he had a personal interest. Getty had no interest in embarrassing one of his MLAs but he had to consider a public already reacting to his fiscal performance. With no laws describing how an investigation into MLA behaviour had to be conducted, the Premier's office did its own private investigation and concluded that Zarusky did nothing improper. Details of the private investigation were never revealed.

Thirdly, sitting governments in Saskatchewan and British Columbia, hammered by scandals of their own making, had the legal means to deal with aberrant political conduct. Until the Conflicts of Interest Act in 1993 and the appointment of an Ethics Commissioner, the Government of Alberta had few means to investigate the activities of politicians and public servants. How could Getty explain why Alberta didn't need a specific law governing MLA conduct when most other provinces and the federal government had one?

Fourthly, conflict of interest allegations hit the Legislative Assembly in 1989 when it was revealed that Forestry Minister Leroy Fjordbotten, owner of some 6,000 shares in Alberta Energy Company, which was 50% owned by the Government of Alberta, did not leave a cabinet discussion involving Alberta Energy's expansion plans. When the matter was raised in the Legislative Assembly, Premier Getty reminded the Assembly that MLAs holding voting shares in Alberta Energy Company were allowed to participate in political discussions and vote on matters involving the company. Such conduct may have been legal in this case, but is it right and proper?

Premier Getty acted before events such as these swamped his government. He asked Judge Ed Wachowich to study the government's approach to conflicts of interest.

Two years later, the Conflicts of Interest Act was introduced in the Legislative

Assembly in 1991. It included rules to govern the conduct of elected members and government officials and set up an office for a Legislature-appointed Ethics Commissioner to enforce the rules.

Two years later, in March 1993, with Getty retired and Ralph Klein running on a clean government ticket, the first Conflicts of Interest Act became law in Alberta.

A LAW IS ONLY AS EFFECTIVE AS THE PEOPLE MONITORING IT

With Alberta's new Conflicts of Interest Act setting minimal standards for MLA conduct, it wasn't long before the new Ethics Commissioner had something to do and something to prove. He had to establish his reputation as a man to respect, an independent official of the Legislative Assembly who meant business. Think about this unique employer/employee relationship: a man hired by the Legislative Assembly had to prove his worth by being tough with the people who hired him. And if he was too aggressive and too tough, would he be rehired for a second term by a government that has little problem being re-elected over and over again? A man who enjoys his work might think about this situation.

A law is only as effective as the people monitoring it. When Bob Clark, a retired Social Credit cabinet minister, was hired by an all-party committee of the Legislative Assembly, an all-MLA committee dominated by the governing Conservatives, a buzz went through Alberta's political community that the appointment was a not-so-subtle move to neutralize what few teeth the Conflicts of Interest Act had.

Because they apply and enforce a law, Ethics Commissioners might have a sense of fair play, a legal background, and either investigative experience or some notion of law enforcement. Retired judges and police officers were prime candidates for Ethics Commissioners or Conflicts of Interest Commissioners. For example, British Columbia has had three commissioners since 1990. Ted Hughes was a judge with a history of investigations, H. A. D. Oliver was a lawyer with experience in military and political intelligence, and his successor, Paul Frasor, was a special prosecutor.

Alberta chose a political veteran who loved the political game and knew its players. Bob Clark, first elected as a Social Credit candidate at age 23 in 1960, sat in the Legislative Assembly for 21 years. As Education Minister, he was the first politician in Alberta to hire a reporter to act as his communications officer. When he retired at age 44, he had spent almost half his life in the Legislative Assembly.

Bob Clark loved politics. I met him first in 1972. I was a reporter with CFRN Television and he was the Official Opposition's Education critic. The young Lougheed Government had released the report of the Worth Commission on Education and we had much to talk about. We met again when I was working as a minister's assistant and he was a political consultant with Hill & Knowlton. He talked endlessly about politics, always wanting to know who was doing what, who was on the inside, and who made the decisions.

I knew Clark loved the game passionately and he respected the people in it. A government seeking a sympathetic Ethics Commissioner, who understands the rigours of political life and won't embarrass MLAs unless absolutely necessary, could not choose better than a man who knows what MLAs have to deal with.

Clark would later describe his job as "90% priest and 10% policeman". He saw educating MLAs on the law as his primary function. He was a very good priest but his record as a policeman would be inconsistent.

Clark knew that MLAs wouldn't take him seriously until they had reason to. He knew that most of them don't bother to read the rules and if they do, they shrug them off. Due to the extensive length of their party's majority, Conservative MLAs tend towards an exaggerated view of themselves and their position. As elected people, they believe they are supreme. As elected officials, they see magical power in their position and elasticity in the rules governing their conduct. I can't count the times that an MLA reminded me that the elected call the shots because only their names are on the ballot in an election. They see themselves answering only to the Premier.

Given that Alberta's political community is small and insular, Clark didn't appear to be the kind of man who would be particularly tough on his old friends. Don Martin, author of *King Ralph: The Political Life and Success of Ralph Klein*, described Clark as "fatherly". Clark's friends would agree. To dispel suggestions that he was a pussycat in a tiger's den, Clark needed a case to establish himself worthy of respect.

Mr. Clark, meet Peter Trynchy, the Conservative MLA for Whitecourt; Mr. Trynchy, meet Mr. Clark, the Ethics Commissioner. They knew each other well; for 10 years, they sat on opposite sides of the Legislative Assembly. Clark was a Social Credit MLA and Trynchy, depending on the year, was either a cabinet minister or a backbencher.

Little did he know it at the time, but Trynchy would help Clark establish his credentials as an Ethics Commissioner who takes his job seriously, not an old political warhorse slowly fading into retirement.

You might think that an MLA such as Trynchy who served 30 consecutive years in the Legislative Assembly and won his largest majority in his last election would be remembered well: perhaps as a citizen dedicated to public service, perhaps for his superior political organizational skills, perhaps for his extraordinary patience to put up with public service for three decades.

If remembered at all, Peter Trynchy will go down in political history for none of those reasons. He will be better remembered as a public servant who didn't change his ideas, his attitudes, or his political style in 30 years. He was an anachronism, a symbol of patronage and bring-home-the-bacon politics. The man always liked to play with fire, and for that he was burned. He loved to boast at how much work and investment he brought into his riding. Trynchy and trouble were soul mates. The evidence is in the facts.

Between 1980 and 1994, Trynchy was the subject of four separate investigations dealing with patronage, loans from a crown corporation, and profiting from a land annexation.

With that history, Trynchy had to know that if the Ethics Commissioner got on his case, he had to go the extra mile to be certain his investigation was thorough. If the matter came down to a question of credibility, Trynchy would not get the benefit of a doubt.

Clark investigated Trynchy, Minister of Transportation & Utilities in 1994, for allegations that he got a special deal from a paving company that did work for the Government of Alberta's Transportation & Utilities department. The same company paved Trynchy's home driveway. Did Trynchy personally profit from the association? After a lengthy investigation, Clark cleared Trynchy of the allegations, although he said that Trynchy may be guilty of bad judgment. Clark found no evidence that the paving job was a gift or that Trynchy used his position to influence the paving contractor. Clark did question a $10,000 cheque dated September 16 that was cashed on November 4. Clark claimed that the cheque was actually written after October 28, a few days after the Liberals raised the paving deal in the Legislative Assembly.

Citing a series of contradictory statements from Trynchy and the contractor, Clark questioned whether money for the paving job was intended to change hands. He concluded that Trynchy used poor judgment and that Trynchy tried to mislead his investigation.

Reading Clark's report carefully, I sensed his anger at Trynchy's attempts to mislead him. When I asked him about the anger, he said that I knew him long enough to understand how he would react to an MLA trying to deceive him.

Trynchy reacted vigourously: he threatened to sue both the Liberals raising the matter in the Assembly and the Ethics Commissioner.

After the Trynchy report, *Insight into Government* complimented Clark: "Ethics Commissioner Bob Clark is to be commended for his work on the Peter Trynchy affair. Clark sent a clear message to MLAs that his office and his personal credibility are serious business. In reading Clark's report, one senses the personal indignation over Trynchy's attempt to change his story midstream. To walk away with his head up, Clark had no choice but to tell the story the way he saw it."

The three incidents occurred in the last part of 1994. That was enough for Premier Klein. Trynchy was booted from cabinet.

MULTICORP AND ITS UNSATISFACTORY CONCLUSION

The Peter Trynchy affair was easy for the Ethics Commissioner compared to what came next, a case that Bob Clark could not have anticipated. Possessing a sensitive political antenna, he certainly did not welcome it.

The facts of the MultiCorp case are straightforward. In October 1993, on a trade mission to the Far East, Premier Klein cut a ribbon to open an office for MultiCorp, a small, ambitious Calgary software company operating in a highly competitive field. Few took particular notice of the event. Although such events occur with great monotony on trade missions led by politicians, the Liberals claimed that this event was not on the Premier's original agenda and therefore he must have had a special reason for participating.

Two years later, MultiCorp became a household word in Alberta, not because its share price has risen some 900% but because of allegations raised by Liberal MLA Frank Bruseker, a school teacher from Calgary. Bruseker introduced the

Legislative Assembly to MultiCorp. He alleged that a number of Conservatives had invested in the company. Ralph Klein's wife, Colleen Klein, was one. She purchased 10,000 shares of the company after the Premier cut the ribbon in Hong Kong. Two others were Rod Love's wife and Premier Getty's former Press Secretary Hugh Dunne who had become head of the Government of Alberta Office in Calgary.

The allegations: Klein had done MultiCorp a favour by opening its shop in Hong Kong and the favour was repaid with company shares. Could a link be proven?

The Ethics Commissioner's investigation had to determine whether the Conflicts of Interest Act that deals with gifts to politicians and their immediate families - such gifts must be declared - was violated.

A crucial element of Clark's first investigation, in November 1995, was the conditions under which Colleen Klein received shares in MultiCorp. The first condition of the sale is that she bought the shares at a considerable discount and she got the shares despite the fact that the private placement was full. The second condition: she didn't pay for them upon receipt. Under the purchase agreement, she paid when she sold. In essence, Colleen Klein bought 10,000 shares that were not available to the public for a buck apiece, well below the market price at the time. No cash up front but the full amount payable when she sold. Carrying charges on the $10,000: 10%.

In his first report, in November 1995, Clark wrote that he was not informed of one condition of the sale, namely that she did not pay for them up front. He then wrote that he hadn't asked the question either. Because he failed to ask the question, he wrote, the Kleins were not at fault.

Clark's first report concluded that the Conflicts of Interest Act was not breached in the limited context of the Act. The Liberals refused to let go.

Bruseker produced information on another trade mission to Hong Kong and China in 1994, again claiming that MultiCorp got special treatment from Premier Klein. The media were all over the case. Some noted that Clark didn't mention the 1994 trade mission in his first report. Clark began his second investigation.

In December 1996, his second report on the Kleins and MultiCorp was released. He said there is "no evidence that the Premier took part in any decision in the course of carrying out his office duties or powers knowing that the decision might further his wife's private interest as a shareholder of MultiCorp."

Insight into Government reported: "The first MultiCorp report, without a thorough investigation by people with investigative experience, satisfied no one. The second, released just before Christmas, isn't receiving good reaction either. However it isn't Clark's decision that is raising eyebrows; it is his investigative methods. He could have called an inquiry at the start and settled this matter once and for all. He could have hired an experienced investigator, but he didn't. The second investigation asked only statutory declarations from certain individuals." Clark was perceived as soft on Ralph Klein.

The MultiCorp case led to an unscheduled review of the Conflicts of Interest Act. Premier Klein asked Clark to do the review. Why would the Premier want a review, other than to act as a strategic diversion from the real issue - the Kleins' conduct? In other words, forget Klein, do a review instead to conclude the matter.

An unscheduled review of a provincial law suggests the law has been found faulty or outdated and requires quick remedy. Klein couldn't have wanted a tougher law. If it had been tougher, if for instance it had an "apparent conflict" clause, Clark would have difficulty exonerating Premier Klein. A review as a strategic diversion makes more sense.

Clark appointed a three-member commission chaired by Alan Tupper, a political science professor at the University of Alberta who had co-authored a book on ethics in politics. The review, *Integrity in Government in Alberta: Towards the 21*[st] *Century,* recommended that "apparent conflict of interest" apply throughout the Conflicts of Interest Act as it does in British Columbia. It also recommended what was dubbed the "Colleen clause": that ignorance as an excuse for financial activities of a spouse no longer be acceptable.

Clark supported the "apparent conflict of interest" clause. The Klein Government did not. Eleven months after Tupper's report was released, Justice Minister Brian Evans said the government "is unable to develop any satisfactory wording that would address the issue of 'apparent' conflicts of interest without interfering with the fundamental right of elected officials to represent their constituents".

ALLEGATIONS OF CORRUPTION; A CHRISTMAS EVE SETTLEMENT

Sometimes events happen in multiples of three, politics included. First the Trynchy Affair. Then MultiCorp. In April 1997, *Banksters & Prairie Boys* hit the bookstores.

Monier Rahall, an angry, bankrupt Edmonton businessman, spared no one for his personal financial problems. *Banksters & Prairie Boys*, a political book unlike anything seen in Alberta, took dead aim at the government-owned Alberta Treasury Branches. Rahall blamed the government-owned bank for his financial problems. He believed that the Klein Government ran the bank and he believed he had the evidence to prove it. Rahall attacked ferociously, named names, cited sources and made numerous serious allegations. No one was excluded, not Premier Klein, not retired Premier Getty, not retired Treasurer Jim Dinning, not veteran MLA Ken Kowalski, not the Auditor General.

Rahall claimed that Alberta's political system was corrupt after more than 25 years of Tory rule; that Provincial Treasurers ran the Alberta Treasury Branches; that its administration was corrupt - and everyone was out to get him.

Rahall claimed that while the Klein Government talked a great game of staying out of business, it used the Alberta Treasury Branches to do its work instead. Rahall published a copy of a memo signed by Premier Klein in 1994 suggesting that the Alberta Treasury Branches strike a deal with West Edmonton Mall to keep ownership of the mall in Alberta. Within months after the memo was written, and after the appointment of an acting superintendent - Alberta Treasury Branches had no Management Board or Board of Directors at the time - West Edmonton Mall had a new loan from the Treasury Branch for $450 million.

All along, there were allegations of bribes, clandestine meetings in parking lots, allegations of bags filled with money, foreign bank accounts and a string of numbered companies.

Because it all ended up to court, politicians were handed the best excuse they could ever have to refrain from comment: "Sorry, I can't comment because the matter is before the courts."

In December 2002, *Insight into Government* reported: "The legal battle between West Edmonton Mall and the Treasury Branch was settled out-of-court two days before Christmas. In other words, when no one was paying attention to politics." The settlement included a media ban that means Albertans will never know how West Edmonton Mall got a $450 million loan from the Treasury Branch, whether there were payoffs, and whether politicians were involved.

While *Banksters & Prairie Boys* made intriguing allegations, I found the reaction to the book by people named in it to be more intriguing. The reaction - or lack of it - defined basic characteristics of Alberta's political and corporate culture.

When *Banksters & Prairie Boys* hit the bookstores, a cloud of silence descended across the province. Not a single person named in the book reacted publicly. No one I talked with admitted to reading the book, including politicians named in it. All refused to talk about it, dismissing the book as the ravings of an angry man.

With no public reaction, the book soon lost the public's interest. When the case between West Edmonton Mall and the Alberta Treasury Branches was settled out of court and the announcement made on Christmas Eve, the matter and the book were buried.

SCANDALS VERSUS SCANDALOUS BEHAVIOUR

If Alberta appeared to be untainted by big-time political scandals, scandalous behaviour was a different matter. The difference between a scandal and scandalous behaviour is that a scandal is wrong and illegal; scandalous behaviour is wrong and stupid.

A real honest-to-goodness political scandal involves personal gain, when the political system is manipulated to pad one's own pocket. Scandalous behaviour can cover a lot of territory and need not be confined to individuals.

The list below is not exhaustive but the examples do demonstrate that Conservative Governments can be lazy, irresponsible, or indulge in behaviour that was scandalous. Untold amounts of money were lost.

Try these:

Scandal or scandalous behaviour?

A series of political decisions cost the taxpayers of Alberta plenty. First, the convoluted case involving NovAtel and what happened to $566 million lost when the Getty Government privatized Alberta Government Telephones in 1990. Could $566 million disappear without a trace? Further, when the Getty Government approved the $566 million loan guarantee, it had no idea how the company was run, whether it had a future, and what that future might be. At the time, it appeared that they were concerned for over 1,000 jobs in the Calgary area.

Second, the Olympia & York case in which the Getty Government signed generous long-term rental leases with the Toronto company in return for office construction in downtown Edmonton in the midst of the recession in the 1980s. The Liberals claimed that Olympia & York were getting more than $22 per square foot to lease 400,000 square feet to provincial government departments when the market rate was $12 per square foot.

Third, after the Klein Government deregulated parts of the electricity industry in the late 1990s, retail prices skyrocketed. There were allegations that the American energy giant Enron manipulated retail electricity prices in Alberta in 1999 (a public inquiry into Enron practices was held in Seattle), helping to drive prices up. Enron became the subject of a major accounting scandal in the U.S. two years later and the company became bankrupt.

Fourth, the Code Inquiry into the bankruptcy of the Principal Group of Companies in the 1980s. After a public inquiry chaired by lawyer Bill Code of Calgary, the Getty Government compensated investors with more than $25 million because Premier Getty acknowledged in the Legislative Assembly that the government was partly to blame for the failure of the Principal Group.

Scandal or scandalous behaviour?
The Klein Government spent several billion on power and natural gas rebates just before the 2001 election to pacify an electorate angry at higher prices due to its flawed electricity deregulation scheme. Meanwhile, schools, hospitals and roads were not being properly maintained. The money was not just about an angry electorate, it was about a Liberal Party led by Klein's adversary Nancy MacBeth. The Klein Government wanted to end her political career and destroy the Liberal Party. Spending was one way to do it. Is that a scandal, or merely scandalous behaviour?

Scandal or scandalous behaviour?
The MLA housing allowance early in the 1990s saw several MLAs living within easy commuting distance of Edmonton nevertheless collect the housing allowance and travel expenses, up to $20,000 tax-free annually.

The purpose of a housing allowance is to pay for a second residence in Edmonton for MLAs living beyond daily commuting distances to the Legislature Building (i.e. Grande Prairie, Peace River, Calgary or Red Deer). To receive the housing allowance, receipts were not required. The rules allowed all MLAs to ask for the allowance, including MLAs living in Edmonton's bedroom communities such as Sherwood Park, St. Albert and Stony Plain from which thousands commuted daily to their work in Edmonton.

While rules for housing allowances and travel expenses that MLAs wrote for themselves weren't broken, the boundaries of ethical behaviour were stretched. The allowance was for a second residence and if an MLA didn't need a second residence, why take the money?

Of MLAs who took the allowance, Peter Elzinga of Sherwood Park did not run in the 1993 election and Dick Fowler of St. Albert was defeated.

Why would MLAs risk their reputations for sums up to a paltry $20,000 a year? If they didn't lose their seats in a province where Conservatives were treated with great tolerance, they certainly lost personal credibility. Scandalous behaviour? Oh yes.

Scandal or scandalous behaviour?

When the Klein Government developed a $700 million disaster assistance program to assist farmers victimized by drought in 2003, it paid according to the amount of land being farmed across the province rather than the land affected by drought. A farmer in northern Alberta not touched by drought got the same government assistance as a farmer in the middle of the drought-stricken area. In the three-year period beginning in 2001, the government paid over $1 billion in drought assistance. Is that a scandal, scandalous behaviour, another back door welfare program for farmers, or a waste of taxpayer's money?

Scandal or scandalous behaviour?

Health Minister Gary Mar, a lawyer by training, gave Kelley Charlebois, his former assistant, a lucrative contract without a defined purpose and without documentation. The contract, worth almost $400,000 over three years, may not have been illegal but it was highly unusual practice.

Scandal or scandalous behaviour?

Sex scandals in Alberta? There were a few.

Sex scandals are titillating and embarrassing but not illegal and occasionally grounds for firing. Sex scandals involving politicians are family tragedies. Some involved MLAs working away from home and getting involved with men and women working in the Legislature. Divorce was the usual outcome. Three cases involved Lyle Oberg of Strathmore-Brooks, Jon Havelock of Calgary Shaw and Mike Cardinal of Athabasca-Redwater. Klein ignored the Oberg and Havelock cases but couldn't ignore allegations that Cardinal used government aircraft to carry on his affair. Cardinal was dumped on the backbench for three years.

Some of these examples created a public reaction, some were scarcely noticed except by a small political newsletter paying close attention to what they were doing. Surprisingly, the Auditor General, while he noted some of these incidents, wasn't appalled. The Ethics Commissioner had little to say.

LESSONS IN KILLING SUSPICIONS OF TROUBLE

Politics and governing are strange businesses in which survival is the ultimate goal. All politicians want to go out a winner and to be able to boast about all the fine accomplishments while they were in public office. To go out a winner means having the political smarts to handle the unexpected events that happen to every government.

I must admit that the three eras of Conservative Government had an impressive ability to deal with the unexpected and to escape virtually unscathed. The public record says that no scandal or examples of scandalous behaviour has jeopardized the re-election of any Conservative Government in Alberta.

Sometimes a resolution of controversy or misdeeds meant allowing the matter to be settled by a court, an action that took it out of the political domain until a resolution was reached or an out-of-court settlement buried. Examples include the Ziad Jaber case in 2001 in which the head of the Alberta Gaming Commission was convicted of influence peddling; and cabinet minister Stockwell Day tapping into the Government of Alberta's Risk Management Fund in 2000 to help pay his legal expenses when charged with defaming a Red Deer school trustee while similar funding was denied to a Liberal MLA in opposition; and the case involving the Treasury Branch and West Edmonton Mall described earlier.

Sometimes, potential scandals were turned over to a government-appointed committee and then mysteriously disappeared from the eye of the media and the public.

Sometimes trouble goes away voluntarily, as when Butch Fischer, Conservative MLA for Wainwright, abruptly resigned in 2001 upon learning that Ethics

Commissioner Bob Clark was investigating his involvement with a company that got loans from the Alberta Treasury Branch. MLAs are forbidden by provincial law from getting loans from the government-owned bank.

Alberta has had two public inquiries in the last 30 years: the Brennan Inquiry into land annexation around Edmonton in 1982, and the Code Inquiry into the Principal Group bankruptcy in the 1989.

Public inquiries are strangers in Alberta because they usually go where politicians don't want them to go. Who expected the federal Gomery Commission to bring down a government? Certainly not the Prime Minister who appointed it. Besides, Albertans don't demand them. Politicians have a built-in bias to protect the system that gives them power and control. Politicians rarely look too hard at poor decisions or misconduct. They look only as hard as is necessary to satisfy the public.

Unlike widespread public attitudes towards politicians elsewhere, Albertans appear to trust the people they send to the Legislative Assembly. "Why" is an interesting question.

While Albertans haven't seen big-time scandals, they have tolerated a mess of bad government decisions that wasted billions of dollars. Then again, is that a scandal, or merely scandalous behaviour?

PEOPLE I MET IN POLITICS

CONNIE OSTERMAN

I wish Connie Osterman had written a book. She took the hit for the collapse of the Principal Group of Companies in 1989. When she abruptly retired in 1992, she said "one day the story will come out". Knowing her as principled and a fighter, I thought she was making a promise.

Connie quietly went away and stayed away, never to reveal what she knew. Quitting was unlike her. In the vernacular, she took a hit for the boys, bit her tongue and kept quiet.

Two decades have passed and the Principal Affair has been forgotten and, I might add, so has Connie Osterman. But we still don't know what happened in the inner circles of the Lougheed and Getty governments that allowed a company as big as the Principal Group of Companies to go bankrupt.

As the minister of the provincial government department that should have been keeping an eye on the Principal Group, she was partly responsible. She was at the cabinet table and those who paid attention at the time know that Premier Lougheed had his fingers into everything. That Lougheed was excused from testifying at the Code Inquiry is insulting.

Politicians in Alberta don't write books describing the internal operations of the government they were part of. They could give the Mafia lessons on silence. They won't even talk at a coffee party about cabinet discussions.

I know of two books on the Lougheed era. *The Lougheed Legacy* was written by David Wood, one of Peter Lougheed's friends, with Lougheed's blessing of course. Wood founded the Public Affairs Bureau. Alan Hustak wrote: *Peter Lougheed: a biography*, in 1985, the year of Lougheed's retirement from politics.

A book that included an insider's account of whether the Principal Group of Companies was discussed in cabinet, when, why and the outcome would be a welcome addition to the public domain.

I wish Connie Osterman had written that book. Ultimately, I wish she had written a book because I, like many others, really want to know what she knows.

9

ALBERTA LIBERALS
A PERSISTENCE IN SELF-DESTRUCTION

Jack Horner was a straight-talking, popular Conservative who was easily elected in east central Alberta - as a Conservative. He won every election from 1958 through 1975 with margins that only Conservatives in Alberta could fathom. In 1977, for reasons only he understood, Horner crossed the floor to sit in Pierre Trudeau's Liberal cabinet. As a Liberal, Horner ran in two more elections and lost both times. Nothing personal, Jack. This was the same man running in the same riding; the single difference was that he switched parties. Trudeau still hadn't introduced the National Energy Program when Horner lost the second and last time. If Jack Horner couldn't get elected as a Liberal, who could?

The National Energy Program of 1980 is considered to be the reason for the Liberals' inability to score with Albertans. Why then have the Liberals done better in provincial elections after the National Energy Program than before? Six years after the National Energy Program, the Liberals elected their first MLA since 1967. By 1993, 35 Liberals were elected.

In Canada's parliamentary system, a political party's measure of success is simple and clear: winning is everything. Only the winners wield power; only the winners write policy; only the winners bring change. In the parliamentary system, the losers are paid to gripe day in and day out, without a break.

For the last 80 years, the Alberta Liberals always lost. They are still losing.

Can you imagine a political plight more frustrating? The Alberta Liberal Party hasn't won an election since 1921. In one streak, they didn't win a single seat for 19 years. They aren't taken seriously across rural Alberta. They have only a smattering of support in the cities. They have had seven leaders in 20 years. They have difficulty attracting good candidates. The media ignores them or just criticizes them. Voters looking for change will stay at home rather than vote Liberal. Yet the Liberals are the major political opposition to the Conservative Government and entertain fantasies of one day forming the government.

Alberta Liberals are the province's favorite whipping boy. They take the brunt of complaints for Alberta's one-party state. When the Conservatives pass tough laws, the Liberal opposition is criticized for allowing it to happen. No matter who the Liberal leader is, the majority of Albertans don't approve. No matter the agenda - be it left, moderate or right - it isn't the right one. No matter the strategy, it won't work. The pundits say the Liberals always do everything wrong: they can't find a charismatic leader, they can't raise significant money, their grassroots organizations are ineffective, and their strategies in election campaigns never work. It seems that the Liberals can't do anything right, that they alone are responsible for the dominance of the Conservatives.

The Liberal Party has been criticized for its inability to capitalize on the sharp right turn the Conservatives took in 1993, a shift that lasted only as long as money was scarce, which was just four years. For this, there is a reason. The Liberal Opposition in the Legislative Assembly had little credibility criticizing the Klein Government for doing what the Liberals had proposed for four years - reduce spending sharply.

As the prime political critics of government policy in a parliamentary democracy, opposition parties usually attract significant media attention. Not in Alberta. Liberal alternative policy papers are usually ignored. Liberal criticisms of Conservative policy rarely rate a headline. Reporters rarely use Liberal MLAs as sources.

Only twice in 80 years did the Liberals have a chance to win an election. They blew it both times. Polls suggested that they had a chance to make gains in 2008 against a Conservative Party led by a lackluster Ed Stelmach but ended up losing half their seats. With Laurence Decore as leader in 1993, the Liberals had a chance to win against Ralph Klein and a discredited Conservative Party but their attempt to be more conservative than the Conservatives didn't work.

The final cut: voters unhappy with the Conservatives would rather stay home than vote Liberal. They stayed home in large numbers in 2001, 2004, and 2008 when election turnouts were abysmal. Unhappy voters no longer had faith in the Conservatives and didn't see the Liberals as an alternative.

Where did the Alberta Liberals go wrong? Today's easy answer is that Liberal failures since 1980 can be blamed on Pierre Trudeau and the National Energy Program that is still reviled in the province. This argument doesn't explain why the Liberals did much better in provincial elections *after* the National Energy Program - their best election result in 50 years came a decade after the National Energy Program - than in elections before it when they had no seats for decades.

Why do the majority of Albertans resist the Liberal Party, the only current alternative to the Conservative Party?

PLIGHT OF THE LIBERALS IN THE CONTEXT OF THE CONSERVATIVES

To understand the plight of the Liberals, you have to understand the rise and continued dominance of the Conservative Party.

Peter Lougheed built an open party from the beginning in the mid 1960s. The men and women with him weren't rabid, radical right wingers or single-minded left wingers with another axe to grind. Men like Dave Russell of Calgary and Lou Hyndman and Don Getty of Edmonton were moderates who believed that the time for political change had arrived and they had to be part of it. They believed in public service and good government. They certainly weren't in it for the money. In 1971, base pay for an MLA in Alberta was around $7,200 in 1971 dollars. To compare, the base salary 38 years later is $78,138 in 2009 dollars. Lougheed found community leaders in rural Alberta and drew them into the Conservative tent.

Lougheed handpicked many of the candidates who contested the 1971 election - people such as Jim Foster of Red Deer, Merv Leitch of Calgary, Al Adair of Peace River and Hugh Horner of Barrhead joined Getty, Russell and Hyndman.

All brought a record of personal and professional success into political life. Driving it all was political leadership. Strong leadership attracts strong people. Lougheed was the key guy. He controlled everything.

Within 10 years of defeating Social Credit in 1971, Lougheed's Conservatives had decimated the opposition parties. A new, bright-eyed, energetic moderate political party had replaced an old, tired immoderate political party. Like Social Credit, Lougheed's Conservatives covered the broad spectrum in the middle. They tilted to the right when necessary - they resisted publicly-funded bilingual education not because it was detrimental to a child's education but because conservative-minded Albertans resisted it, as they resisted everything to do with bilingualism. The Conservatives veered to the left when necessary - their social assistance programs were the best in the country and Lougheed didn't hesitate to dabble in the private sector: invest in an airline, buy debentures in a utility company, and loan money to a pulp mill.

In the course of a four-year term, they managed to do something for everyone. They identified themselves as Alberta's champions by fighting the Trudeau Government in Ottawa on two image-building issues: the constitution and oil prices. Lougheed successfully turned the battles into "us" (the Alberta family) against "them" (the eastern intruders). The Conservatives were Alberta; other political parties in the province were mere spectators.

There was money to spend, lots of it. And the Conservatives spent it. No Liberal Government, however loose with money, could spend like Alberta's Conservatives. What other government on the North American continent had the money to help every homeowner pay their mortgage when interest rates rose to 20%? Only Alberta, and Lougheed paid in one of the most generous direct assistance programs in history. It was welfare on a grand scale. Money was so plentiful that it was done without running a deficit. Complaints were few and far between. Who complains about a free-spending government when they are getting a piece of it?

At no time in their first 15 years did the Conservatives appear to be vulnerable. When Lougheed retired in 1985, the party he built had become so dominant that an aspiring politician, regardless of political leanings, looked to the Conservatives before anywhere else. In 1985, only a fool would try to build a political party to rival the still youthful and vigourous Conservative Party. Die-hard New Democrats were reduced to a few men and women with common left wing ideology, the Liberals were still on their hands and knees from decades of trouncings. Social Credit, a power barely threatened for 35 years, had virtually disappeared a decade after losing its first election.

Ralph Klein broadened the Conservative tent even wider. Flirting with the Liberals only a year before joining the Conservatives in 1988, he had no trouble making the switch to the winning side. If Klein had a political ideology, he hid it well. Klein would do whatever it took to get elected. He was, shall we say, flexible in political matters. He could be a deficit slayer one year and a flagrant spender the next - it didn't matter as long as voters agreed.

Right-wingers were welcomed and some were given positions of power. Stockwell Day of Red Deer with his narrow view of morality belonged in a right wing party, but his ego and agenda didn't include shouting from the opposition benches. Victor Doerksen, also of Red Deer, was better suited to a right-wing party. Steve West of Vermilion, who made Day and Doerksen look like liberals, joined. Connie Osterman of Three Hills was a true fiscal conservative but unlike many conservatives, she had a social conscience. All ended up as Conservatives for the simple reason that Alberta had no viable right-wing alternative. Lyle Oberg and Lorne Taylor, both rigid ideological conservatives from southeastern Alberta, joined the Conservatives when they would have been more at home in a Reform Party. Tony Abbott of Drayton Valley, while mostly a nuisance properly buried on the backbench, was better suited to a narrow-minded right-wing party.

Klein's Conservative caucus was broad enough to attract moderates. Here came moderate thinkers like David Hancock of Edmonton, Iris Evans of Sherwood Park and the two Calgary lawyers, Gary Mar and Ron Stevens, all of whom could sit comfortably in a centralist Liberal Party. So could about a quarter of Ralph Klein's caucus.

Remarkably, they got along in public. They may have fought bitterly in the Conservative caucus, far from the curious eyes of the media and the electorate, but in public, the Conservatives were one big, happy family. Like most happy families, they may fight amongst themselves but when an outsider threatens the family unit, it sticks together until the outside threat is repulsed.

Right wingers or moderates - the choice was not about political party but whether to sit on the governing side or in opposition. Sitting in opposition complaining about the government isn't the best reason to get up in the morning. Better to go where the power is. Better to join a successful party and try to take it over from within.

Peter Lougheed's Conservative Party, with its politically moderate nucleus, had become Ralph Klein's Conservatives, a tent big enough to accommodate all views, even Lougheed Tories like Jim Dinning. Another Lougheed Tory - Nancy MacBeth - ended up as a Liberal only after she exhausted her political capital as a Conservative.

With a broad range of candidates, the Conservatives were ideologically flexible. In one era, they are social activists who interfere in the private sector; in another era they dismantle the foundations of everything done by the same party in the previous 15 years; and in yet another era, they go on another wild spending spree. In 35 years, the Conservative Government under three leaders covered the entire political spectrum. Makes one wonder what an Alberta-style Conservative stands for.

In this one-party state where the Conservatives draw from across the spectrum, there wasn't much left for the Liberals.

THEY SAID THEY WERE LIBERALS - BUT WHAT WAS AN ALBERTA LIBERAL?

Contrary to popular sentiment outside the province, Liberals do exist in Alberta. Honest. Liberals formed the provincial government from 1905 when Alberta joined Confederation through 1921, winning four straight elections. History also shows that the Liberal Party's well went dry for the next 65 years. But Alberta politics were dry for all parties not called Social Credit or Conservative. The Liberals bottomed out in 1971, when Lougheed's Conservatives defeated the Social Credit, who won just 1% of the votes cast.

Part of the Alberta angst against everything Liberal stems from the actions of the federal Liberal governments. Historical slights - Albertans can hold a grudge as well as anyone - broadly lumped under the term "western alienation" and including the Crow Rate and the National Energy Program, have given Albertans ample reason to despise any Liberal. If that wasn't enough, federally-mandated bilingualism - why should a Westerner have to look at French on a corn flakes box? - clinched the deal.

In 1989, something changed. Maybe it was the sad performance of the Getty

Government and its myriad of failed investments culminating with the collapse of the Principal Group. Maybe it was the emergence of Edmonton Mayor Laurence Decore as leader of the Liberal Party. Maybe it was a combination of both. Whatever the case, the Liberal vote tripled to 237,787 votes in 1989 (28.7%). In 1993, the Liberals did still better with 392,899 votes (39.7%) and came close to winning the election. As of 2008, they are back to 26% of the vote and in the 15 years between 1993 and 2008, they lost 131,000 votes.

OK, so many Albertans don't care for Liberals. Lots of Albertans don't like the Conservatives either. That's politics. But … if a Liberal runs as an individual, the outcome is sometimes different. For more than 20 years, the mayors of Calgary, the bastion of anti-Liberal rhetoric in the so-called "new" West, have all been Liberals. Ralph Klein as mayor was a Liberal. Al Duerr, another Liberal, succeeded Klein and was even more popular. The current mayor, David Bronconnier, ran and lost as a federal Liberal candidate in Calgary. As just plain David, he won the mayoralty easily. Medicine Hat, another rabid anti-Liberal city in southeastern Alberta, elected a Liberal as mayor. Confessed Liberals were elected as mayors in Drayton Valley, Claresholm and Grande Prairie. Liberals are elected to municipal councils and to school boards.

If you must lay blame for Alberta's one-party state since Lougheed retired in 1985, the behaviour of the Liberals themselves is a good place to start. If the Liberals are good at anything, it is making a mess of their party. To use a trite phrase, the Liberals are their own worst enemy. Before they won seats in 1986, no one cared; after they won seats, everyone noticed. The Liberal story is laden with internal bickering, policy disputes, MLA defections, and an unwillingness to support the leader in tough times. All of it is encased in a defective brand name courtesy of the federal Liberals.

They said they were Liberals - but what was an Alberta Liberal? They experimented liberally - the old-time Liberal Nick Taylor who believed in the liberalism of Louis St. Laurent and Lester Pearson; the fiscally conservative Laurence Decore who talked as if he were a member of the Reform Party; the traditional liberalism of Grant Mitchell; the ambiguous politics of Nancy MacBeth (formerly Betkowski) who reminded me both of a conservative and a liberal depending on the issue; the pragmatism of an intellectual such as Kevin Taft?

The Liberals tried them all, didn't win with any of them and will no doubt be looking for something different again, something - anything - that Albertans might buy.

The Liberal membership is always searching for that perfect leader to rescue them from opposition. When the Liberals finished with Decore, they prayed for Calgary mayor Al Duerr but settled for Grant Mitchell. When the Liberals found themselves with Kevin Taft, they looked south hoping that another Calgary Mayor, David Bronconnier would be available.

While Don Getty and Ralph Klein were inviting anybody to seek a Conservative nomination and determine policy afterwards, the Liberals were trying to squeeze their candidates into the Liberal platform of the day. Seen another way: the Conservatives sought candidates and wrote policy later; the Liberals wrote policy and looked for candidates to fit.

LIBERALS TURNED SHARPLY TO THE RIGHT

Laurence Decore, another long-time Liberal and mayor of Edmonton at the time, succeeded Nick Taylor. Decore was a smart guy. He knew the enemy - the Conservatives. He wasn't sure that he could beat them himself, so he went looking for allies. There are two versions to what comes next - the Alex Macdonald version and the Rod Love version. Macdonald worked with Decore throughout his municipal career and followed him into the Legislature. He told me that in 1988 Decore talked to Mayor Klein in Calgary about running together as Liberals - Decore as the northern champion and Klein as the southern champion. Macdonald swears the conversation took place. Love denies it.

In the grand Alberta tradition of flexible political ideologies, Liberal Decore soon became conservative Decore. At a Liberal fund-raising dinner in 1990, he unveiled a platform that could have been written by Reform leader Preston Manning. It demanded balanced budgets, a stabilization fund, cash-only for capital projects, efficiency audits, a host of Legislature reforms, and he even wanted to sell the Heritage Fund to reduce the rapidly-rising provincial debt. Significantly, he barely mentioned that traditional foundation of Liberal policy: social programs.

Within months, Decore's program was packaged in a brief four-page brochure entitled "Alberta's Biggest Problem: The System Itself". Decore claimed Alberta had a spending problem, not a revenue problem. The line would find itself in soon-to-be Conservative Treasurer Jim Dinning's lexicon.

Speaking of fiscal reform, Decore said: "There is no doubt that this approach will mean some government programs will have to be cut, resulting in critical reaction from certain segments of the public. But our political resolve will come from the knowledge that a far greater proportion of our society will agree with us spending more wisely, more in tune with what we can afford."

Despite leaning to the right, which is where Decore believed the majority of Albertans were most comfortable, he wasn't catching on. In February 1992, I reported in *Insight into Government*: "In all my travels throughout Alberta, I have yet to find a deep commitment either to the man or his party. He isn't being written off but neither is he attracting large numbers of supporters. Some say they'd vote for him if he weren't a Liberal. Others say they still aren't sure what an Alberta Liberal stands for. Still others say they will not support Don Getty, are leaning Liberal, but haven't decided whether to vote Liberal or stay home."

Why would farmers in south central Alberta, who wouldn't vote for their own Jack Horner as a Liberal, vote for a Liberal from Edmonton they don't know?

THE RURAL ANTI-LIBERAL BIAS

Alberta's geography works against an urban-based party. Geographically, Alberta has three natural political zones: Edmonton, Calgary and rural Alberta. The party that wins a majority in two of the three zones forms the government. Edmonton is the most politically moderate of the three zones. Liberals and New Democrats have a better chance to win in Edmonton than anywhere else in the province.

With ambitious right wingers sitting in the Conservative Party, the Conservatives start every election campaign with no competitors for rural Alberta's 35 seats and better than an even chance in Calgary. No party can concede about 40% of 83 seats in the Legislative Assembly to the Conservatives and expect to win.

With moderates in the caucus as well, the Conservatives always have a fighting chance in every Edmonton seat. Sometimes they have a majority in the city and sometimes not, but the existence of moderates in the Conservative caucus guarantees that the Liberals will not dominate the centre and will never be the sole moderate alternative.

The Conservative Party, with a coalition covering two-thirds of the political spectrum, assures that it will govern for a long time.

Why do voters in rural Alberta constantly reject the Liberal Party? Alberta hasn't had a Liberal Government since before the Great Depression in the 1930s, so it can't be their record in provincial politics.

The fault of Pierre Trudeau's federal Liberal Government and its National Energy Program in 1980? Jack Horner was rejected long before the National Energy Program. Controversy over cancellation of the Crow Rate that subsidized grain shipments for western farmers led to cries of "western alienation" on the prairies, and it seems that western farmers haven't forgotten a controversy with roots dating back to World War I. Historically, the western view is that the Liberal Party governed for the east, particularly to preserve its Quebec base, at the expense of the west.

At the risk of stereotyping rural life, rural values and rural politics, rural voters see themselves as straightforward in word and deed and bound to tradition and traditional values, however they may be defined. They like things to continue to be as they are and the way they have always been. And they have never voted Liberal. It appears that rural voters in Alberta just don't like Liberals.

What we know about rural provincial politics in Alberta is that it votes Conservative election after election, rarely deviating even for right-wing movements such as the separatist Western Canada Concept in the 1980s or, more recently, the Alliance. And when rural voters can't support the current Conservative regime, as in the elections in 1989 and 2004, they stay home rather than change their vote. If they don't vote Conservative, they don't vote at all.

In the last 30 years, you can count the number of rural seats that rejected Conservative candidates on one hand and have a finger or two left over. Bonnyville and Vegreville flirted briefly with the Liberals and New Democrats, but soon returned to the Conservatives. Three Hills in Central Alberta voted Liberal in a by-election during the Getty Regime but in the next general election, went back to the Conservatives.

Rural voters have discovered that if they continue to support the Conservatives, they will run the province. The single largest group in the Conservative caucus is the rural caucus, with 30 to 35 members who make up between one-third and half the Conservative caucus. Calgary and Edmonton MLAs rarely agree on anything. The urban split makes the single-minded rural caucus very powerful.

Rural Alberta has found a cow that never stops giving, and they milk it every day.

Later, in February 1992, Liberal policy took a distant second to the discovery that Laurence Decore had a cancerous growth on his liver. It was his second bout with cancer. There is a school of thought that this was the *de facto* end of Laurence Decore's ambitions to become Premier of Alberta. Maybe. Maybe not. Ralph Klein was still Environment Minister in the Getty Government and there was no sign that Premier Getty would leave before an election. Whether public concern about a Premier with a history of cancer (Will he have the energy to do the job? Will he survive even one term?) or the emergence of Ralph Klein as the principal cause for his defeat in 1993 is open to argument. But - the two events together, both in 1992 - were enough to create doubt in the public mind.

The Liberal climb to power and respectability had become much steeper. Decore persisted in the belief that as long as Don Getty was Premier, he would have the edge by running against Getty's fiscal disasters. Polls showed that the Decore Liberals were running neck-and-neck with Getty's Conservatives.

LIBERALS BLOW THEIR BEST CHANCE TO WIN

The 1993 election changed Alberta politics. Some say for the better; some say not. But Alberta did change. The Liberal campaign strategy blew a tire half way through. Decore was sucked into talking about abortion, which he described as "repugnant" thereby alienating the liberal-minded women working on his campaign and New Democrats who planned to park their vote with the Liberals this time to get rid of the Conservatives. Decore apologized for his comments but the damage had been done.

Insight into Government assessed the Liberal campaign midway through the 1993 campaign: "Decore has failed so far to change public perception of his personality often described as distant and arrogant. Some will tell you that Decore, like former Treasurer Dick Johnston, is a warm, engaging fellow in private. Perhaps, but Decore's comment to the *Edmonton Journal* editorial board last week did nothing to dispel that. He said that he holds 'Edmonton in the palm of his hand'. After his careless comments on abortion, he should have known better."

Put all together and add the very significant fact that in an era where so much of politics is theatre - Ralph Klein was a superior political actor - and you have the end of the Decore era. Klein simply ran a better campaign. From *Insight into*

Government: "The clear, simple fact is that Klein mopped the floor with Decore. As a campaigner, the Liberal leader isn't in the same league. He wasn't this time and the more clear-minded Liberal thinkers know that in four years, Klein will do it again. Put Klein and Decore on a platform together and before either utters ten words, the audience has made up its mind. No need for deep intellectual analysis: Klein connects with people; Decore doesn't."

Peter Horcica, an astute political analyst, described Decore as "a bad political actor. Politics is theater and if you can't act, you don't get good reviews."

Liberal knives were unsheathed almost immediately even though they got 39% of the vote and 32 of 83 seats, about half of them in Edmonton. The anticipated rural break-through didn't happen. The Liberal caucus and the party membership began to bicker amongst themselves again. The Liberal convention in January 1994 wasn't a happy place. In April, Liberal MLA Paul Langevin bolted to sit as an independent. In two years, Decore was gone, replaced by Grant Mitchell, described by his supporters as "a little Lougheed".

THE GRANT MITCHELL ERA

Political sense suggests that with the fiscal conservative regime led by Decore done, the Liberal membership would welcome a traditional liberal like Grant Mitchell with his belief that government has a vital role in making life better for people. He won the leadership in November 1994 but the innovative tele-vote mechanism that allowed members to vote by telephone broke, forever tarnishing his leadership. Some Liberal leadership candidates, like Sine Chadi of Edmonton, refused to let it go. Chadi believed that if the televote had been done correctly, he would have won. The holdovers from the Decore era were unforgiving. And since nothing attracts journalists more than political controversy, they became preoccupied with the internal squabbling that never stops in the Liberal Party.

Mitchell survived it all and despite polls suggesting that the Liberals would be wiped out in the 1997 election, he got 33% of the popular vote - down 7 points from 1993 - and held on to 18 seats. But he wasn't destined for the Premier's office and he knew it. Regardless of the internal party bickering and his Liberal roots, Mitchell carried another handicap. In 1996, during a speech to a realtors' convention in Calgary, I asked delegates what they knew about Grant Mitchell. The response was instantaneous and near unanimous: "He worked for Principal." Nothing else about Grant Mitchell had registered. Several months later, while leading a political seminar in Claresholm, I asked the same question. The answer was identical: Mitchell was with Principal when it went bankrupt.

Mitchell's career with the Principal Group dogged him, with good reason. The Principal Group of Companies, with its high pressure sales tactics, snared about 65,000 investors on the Prairies, many of them in rural Alberta. The Alberta Government pulled its license in 1987, which was followed by a lengthy public inquiry. Nothing sticks in memory like failed investments with fraudulent companies. Mitchell, an executive with the company from 1979 to 1986, claimed to know nothing about the company's dubious operations. Not everybody believed him but many, many remembered that he was there when it happened. Rural Alberta simply ignored him.

Mitchell retired from provincial politics in 1998 and joined Wood Gundy as a stockbroker. He is now one of Alberta's Senators on Parliament Hill in Ottawa.

LIBERALS TURN TO CONSERVATIVE NANCY MACBETH

Whatever possessed Conservative Nancy MacBeth to think she should be the leader of Alberta's Liberal Party? She had been a loyal Conservative for two decades. Perhaps the Conservative Party changed and she didn't fit anymore. But her one-time political soulmate Jim Dinning fit in just fine. She didn't explain herself well, telling the media that her husband and her son told her "to go for it". If there was a more important reason to return to politics, she didn't say. The speculation however was rampant. This was revenge; she would get even for whatever Ralph Klein did to her in the Conservative leadership race in 1992.

Whatever possessed the Liberal Party to expect that an unhappy Conservative was their road to the government side of the Legislature? As the expression says: given a choice between a real Liberal and a facsimile, voters will choose the real Liberal. Not so, not this time. The Liberal membership had to know that few Conservatives would switch their vote because MacBeth switched parties. Conversely, the Liberals might have suspected that some of their own supporters would vote Tory because they couldn't tolerate what their party had done.

MacBeth tried - she even sought advice from Peter Lougheed - but she couldn't attract fresh, new faces to run as Liberals. Only Kevin Taft succumbed. Then she tried old faces: David King, the former Conservative cabinet minister who left the party because of Ralph Klein, declined.

In an interview months before the 2001 election, I pressed her on candidate recruitment. I hadn't seen the new candidates she had promised and asked whether she had been able to attract new faces. She said she had new candidates but they didn't want to come out too soon before the election was called. When I said that new Liberal candidates should start to campaign years, not months, before an election, she shrugged and said each candidate had to make his or her own decisions. No nomination meetings in the ridings, no campaign strategies - her Liberals didn't look ready for an election.

In the 2001 election, Albertans had a choice that could only happen in Alberta: a Conservative leader who had been a Liberal and a Liberal leader who had been a Conservative. The Liberal vote dropped by another 30,000, to 27%. MacBeth lost her own seat and immediately resigned, leaving the Liberal party deeply in debt and in yet another state of disarray. Since 1993, the Liberals had lost 130,000 votes. This time, there was no obvious successor to save the party's image.

KEVIN TAFT'S TURN

Kevin Taft talked himself into a run at the leadership when Ken Nicol of Lethbridge resigned in 2004 after a short unsuccessful term. Taft is articulate and intelligent - an academic who wrote books - but woefully short on political experience and political savvy. He was, it should be noted, easily the best of the few people who would put themselves on the line in the leadership contest.

To succeed, Taft needed help. He had no network outside Edmonton and despite touring rural Alberta extensively, wasn't able to connect. Rural Alberta likes their politicians simple, humble and local. As an academic, Taft was a tough sell in rural Alberta where intellectuals are as welcome as bad weather. He's a city boy, and he looked like one and talked like one. Unable to connect with rural folks, he was giving up almost 40 seats in the 83-seat legislative Assembly before an election was called.

Like other Liberal leaders before him, Taft wasn't able to attract a stable of credible candidates and build the party outside Edmonton, riding by riding, and the Liberal membership didn't help him.

In the 1960s, Peter Lougheed built a party, farm by farm, town by town, riding by riding. He knew he couldn't win without strong organizations in every riding -

built from the bottom up. The Liberals seem to think that a party is built from the top down. Strong local organizations produce candidates and attract support. Without them, a party ends up exactly where the Liberals are today - scratching their heads, looking for their next miracle-maker.

In the 2008 election, the second with Taft as leader, the Liberals lost another 15,000 votes and half of their caucus. It was the fourth consecutive election in which the Liberal vote declined. Vote-wise, the Liberals are now back to where they were after the 1989 election. The story is familiar: the media have dumped all over them for the way the campaign was run, Taft was being blamed for everything and resigned as leader, the membership is not happy. The Liberals have only themselves to blame. Why would David Bronconnier, the popular mayor of Calgary who is a federal Liberal, want any part of it?

Grant Mitchell summed up his party's attitude towards its leaders in his farewell speech in 1997: "If the party doesn't like its leader, why should the public?" Nick Taylor and Laurence Decore would have agreed.

Will the Alberta Liberals ever form a government? I think not. Under Taft, the party mused that perhaps the Liberal brand name was their problem. That certainly is their problem in rural Alberta where the Liberal name is despised. No party will form the government in Alberta unless it can win at least half the rural seats. History says that can't and won't be the Liberals.

More likely, a new, fresh moderate party will rise, as Social Credit did in 1935 and the Lougheed Conservatives in 1971. New look, new agenda and most important, fresh faces to replace the tired Conservative Government. The Liberal Party has never been able to put them all together.

It was so before and will be so again.

PEOPLE I MET IN POLITICS

GRANT MITCHELL

When Grant Mitchell was elected as Liberal in West Edmonton in 1986, a friend told me to interview him because, he said, "I guarantee you that this guy is a little Lougheed. Everyone is saying it. To be elected as a Liberal in Alberta five years after the National Energy Program - this guy is something special."

I drove out to his constituency office to talk with him. He certainly wasn't a "little Lougheed". Peter Lougheed wasn't tall and Grant wasn't either. Not having seen them side-by-side but measuring by eye, I'd say they were about the same height. Both could walk under a decent-sized table.

For a politician, Grant was a different interview. When I asked a question, he would give a vague answer and always finish by asking what I thought. Driving back to the office reflecting on the interview, I discovered that I did as much talking as he did. Later I learned that Grant was a terrific listener, a rarity in politics.

Grant was articulate - he could deliver a stump speech with the best of them -

and he loved politics. You won't meet a more congenial person. He was a true liberal who believed that when managed properly, government could be a positive force in society. He believed that government could do good things to make life better for people.

Grant Mitchell was in the wrong province at the wrong time. Laurence Decore, the new leader of the Liberal Party, was running on a platform that was part Reform Party. Voters were angry at government spending under Premier Don Getty. A Liberal who believed in the power of government to do good was always out of place in Alberta. Yet he won re-election three times and served 12 years in the Legislative Assembly, largely on the strength of his gregarious personality.

After his recent appointment to the Senate, we met in Ottawa and he offered a tour of the Parliament Buildings. His passion for politics and his love of Canadian political institutions was contagious.

In Ottawa, Grant Mitchell is finally in his element.

10

JIM DINNING
DEATH OF A POLITICAL DREAM

"I want to be in there," Jim Dinning said one morning in 1981. He was Treasurer Lou Hyndman's assistant and I was Education Minister David King's assistant. Our offices were in the same wing of the Legislature Building. Over a coffee, I casually asked him what he intended to do after politics. Dinning had pointed at Hyndman's office. "I want to be in there." There was no "after politics" in his thoughts. He was all politics.

Iris Evans has been a friend for 25 years and I know that she has good political instincts. She understands people. In July of 2005, she was in the kitchen of our home in the Edmonton Highlands neighbourhood talking about the Conservative leadership race that was expected within two years. "Jim Dinning won't win," she said emphatically. "He has too much going against him. Not enough people like him. And he's from Calgary. The next Premier will not be from Calgary."

I was in Kingston, Ontario, 18 months after my retirement from political reporting, when I read that Ed Stelmach had won the Conservative leadership race in Alberta.

I wasn't surprised that Stelmach had won; I was stunned that Jim Dinning had lost. How in the hell did Dinning lose it? I asked myself. He had ten years to plan, more than enough money to finance a serious campaign, and he had friends everywhere.

Dinning was a stronger candidate than Ed Stelmach. He had a superior record in politics, was better known around the province, and was far more articulate. Dinning had been the architect of a high-profile political solution to the province's financial condition that had become a fiscal calamity; Stelmach was invisible for more than a decade in provincial politics. Stelmach had so little confidence in his ability to win the race that he hadn't bothered to assemble a transition team in case he won. Yet Dinning lost.

The leadership race in 2006 was Dinning's to lose from the start - and he did. For ten years working in the private sector out of Calgary, he patiently waited for Premier Ralph Klein to retire. Ever mindful that a retired politician, even one temporarily retired, will be forgotten quickly, he tried to balance subtle political involvement from the fringes with keeping his nose out of politics for fear that he would be seen as undercutting the slowly fading Ralph Klein.

Dinning managed the balancing act well. In a reader survey shortly after the 2001 election, I asked my readers who would be the best choice to succeed Ralph Klein. Dinning was the easy winner.

So, how in the hell did Jim Dinning, arguably the best Provincial Treasurer in the province's last 50 years, the principal architect of the balanced budget strategy for which Klein happily took credit, lose the Conservative leadership race?

From the beginning, the race was different from other leadership competitions. Life in Alberta was so good for so many that no political issue dominated. The province was rich again: the money flowed, people had money to spend, and the belief was that it would continue to flow forever because the global thirst for oil could only grow. In Alberta, money brings happiness. The leadership contest was not about ideas or ideals - Alberta hasn't had a government of ideas and ideals since the Lougheed Government of the mid-1970s - the last 20 years of Conservative

Government have been all about money. Even a plan to manage the riches from the latest energy price explosion didn't seem to be important.

Life in Alberta had become so damn good that the people, who bought a Conservative Party membership and a vote in choosing the next Conservative leader, had the luxury of choosing the candidate based not on vision, personal strengths, political record, ideology or likability but on simple geography.

The majority view from the regions north of Red Deer was that a Calgarian had held the Premier's office for 28 of 35 years of Conservative rule and that was more than enough. The time for a Conservative leader, and Premier, from the northern half of the province had arrived. In a sentence, it was Northern Alberta's turn. That there was no exceptional candidate from Northern Alberta didn't matter; it was Northern Alberta's turn.

Dinning's mission was clear: to convince the people who paid to vote that hometown didn't matter. If he neutralized the hometown issue, he'd win. On that simple assignment, he failed.

THE MISTAKES STARTED EARLY

Jim Dinning - JD to his friends - should have known better. Here was an ambitious, intelligent young man with nothing but politics on his mind using his Calgary Shaw constituency newsletter to ask his constituents whether the man he worked for - Premier Don Getty - was doing a satisfactory job of governing the province. When the question is asked, readers expect an answer. In December 1990, Dinning, who was appointed to the provincial cabinet by Don Getty, reported to his constituents and the entire province that Premier Getty's performance was, on a scale of 1 (low) to 5 (high), a modest 1.62.

Premier Getty was not particularly popular at that time but he didn't need his Education Minister reminding everybody just how unpopular he was. At that point, whether Dinning had a future in politics was a fair question. For an intelligent young man in politics so long, he should have known better than to ask the question in the first place.

Getty spared him, but the young man was a slow learner. Six months later, in June of 1991, Dinning jumped into hot water again. His friends organized a golf tournament to raise money to help pay travel expenses between his Calgary home and his Edmonton job. The Legislative Assembly already provides travel and living costs for MLAs who reside outside Edmonton. Dinning offered no explanation for requiring additional money.

Dinning's problem was not that the funds were raised - that's normal politics - but that the names of his donors and the amounts of their donations for a political cause were not filed with the province's Chief Electoral Officer. Dinning merely had to file a return with the Chief Electoral Officer, list his travel expenses as expenditures and everything would be legal and proper. To do otherwise is just plain dumb. Dinning should have known better.

Skip ahead to the spring of 1997. Dinning, after four strenuous but successful years as Ralph Klein's Provincial Treasurer, decided to retire after the March election. Klein's campaign staff, fighting an election the polls suggested they would sweep, was looking for a greater edge. What better way than using Liberal leader Grant Mitchell's campaign platform against him? First the Conservatives had to know the platform's costs.

During an election campaign, the Conservatives should do their own calculations. This time, they got a gift. According to the report prepared by the Ethics Commissioner, Treasurer Jim Dinning had asked the Treasury department to calculate the costs of Liberal election promises and passed the report to Conservative Party strategists Rod Love and Peter Elzinga. Armed with the numbers produced by the Treasury department, Klein hammered the Liberals throughout the campaign as flagrant spenders.

Mitchell appealed to Ethics Commissioner Bob Clark claiming that the public service had been used for partisan political purposes. Clark investigated when the election was over - Klein won big - and reported that Treasury did crunch the numbers at the behest of Dinning who, Clark reported, didn't benefit personally. Clark said that while poor judgment may be apparent, no law was broken. Adhering to a strict interpretation of Alberta's Conflicts of Interest Act, Clark said that the Conflicts of Interest Act doesn't apply during an election period. Hence nothing prevents the public service from being used by the governing party during an election period. The public service certainly won't respond to a similar request from an opposition party. Clark further suggested that winning an election isn't considered to be advancement of "a private interest".

Clark's interpretations may make sense to a lawyer but they don't make sense to me. Using the public service for partisan political interests during an election period is wrong. The leader of the political party is accountable for the party's conduct in an election period. Otherwise, no one is accountable for anything because no rules apply.

Clark was lenient. Did he not consider that if Klein had lost the election, Dinning's employment prospects in the private sector would not have been nearly so good? Regardless, Dinning, already a political veteran, knew what he was doing. He should have known better than to use the apolitical public service for partisan political purposes during an election campaign.

Although he was retiring from provincial politics, Dinning would go on to make a series of more fatal political errors, errors that cost him the job he yearned for all his adult life.

But ... in between Dinning's wrong-headed golf tournament and the Conservative leadership race 17 years later is one of the strongest fiscal performances by any provincial politician in the country. Dinning took the fiscal mess left by the Don Getty Government - growing annual deficits and accumulated debt, a billion or two in public money wasted in disastrous investment in private companies, no fiscal plan other than a commitment to resist cuts to key programs such as health and education - and brought order to it.

By the time Dinning left in 1997, Alberta's fiscal picture was among the best in the country. Whether the extreme cost cutting and government restructuring were necessary is another story.

A FISCAL HAWK BEFORE IT WAS TRENDY

The Jim Dinning story is a curious story, and a tragic one to the extent that political failure can be described as tragic. It is not easy to see a friend who wants something so badly and works so hard at it, unexpectedly fail. It is worse when he is the principal cause of his own failure.

I am not one of Jim Dinning's close friends but I know him well enough. We met in 1981 when he was Provincial Treasurer Lou Hyndman's assistant. I worked across the hall on the third floor of the Legislature Building as Education Minister David King's assistant. In the year Dinning was elected as the Conservative MLA for Calgary Shaw, 1986, I began publishing the political newsletter *Insight into Government* on my own. He was back in politics where he wanted to be and I was in the private sector with my own company, which is where I wanted to be. We talked often, both privately and politically, well beyond his political retirement in 1997 and my professional retirement in 2005.

Dinning was articulate, efficient, and gregarious; he was serious and ambitious; he was always gracious in public and often ruthless in private. I couldn't help but see something of Peter Lougheed, his first political mentor, in him. Aside from a determination to succeed politically, both had one essential trait: they told you only what they wanted you to know and not one thought or word more. Even idle conversation was controlled. And both were autocrats, defined here as a politician who tells you what to think rather than asks what you think.

Like Lougheed, Dinning knew what he wanted and how to get it. What Dinning wanted in 1981 was to get elected and sit in Provincial Treasurer Lou Hyndman's chair. While I expected to spend no more than five years in politics as a cabinet minister's assistant - politics was my stepping stone to something better - Dinning saw only politics in his future. "I want to be in there," he said one afternoon in 1981 when we were talking about where we were going in our lives. He pointed over his shoulder to Hyndman's office. There was no mistaking his purpose and ambition. I didn't know at the time that Dinning was really talking about the Premier's office.

In 1981, Dinning, at 29 years of age, had already been inside the Lougheed administration for four years and learned the inner workings of a government. Always thinking ahead and always with his eye on cabinet, he went into the private sector for experience. It didn't last long; within a year he had bounced back into public administration as the Deputy Minister of the province's Federal & Intergovernmental Affairs department. If he was going to be a cabinet minister, he should know what a deputy minister should do. When he had the deputy minister's job down cold, he didn't waste any more time in it. He went straight into elected office as the Conservative MLA for Calgary Shaw, taking a healthy 61% of the popular vote.

Peter Lougheed retired in 1985 and Don Getty, a famous Edmonton Eskimos football player and one of the six original Conservatives elected in 1966, succeeded him. Dinning jumped into Getty's cabinet as the Minister of Community & Occupational Health. He was barely noticed. Public attention went to the fiscal picture after oil prices collapsed in 1986. The province's energy royalties dropped by more than 60%, plunging Alberta into deficits the province hadn't experienced in more than a decade. While natural resource royalties were going through the floor, interest rates were going through the roof and the provincial economy followed the rest of the world into recession. In this condition, who cared about another rookie cabinet minister? No matter, Dinning was where he wanted to be.

After the 1989 provincial election, Dinning was promoted to Education. He was barely noticed in that portfolio too, not because he didn't do anything, but because the focus of the Getty Government was the continuing sorry plight of oil prices and the string of failed investments in private sector companies. The deficits were continuing while voters were becoming increasingly concerned and angry about the state of the province's finances. Getty's personal popularity was suffering. The recently formed Reform Party under Preston Manning was making a strong case for tougher fiscal management across the country and even Alberta's Liberal Party, then led by former Edmonton Mayor Laurence Decore, was talking a tough fiscal story. Getty was boxed in.

Jim Dinning suspected what was coming.

In September 1992, before Getty retired and before Ralph Klein said a word about deficits, Dinning was talking a tough fiscal line. As the Education Minister in a Conservative Government experiencing large budget deficits, Dinning told educators that strong measures had to be taken to restore balanced budgets and the education system would have to do its part. He was a lone voice in Getty's cabinet.

Insight into Government told subscribers that they should take a close look at Dinning's fiscal realities package: "The government and the opposition have been less than frank about the fiscal situation. The Conservatives tend to think that revenues will one day explode and all will be well. The opposition, particularly the Liberals, trash every cost-cutting measure while preaching fiscal restraint and balanced budgets. Dinning, sometimes a rebel in his own Party, has laid it out honestly, cleanly and neatly. Using government fiscal policy and legislated spending limits, he figures that provincial grants to education will drop in each of the next four years."

His message was decidedly different compared to what had happened after royalties collapsed in 1986 - government grants to education increased every year, small increases but increases nonetheless. In the seven budgets from 1986 through 1992, the total education budget - elementary, high school and the universities -

had risen almost 35% while revenues increased a mere 7%.

WHY BETKOWSKI RATHER THAN DINNING?

Within a month, Getty would resign and a leadership race set in motion.

Ralph Klein was out of the gate early. Nancy Betkowski, whose political rise was uncannily similar to Dinning's, was next.

Dinning was an early Betkowski supporter and they had similar apprenticeships. They both studied at universities in Eastern Canada, both were attracted to politics by Peter Lougheed, both worked in Lougheed's office, both worked as assistants to Provincial Treasurer Lou Hyndman, both were elected to the Legislative Assembly in 1986, both went straight into cabinet as rookies, both held the Education portfolio in a Getty Government, and both rejected what they saw as Ralph Klein's "reward and punishment" style of politics. The essential difference between the two is that Betkowski was from Edmonton and Dinning from Calgary.

Two bright, young ambitious people, one male and the other female, with the same political mentor, and two similar political careers - why did one end up supporting the other in a leadership race? Who decided which one would be the leadership candidate? Certainly Dinning was every bit as capable and as charismatic as Betkowski. He was as well educated, as politically experienced and he was arguably much better at relating to people than she was. Perhaps more important in Alberta's regional politics, he was from Calgary, and after two terms of Edmonton's Don Getty, the leadership of the Conservative Party should return to Calgary. One common denominator: rural members of the Conservative caucus saw both as closet liberals.

No journalist or academic has pursued the story of why Betkowski rather than Dinning became the candidate representing the Conservative Party heritage, i.e. the Lougheed school. I've not heard an argument anywhere suggesting the matter was debated. Yet, regional politics favoured Dinning and so did gender politics.

Connie Osterman, the fired Conservative MLA from central Alberta, told me at the time that Alberta wasn't ready for a female Premier. She didn't understand the reasons but she said her instincts told her that Albertans "don't want to go there." When I reminded her that male-dominated countries such as Turkey, India, Israel and Argentina had already elected women as leaders, she shrugged and repeated that Albertans hadn't reached that stage of political enlightenment yet.

Tactfully, she didn't mention that when politicians in a government dominated by males looked for a scapegoat, a woman would serve nicely - as Osterman did for the Getty and Lougheed government's failures to regulate the Principal Group of Companies.

Dinning's political credentials were critical at the time, for good reasons. He had shown questionable judgment in asking his constituents to assess Premier Don Getty's popularity and in organizing a fund-raising golf tournament without reporting the outcome to the Chief Electoral Officer. While not career-wreckers, such activities aren't career builders either. In 1992, both incidents were still fresh in the minds of the Conservative Party. Betkowski, however, was clean. At a time when political judgment is a campaign issue, Dinning was a liability. He wouldn't get his chance for another 15 years. The outcome wouldn't be much different.

On that December 1992 night outside the Northlands Agricom in Edmonton, Jim Dinning was walking rapidly to his vehicle. Ralph Klein had just won the Conservative leadership and Dinning may have feared his political career was over.

I saw him across the parking lot and asked if we could talk. He waved me off, saying that we could talk another time. All the organizing work he did for Betkowski in Calgary and his contributions to *200 Days of Change*, the bible for Betkowski's leadership bid, was going down the drain. He sat in limbo for a week, not summoned to Klein's office to hear of his future - most likely the ignominy on the backbench - and not talking to anyone else either.

BE ASSERTIVE, YOUNG MAN

Betkowski's inability to face up to the fact that she lost the race and her immaturity in dealing with the consequences saved Dinning's political life. She wanted too much from Klein. How much? The versions differ according to the source. Bottom line seems to be the Provincial Treasurer's job - one version says Klein offered it to her and another says she asked for it. She also insisted on Deputy Premier. She could have Treasury, Klein reportedly said, but Deputy Premier had already been promised to one of his supporters. Betkowski wouldn't settle for less and because winners make the decisions, she was escorted to the backbench.

As much as the new Premier was happy not to have to deal on a daily basis with Betkowski and the elitism he thought she represented (Klein's team branded her as a member of the "white wine crowd" during the leadership race), the Provincial Treasurer's job was still open and Klein had no link to Betkowski's campaign team. Although she lost, she had considerable support in Edmonton and Klein would need all the support he could get to fight the coming election. No one in his gang wanted Treasury, not with the very tough medicine that Klein had promised and the public expected.

Most of Klein's early MLA supporters were from rural Alberta: Ernie Isley of Bonnyville, Ken Kowalski of Barrhead, Peter Trynchy of Whitecourt and Don Sparrow from south of Leduc. Each and every one was better known for spending money than conserving it. Not one of Klein's legion of MLA supporters had the stomach to be Provincial Treasurer and Klein knew it.

A second factor was at play. The job would be tough but if it didn't work, Klein needed someone to blame. He had a habit of blaming others for his failures - repeated efforts to reform health went nowhere and as late as 2008, he was still blaming the federal government for refusing to amend the Canada Health Act as he alone wanted. Klein blamed the media when his polls dipped. He blamed interest groups when there was a strong reaction to his policies. And if the deficit elimination plan went badly, he needed someone to blame - someone like Dinning who was an insider on the Betkowski team.

As for Klein keeping incumbent Provincial Treasurer Dick Johnston in the Treasury portfolio - better to eat razor blades. Johnston, who had supported Energy Minister Rick Orman, hung around his office calculating that no one in Klein's gang possessed the guts and skills required for Treasury and he would be reappointed. Johnston had counselled his office staff to stay in their chairs because he believed there was a chance he would be back. Wrong.

After the leadership race, Jim Dinning had been stewing in his Legislature office for a week, not knowing what was happening in the Premier's office where MLAs were streaming in and out and nobody was talking. The Klein-Betkowski speculation was all over the newspapers but the real story depends on whom you want to believe.

The real story didn't matter to Dinning who was more concerned with his own future. He correctly figured that if Betkowski wasn't Provincial Treasurer, he had a chance. Had Betkowski won the leadership, Treasury would have been his choice.

One of Dinning's close friends confided that the strategy as Dinning waited for Premier Klein's office to call could be summed up in a short paragraph: Tell Klein what you want; don't wait for him to tell you what you can have. Show a determination to help him do what he promised to do.

When Klein's office finally called, Dinning had talked himself into being aggressive with the new Premier, promoting himself as the best choice for Provincial Treasurer rather than allowing Klein to dominate the meeting. The strategy was risky but he had nothing to lose because he probably wasn't going to get much from a group that loved to punish its vanquished opponents.

Dinning would tell Klein that he wanted to be Provincial Treasurer, he had devised a tough fiscal plan to implement Klein's agenda, and he would happily take the heat when the heavy spending cuts came. The fiscal plan, as I learned later, was based on *200 Days of Change*, the plan that he had written for Nancy Betkowski's campaign.

Dinning was all smiles the next day. Klein had listened and agreed with his approach. Dinning had the same job as Lou Hyndman had. It would be the start of a four-year term that would turn government operations upside down, restore fiscal sanity to the budget books and restore his personal political credibility.

In 1997, when Dinning retired from politics, he was at the pinnacle of his career.

Ideas to restructure Alberta's public service were in ample supply. The Reform Party had laid out a masterful hard-core conservative fiscal program seven years earlier. The Reform platform was so popular in Alberta that Laurence Decore, the Alberta Liberal leader in 1988, stole many of its ideas, repackaged them as a Liberal plan, and used it as the basis for his 1993 election strategy.

As popular as the Reform fiscal plan was, no one had tried to implement it because no government in power was interested in anything so radical and so threatening to social programs. Besides, turning ideas into action requires a different set of skills and an ability to wield political power.

200 Days of Change, a bold, aggressive plan for the first 200 days of a Betkowski Government had taken elements from various platforms and packaged it as the new way. To accompany *200 Days of Change*, Dinning was a fan of *Reinventing Government: How the Entrepreneurial Spirit is Transforming the Public*

Sector, by David Osborne and Ted Gaebler, the latest American fad to restructure public services. Copies began showing up in MLAs offices in 1993, some copies courtesy of Elaine McCoy. Every Conservative MLA who liked to read, by no means all of them, had a copy. Murray Smith, a rookie backbencher and entrepreneur from Calgary, carried a well-thumbed copy in his back pocket. Dinning was a fan.

Sir Roger Douglas' *Unfinished Business*, his own tale of how he helped save New Zealand's economy from the socialist hordes, was another favourite. Douglas introduced the Conservative caucus to strategies to keep opponents disorganized: quantum leaps (rewritten in Alberta to come off as "you can't cross a chasm in two leaps"), large packages released simultaneously to lump the good with the bad and prevent opponents from focussing on one item, and that speed of change is essential to keeping opponents off balance.

Dinning studied another less-known political classic: *Not Without Cause: David Peterson's Fall From Grace*. Co-written by Georgette Gagnon of Calgary, it was a well-documented treatise of the numerous mistakes Liberal Premier David Peterson made on the road to losing a majority government in Ontario in 1990. Dinning read it, highlighted sections and tabbed pages. Why would a politician considering retirement in 1997 read about political strategies? The book would be more helpful to a fellow considering a leadership race sometime in the future.

And what about those ideas of running government as a business accredited to Ralph Klein? Note that Elaine McCoy, as Minister of Consumer & Corporate Affairs and Minister of Labour in the Getty Government, ran her departments as if they were businesses long before Klein had even heard of the term. Dinning as Minister of Education wasn't interested at the time either.

IS THAT A SPENDING PROBLEM? OR A REVENUE PROBLEM?
Because the province's economy took off with the oil sands investment explosion that began in 1997, few questioned Dinning's controversial deficit and debt reduction strategy. Was it smart to eliminate the deficit on the backs of health, education and other public services? Was it smart to accelerate the debt elimination plan rather than reinvest in public services such as roads, schools and hospitals? The spending cuts lasted barely four years. I often wonder whether Klein would have survived another election if the spending cuts had continued into his second term and people began to understand the implications of lower public services on

themselves and their communities.

Headaches from accelerated deficit reduction remain to this day, notably the large infrastructure deficit that has accumulated over the years because infrastructure spending was hit hard so the budget could be balanced.

Dinning claimed that the Government of Alberta had a spending problem, not a revenue problem as he took an axe to spending. Liberal leader Laurence Decore had coined the phrase several years earlier in a policy paper on how the government's budget process should be reformed.

Did Alberta have a spending problem or a revenue problem? The fact is that the Government of Alberta's spending had been under control for more than a decade. Deficits occurred not because spending on public programs suddenly got out of hand but because energy royalties suddenly collapsed. That looked like a revenue problem to me.

How did Dinning determine that the government had a spending problem? Was spending high compared to revenues, or compared to the cost of essential programs? In 1993, Klein told the Alberta Weekly Newspapers Association that $11.4 billion was enough to run the province. By 1999, just three years after the deficit was eliminated, spending had returned to its pre-Klein level of over $16 billion, a level that constituted a spending problem in Dinning's world.

If Klein and Dinning believed that government spending on essential public programs should follow a revenue path in a resource-based economy, it would lead to fiscal chaos. To spend large amounts of money in health and education one year because energy prices are high and remove the money the next year because prices are down is nonsense.

Government's responsibility is to provide stability in programs such as health and education and to set aside monies to provide stability when revenues are down. Yet it took that Conservative Government more than a decade to set up a stabilization mechanism. As it was, they ignored the one stable financial resource in its budget - the Heritage Savings Trust Fund. Essential public programs - health, education and infrastructure - could have been spared had the Heritage Fund been used to slowly and methodically reduce the deficit.

The price is being paid today with too many substandard school buildings, not enough new schools, too many highways in poor condition, and the questionable physical condition of health facilities.

BEING VISIBLE AND INVISIBLE - AT THE SAME TIME

When Dinning announced his retirement from provincial politics in 1996, *Insight into Government* summed up his term this way: "With due respect to those MLAs who are retiring and those who will retire shortly, no departure is as significant as Treasurer Jim Dinning. His term must be critically reviewed not to judge the man but because the changes he brought dramatically changed the style and operations of the province's fiscal regime. Many of the changes will be standard operating procedure well beyond the life of the Klein Government: a reduced, well-focussed role for the provincial government; balanced budget legislation; a formula for more conservative - but hardly more accurate - forecasts of oil and natural gas revenues; consolidated financial statements; improved budget information; and three-year business plans and performance measures for each department."

Dinning went on to a lucrative career in the private sector. He remarried after his first marriage ended in divorce, his four children grew up with him in Calgary and life was good. But the young assistant who aspired to the minister's office now aspired to the Premier's office. The political fires were still burning. Dinning never made a secret of his ambitions, and, in retrospect, perhaps he should have. Maybe he worried that he would be forgotten. Whatever the reason, he kept his head down, but not far enough.

"He was getting around," I wrote in an article for *Alberta Views*. "He's visible while being invisible but he keeps his nose clean. He takes speaking engagements carefully - business groups, think tanks - and he shows up occasionally in rural ridings. His public statements are crafted carefully to suggest that he has new ideas while avoiding direct criticisms. Try this one to the C.D. Howe Institute in June 2001: 'If I had my druthers, the next agenda would be an agenda for change to shake things up - where government becomes an agitator for change, refusing to become complacent or accept the status quo ...'"

Dinning stayed out of politics until Ralph Klein was forced into retirement by his own party in 2006. Dinning, to no one's surprise, was a candidate. He had money, support and profile. The race was his to lose. And he did. Why didn't he win?

Dinning isn't talking. He and I met in Calgary in August 2007, two old political friends rehashing Alberta politics, and I asked about the race. He didn't appear to be surprised by my question - he had heard it a thousand times before I asked it.

Nor did he seem annoyed at a question about a subject that I quickly learned he didn't want to discuss.

"I'm not talking about that," he said matter-of-factly over a cup of coffee at the Westin Hotel. "That part of my life is over and I'm moving on."

I persisted. "You must have some thoughts about what happened."

"You will have to find out from someone else," he said. "Maybe someone will write a book, if anyone is still interested, that will tell the story. As far as I am concerned, it was not to be. It is over and my life will go on. It's the past and I am thinking only about the future. Politics is no longer my future. Let's see what happens. Life is good, the family is fine."

More than two years after the leadership race was lost, Dinning still won't talk. When I asked a close friend who knows and understands Alberta politics as well as anyone about Dinning's failed campaign, he responded, "Dinning will not talk. The last comment he made on the leadership race that I heard from a close personal friend of his quoted Jim saying 'I spent five years and $7 million of my friends' money and have nothing to show for it.'"

The race was real and it was over. Dinning's behaviour is remarkably similar to Nancy Betkowski's behaviour when she lost the Conservative leadership race to Ralph Klein in 1992. She went into a snit that lasted for years. Dinning isn't hiding but he certainly is in denial.

Dinning won't talk but other well-connected Conservatives will - sort of. Taking bits and pieces from contacts I trusted for many years and putting them all together, here's how Dinning's failed leadership bid went down.

MORE MISTAKES AT THE WRONG TIME

For Dinning's campaign, the race came down to two decisions after the first ballot. Based largely on his inability to neutralize the hometown issue, he led on the first ballot but didn't have the necessary 50% majority.

His first mistake was not to strike a deal with a northern candidate such as David Hancock of Edmonton who had been eliminated on the first ballot. Striking deals with other candidates in the middle of a leadership race is common practice and good politics; it is much smarter to make a deal before it is necessary. Good and unexpected things happen when a politician has the smarts to make a deal - witness Stephane Dion in the federal Liberal leadership race.

Dinning's people figured they could win without making deals and without expanding his key campaign staff beyond the Calgary crowd, and they were wrong.

From the beginning of his drive for the Premier's office, Dinning knew he had an Edmonton problem. That he wasn't able to overcome it is one more reason he is out of politics.

In 2004, I listened to him try to convince a blue-ribbon crowd at the Petroleum Club in Edmonton that he "lived in Edmonton, worked in Edmonton and his children were born in Edmonton". All accurate statements but the argument made scant impact on the crowd.

I was standing in a corner and noted that few were listening while Dinning spoke. When his speech was over, I asked the question to friends on the way out: "Is Dinning right about his Edmonton heritage?" Not a single person agreed. Did they think another Calgarian would win? Same answer: no. The reason given: as soon as Dinning left the Legislature, he returned to Calgary, his home before and after politics. In Edmonton, Dinning was considered a Calgarian; this was Edmonton's turn.

Hancock's supporters would have given Dinning that vital Edmonton boost he needed to win. The offer was made after the first ballot and it included an offer, perceived as arrogant, to pay Hancock's campaign debts, but the offer came too late. Hancock and Ed Stelmach had already struck a deal where they would combine support behind the candidate leading after the first ballot. There is a big difference in politics between *wanting* a relationship and *needing* it. Politicians prefer to be *wanted*.

Dinning's campaign was a series of miscalculations in the early going. He overestimated his support in Calgary and the ability of rural MLAs to get the vote out. He seriously underestimated the rural pull of Ed Stelmach and Ted Morton.

Dinning's second mistake late in the leadership race was to attack right-wing candidate Ted Morton. Negative politics aren't popular in Alberta unless it is another rant against the federal government. People thinking of moving to Dinning on the second ballot didn't appreciate his ruthless attack - "fear-mongering", some said - and went to boring, safe Ed Stelmach instead.

The third mistake: dragging out old Peter Lougheed, who had retired from provincial politics 22 years earlier. Lougheed smacked of Calgary elitism and the past; Conservatives wanted a glimpse of the future from somebody outside Calgary.

Strike three: game over for Jim Dinning. Three critical mistakes in one week. Dinning should have known better.

A smart politician can turn negative situations into opportunities. It's a matter of reading the situation accurately and responding with intelligence and force. That's what separates success from failure in politics.

Jim Dinning has two sides: the successful side that did so well as Provincial Treasurer and the side that made critical mistakes at critical times. At the most crucial point in his political life, the mistake-prone side showed itself.

INTERNAL BICKERING AND A PURGE IN THE PREMIER'S OFFICE

Two other incidents, both out of the public eye, were a factor in what Conservative Party members thought about Jim Dinning and the people who supported him.

First, the outcome of the 2004 provincial election in which the Conservatives lost 12 seats, dropped 210,000 votes and allowed the right-wing Alberta Alliance to win one seat, demonstrated to the membership that the Conservative Party hierarchy was in disarray.

Premier Klein admitted the Conservative Party was broken and promised to "fix it" with a "Renewal Initiative." By the time the "Renewal Initiative" had reported, Drew Hutton, its co-chair and Executive Director of the party, had taken stress leave caused, in no small measure, by the effort to "fix" the party.

Hal Danchilla, a Dinning supporter, co-chaired the "Renewal Initiative" with Hutton. It did not go well from the start.

Danchilla was accused by party members of trying to install a number of Dinning supporters in the Conservative Party's administration office. If he succeeded, the Dinning campaign would have access to Conservative Party files and membership lists. Internal bickering was vicious and a period of lethargy followed. Remember that it was Conservative Party members, not the voting public, who dumped Klein in 2006. Klein allowed the Party machinery to deteriorate and Dinning supporters were alleged to be behind a take-over to restore the Party.

Second, after the 2004 election, a small but immensely important purge occurred in the Premier's Office. The Premier's personally-appointed Chief of Staff controls the people, the tone, access to the Premier, and the flow of information in the Premier's Office. The Chief of Staff has access to everything including the most politically sensitive information. A Chief of Staff can make or break political careers by advising the Premier on who should and should not be in his cabinet. A leadership candidate with access to that information has a distinct advantage.

Chief of Staff Steve West, loyal to no one but Ralph Klein, was outright fired days after the 2004 election. Chief Deputy Minister Julian Nowicki, who had been West's deputy minister in two departments, was transferred to the Alberta Gaming & Liquor Commission office in St. Albert. Jack Davis, CEO of the Calgary Health Authority and former Chief of Staff, Klein confidant and Dinning supporter, had a hand in West's firing. Davis had been West's deputy minister in two departments. Rod Love, who returned as West's temporary successor, also had a hand in it. Love was another Dinning supporter. They wanted to install Robert Day, Dinning's good friend, in the Chief of Staff's chair. Day rejected the offer. Another Dinning supporter, Peter Kruselnicki, former Deputy Finance Minister, was the last alternative.

The stench of power manipulation was overpowering. Who was running this outfit? A contact in the Legislature, when I asked for an assessment, said: "Peter Elzinga vouched for Kruselnicki. Klein was OK with that because he knew Kruselnicki as Deputy Finance Minister. As for Robert Day as Dinning's guy? I only heard about that but I do know that Colleen Klein desperately wanted Day. With all the politics and treachery, the atmosphere became poisonous. Kruselnicki wanted to fire some of the deputies he didn't like and Ron Hicks, the Chief Deputy hired by Klein, didn't know what to do or who to listen to. Klein was absent as usual. I doubt that it will ever get deciphered even if Klein writes a tell-all, which he won't."

Alberta, despite its geography, is a small political community in which rumours travel quickly. Political manipulation of this kind, real or imagined, by a small group of insiders, sent a strong message to the Conservative membership that wholesale change would be necessary. The first chance the members got - the Conservative leadership review two years later - they expressed their demand for change.

Surprisingly, almost 45% of the members asked for a leadership review. The once politically invincible Ralph Klein, the darling of conservative Alberta, was no longer so popular with Conservative Party members.

Theories explaining Klein's demise are as varied as the people expressing them but the bottom line is that the Conservative Party was concerned about its future if Klein continued to lead as he had in the past five years.

Conservative party members expressed their concern again during the leadership race by turning their backs on Dinning.

A curious story lingered in Calgary for months after Ed Stelmach's win. In Alberta's small, inclusive and ever-gossiping political community, one never knows where these stories start or who perpetuates them, but I heard slightly different versions of this story several times.

As Ed Stelmach's Premiership drew negative media reports for a lackluster start and Conservative supporters were thinking that the Conservative Party made a mistake, the story said that Dinning should patiently wait, that Stelmach was the wrong choice and he'll probably blow the election. The Party, this story goes, will have little choice but to encourage Dinning to try again.

Harry Strom is familiar name to people who know Alberta politics. Strom, a veteran minister in a tired Social Credit government, succeeded Ernest Manning and lost the election in 1971, ending 36 continuous years of Social Credit Government. In those few months after the Conservative leadership race, some Conservatives feared that Stelmach would be another Harry Strom. Stelmach fooled them. By winning a large majority, Stelmach is looking more like Ernest Manning.

Stelmach will be around for a long time. He may be as dull as watching paint dry, but he will be safe in the Premier's office until a credible alternative emerges that gives voters a serious choice on election day. To date, none has.

Jim Dinning missed his chance. Too many mistakes did him in.

PEOPLE I MET IN POLITICS

IRIS EVANS

I have known Iris Evans since the early 1980s when I was Education Minister David King's assistant and she was head of the Alberta School Trustees' Association. You get to know a lady quite well when dealing with her for a quarter of a century.

Iris went on to be the Reeve of Strathcona County and hold three portfolios including Health in Ralph Klein's Government. In 2009, she is the Stelmach Government's Finance Minister, a lofty position by any sensible political standard.

My view of her hasn't changed. She was a fine lady before politics, a fine lady in politics, and she is a fine lady still. If she told me something, I believed it was true and accurate. She always came straight to the point, much like Connie Osterman. And like Connie, Iris wore her heart on her sleeve.

Politics did not change Iris Evans. She was as honest and forthright then as she is now. And she was a helluva interview. In one interview, I opened by saying "Hi, how are you?" She talked non-stop for 45 minutes about what was going on in her life and in the government she represented. I didn't ask a second question yet got most of the information I came for.

Iris cares about people and children in particular. That's the reason she was the first minister of the new Children's Services portfolio. She had the sense to get people talking about children and had the smarts to know that to focus Premier Klein's attention on children, she had to win over Colleen Klein. The outcome was the Children's Forum chaired by Colleen Klein and The Alberta Promise.

I saw Iris stuck for words just once. Speaking to the Alberta Congress Board, she casually mentioned that when first appointed to cabinet in 1997, she was asked to sign an undated letter of resignation. I told her afterwards that I knew at least one minister who wasn't asked to sign one. She was surprised – she thought everyone was treated the same.

Iris often left a mark of her visit. She had framed multiple copies of a painting of an iris. I don't know how many she gave but we have one in our home.

11

ENERGY, THE ECONOMY & THE ENVIRONMENT

THE WET DREAM THAT IS THE ATHABASCA OIL SANDS

In 1995, the National Task Force on Oil Sands Strategies predicted $25 billion in investment in the Athabasca Oil Sands over 20 years - if the Government of Alberta gave them what they wanted. They were wrong - investment topped $80 billion in ten years and if you think the royalty rate and the rest of the agreement weren't extremely one-sided, you aren't thinking. Literally, oil was given away in exchange for the right to mine it. Alberta's next energy boom was on.

In 2003, the Klein Government had three different "visions" running concurrently: the three P's: People, Prosperity and Preservation; the three E's: Education, Environment and the Economy; and a third "to unleash innovation, to lead in learning, to help Alberta compete in the global marketplace, and to make Alberta the best place to live, work and visit."

Oil built Alberta. Oil with its immense treasure in the Athabasca Oil Sands is Alberta's future. Are the people elected to govern the province smart enough to manage the treasure properly?

Given their management record since the oil sands boom began in 1997, the people of Alberta should have serious reservations about leaving this immense responsibility to the elected.

The discovery of oil at Leduc in 1947 changed Alberta from a cattle and agriculture-based province into an energy giant. Thanks to oil and natural gas, Alberta is an economic powerhouse with the strongest economy in the country - when energy prices are high. The rest of the time, the Alberta economy manages to survive until the next round of high prices.

The Athabasca Oil Sands generated the latest boom. It came at a good time for the province. Conventional supplies of crude oil were petering out and natural gas production was at capacity. Attempts to diversify the provincial economy were never taken seriously. The economy badly needed a new engine.

Much has been written about Ralph Klein's first term and how he turned the economy around by slashing government spending and trimming the public service. If you listen to his supporters, Premier Klein did something quite magical to bring order and discipline to the provincial government and thus, with government straightened out, he revived the economy. Such are the myths on which legends are built.

In truth, Klein's magic wasn't so magical. The energy industry did it for him. In late 1995, in the midst of deep deficit cutting, along came the National Task Force on Oil Sands Strategies bearing a gift: if the provincial royalty rate on oil sands production were reduced to a mere 1% from 25% until capital investment was recovered, investment would flow into the province.

The Klein Government was so excited to receive this gift to economic revival that the Task Force's report was accepted exactly as the energy sector wrote it - a Faustian bargain if there ever was one. Klein and his cabinet didn't even quibble about the royalty rate, which was the next whole number above zero. The National Task Force couldn't write a lower whole number than 1% and its authors must have been giddy when they wrote it. A low royalty rate made sense, but a royalty rate at a meager 4% of the conventional rate? Admit it - who would have the nerve to propose a 96% reduction in anything? Energy companies weren't going into this cold, barren land to mine expensive oil without substantial economic incentives, especially when a government was desperate to kick-start the economy. Smart and motivated strictly by profits, they weren't going in unless substantial profits were guaranteed.

Klein gave the energy sector everything it wanted - the royalty rate, few environmental caveats, and a virtually unregulated pace of growth. With bargaining savvy, the royalty rate could have been negotiated to 3%, 5% or perhaps 7%. All of these numbers are far below the conventional rate of 25%. But Klein chose to accept the Task Force's recommendation of a measly 1%.

Klein's magic in turning the economy around was the 1% royalty rate, the lowest rate in the world for oil production.

In 1995, the National Task Force on Oil Sands Strategies predicted $25 billion in investment in the Athabasca Oil Sands over 20 years - if the Government of Alberta gave them what they wanted. They were wrong - investment topped $80 billion in 10 years and if you think the royalty rate and the remainder of the agreement weren't one-sided, you aren't thinking. Literally, oil was given away in exchange for the right to mine it.

The next energy boom was on. The political and economic equivalent of a wet dream. The Klein Government had only to learn to manage the economic growth that came with $80 billion.

Don't blame the energy companies for proposing the next lowest number to zero - profits are their business. The government's business is to get a fair share for the owners of the oil - the people of Alberta. Oil is strictly business.

A MANAGEMENT JOB TOO BIG FOR POLITICIANS

All of which leads to the question of whether overall management of an immense, strategically-important oil sands development should be left to mere politicians.

Good business management always gets a fair return for its partners. In this case, has the Conservative Government received a "fair share" for the people of Alberta?

Our Fair Share, Report of the Alberta Royalty Review Panel, the committee appointed by the Stelmach Government to review the entire energy royalty structure in 2007, answered the question in the final report's first three sentences: "Albertans do not receive their fair share from energy development. The royalty rates and formulas have not kept pace with changes to the resource base and world energy markets. The onus is on their government to rebalance the royalty and tax system so that a fair share is collected."

It recommended that the total government "take" from the oil sands, all aspects included, should be 64% rather than the current 47%. This new regime, the report said, will still be lower than several competing jurisdictions. There's more. It said that because of the royalty structure, "Alberta faces lower potential royalties in future years, even if energy prices continue to climb."

Premier Ed Stelmach dabbled with the royalty structure, removing what some considered to be its single biggest flaw - that royalties didn't rise with prices and production. Stelmach was reluctant to get too tough for fear that the energy companies would go elsewhere if Alberta's royalties rates increased. That has always been a fear in Alberta where the international demand for oil is often underestimated - that energy companies would look elsewhere if their treatment in Alberta wasn't what they wanted. It is why, I suggest, that Klein gave them everything they asked for in the National Task Force on Oil Sands Strategies report in 1995. The political attitude is that it is better to try to manage a robust economy based on low royalty rates than explain a troubled economy with higher royalty rates. A tough negotiator would look at the royalty regime and call the Conservative Government "soft".

To make matters worse, the *Our Fair Share* report said that the Government of Alberta hasn't the means or the mechanisms to determine whether the energy industry was paying what it should. Fixing the problem, the report emphasized, was of paramount importance. The fact is that the weaknesses in the reporting system have been known for years, highlighted mostly by the Auditor General. While the Conservative Government regularly boasted that it was accepting the Auditor General's recommendations, *Our Fair Share* says the problem is worse than ever.

If that isn't enough, the report said that Albertans should be told the current status of energy royalties fully, openly and regularly. In other words, no more hiding behind the Freedom Of Information & Protection Of Privacy Act that, by its own wording, discourages open communication.

When the Conservative Government's ability to manage the oil sands is considered, its attitude towards the environment must be included. Frankly, environmental laws and regulations in Alberta have been written so as not to disturb economic development. Energy companies mining the oil sands have not been subjected to tough regulation or tough monitoring. The Klein Government boasted that the energy sector could be trusted to voluntarily monitor themselves. Alberta journalist Andrew Nikiforuk, in his new book *Tar Sands: Dirty Oil and the Future of a Continent*, quotes Alberta Environment Minister Rob Renner: "It's not the role of Alberta Environment to advocate on behalf of the environment." If not the government that writes the laws, then who?

When the ability to manage is debated, honesty is good; honesty creates trust. The generally accepted measure for greenhouse gas emissions is gross emissions. The Kyoto Protocol used gross emissions. Gross emissions didn't fit Alberta's situation - gross emissions in the province would never decline in this century without major changes to oil sands development - so the Government of Alberta changed the measurement. Rather than gross emissions, "emissions intensity" was employed.

Emissions intensity is the ratio of gross emissions to Gross Domestic Product. Simply, if gross emissions rise 5% and the gross domestic product rises 6%, emissions intensity has dropped despite the fact that greenhouse gas emissions into the atmosphere increased. More than once, I noticed that Alberta's Environment department reported a drop in emissions intensity which it translated as Alberta moving to meet Kyoto's targets.

Finally, rapid development isn't everything. The run to the oil sands created environmental and infrastructure concerns. The Conservative Government closed its eyes to environmental concerns but could not ignore the pressures on public infrastructure. Relying on rail and road to move people and goods, public infrastructure could barely cope. Yet no attempt has been made to control the rate of development of the oil sands. Shouldn't the rate of development at least be discussed openly?

Are elected politicians the best managers of this immense resource? Arguments in their favour aren't that strong.

ENERGY AND PEOPLE: RETAIL SALES TELL A STORY

To describe the impact of the energy sector on the province, forget about the monuments and government wealth and the sense of confidence that energy money brings. Although if you do think about it, where are the great public monuments paid for by the riches from energy resources - the concert halls, the art galleries and the museums?

But of greater interest is what the energy sector does directly for the people of the province. The energy sector puts people to work and puts money in their pockets. It helps create a material quality of life that others can only imagine. Businesses were created to support economic activity from the energy sector that in turn brought even more work.

Can statistics assess the impact of the energy sector? Numbers in the millions and billions make little sense to anyone except economists, accountants and, at budget time, the politicians. We need numbers that describe what is happening in the living rooms of the province, not in the corporate board rooms, numbers that tell of the impact on the lives of people who struggle to make ends meet. The best numbers show how much money people are spending because when Albertans have money, they spend it. And if they earn lots of money, they spend lots of money.

Insight into Government followed monthly reports of retail sales to gauge the impact of an energy boom on the streets of the villages, towns and cities. Retail sales was one statistic that I believed could describe the impact of the Athabasca Oil Sands boom on individuals.

In February 2005, just months before I retired, annual per capita retail sales in Alberta were $11,200 compared to $9,280 in British Columbia. In Ontario and Quebec, per capita retail sales were under $9,000. In the eight years after the oil sands project took off, per capita retail sales in Alberta increased 82%, an average annual increase of over 10%.

In 2002, 2003, and 2004, an average of 200,000 new vehicles were sold in Alberta in each year. That's a new vehicle for every 15 men, women and children in the province each year for three consecutive years. Seen another way, one in five Albertans bought a new vehicle every three years.

Energy made many Albertans very happy people, with money in their pockets, nice vehicles to drive, nice houses to live in, and money to spend to escape the seemingly endless winters. True, a roaring economy has its drawbacks: high housing costs, shortages of affordable housing, increased depths of poverty for those who can't take advantage of the economic boom, increased reports of petty and violent crime, and crowds everywhere.

All due to economic activity generated by extracting a barrel of oil or a cubic foot of natural gas out of the ground.

You have to travel elsewhere to appreciate the superior quality of life most Albertans enjoy. An Albertan complaining about the local school or hospital or the roads should spend a few weeks in other provinces to get a taste of real life without oil and natural gas driving the economy.

The energy sector is that good to the people who live in Alberta today. Whether the deal that drove investment in the oil sands will be as good for the next generation is a different story, one that will be told much later when the oil sands royalty rate rises to the maximum and production increases. If money continues to flow into the Provincial Treasury, the deal was a good one. If the chaos of poor government oversight and unlimited environmental degradation persists, the Athabasca Oil Sands may be something quite different.

Sound, sensible management of all aspects of the Athabasca Oil Sands is the key. The oil will always be there; no one can move it to a different location. Oil will always have value and will always be a necessity. Oil doesn't have to be given away in this generation. It can be exploited incrementally while a broader economy is being built that can either thrive with a strong energy sector or supplant it as Alberta's economic driver.

TWO ECONOMIES: BOOM AND NOT-BOOM

In May 2005, in a comfortable meeting room on the University of Alberta campus, Todd Hirsch, Chief Economist with the Canada West Foundation, was talking to a small group about the latest economic boom in Alberta that was at its peak.

This was no ordinary group. While small, it packed considerable power. Among them: Jim Edwards, former Conservative MP and chair of the Board of Governors at the University of Alberta, Eric Newell, Chancellor of the University of Alberta and a kingpin in oil sands development, Allan Scott, CEO of Economic Development Edmonton, and Allan Warrack, former Conservative MLA, retired economic professor turned international consultant, and a man who knew more about the current condition of the Heritage Savings Trust Fund than Peter Lougheed, the Premier who created it.

A man talking to an influential group like this had to know what he was talking about.

Hirsch acknowledged that the oil sands-fired economy was, as he put it, "firing on all cylinders." Generally the economy is terrific, he said, but there are worrying trends in an economy that he described as "boom and not-boom."

Hirsch's first concern was a provincial government that relies on oil sands royalties and natural gas production for the bulk of its revenues.

Lack of economic diversification was another. Hirsch said the economy is less diversified than ever and no sector is growing anywhere near the growth rate in the energy sector. Manufacturing is doing well, he said, but much of its growth was directly related to the energy sector. The story is similar for other industries.

Clearly, despite the health of the provincial economy, he was concerned about an economy tied so strongly to a single industry. History shows that Hirsch's concern was valid.

In 1980, Alberta's economy was propelled by a roaring energy sector. The price of oil threatened to reach $80 a barrel, a price unheard of in 1980. Huge amounts of money were flowing into the province. Within five years, by 1985, the international price of oil dropped to a single digit, interest rates went to double digits, and the world's economy went into recession. So did Alberta's economy.

The Government of Alberta, unable to respond to the times, cynically blamed the federal government's National Energy Program because, for the Government of Alberta, the federal government is easy to blame for economic problems in the province.

Albertans have heard many times before that the province's economy should be more diversified. They have heard the argument that raw materials should not be shipped out of the province. Better to process raw materials to create jobs in the province and help lessen the province's reliance on the energy sector. A simple, logical argument that requires economic leadership and a government with vision.

Provincial politicians know this. I don't have enough fingers on one hand, maybe even two hands, to count the economic diversification strategies that have come out of the Lougheed, Getty and Klein governments.

Let's begin with Peter Lougheed, the Conservative Premier who brought Alberta into the 20th century after 36 consecutive years of Social Credit. In the 1970s, Lougheed complained about large exports of raw products to eastern Canada and the United States. We shouldn't be doing that, he said. We should be building the refining and processing industries in Alberta and creating jobs for our own people. Unprocessed oil products shouldn't be shipped elsewhere; live cattle shouldn't be shipped when a competitive meatpacking industry could be built in Alberta, he said. That was 30 years ago.

To back his talk, Lougheed wrote the *White Paper On Science & Technology* in 1983. Lougheed retired before he did much more than talk about it. His friend and successor Don Getty didn't bother to read the *White Paper*. Instead, Getty launched his own province-wide consultative process in 1991 entitled *Towards 2000 Together* that laid out another strategy to diversify the economy. Like Lougheed, Getty retired before he did much more than talk about his strategy. Getty's successor, Premier Klein, didn't read either paper. Instead, in 1993, his people lifted sections from both of them, added a few of their own ideas, and repackaged the outcome as *Seizing Opportunity*, another economic diversification strategy.

After the 1993 election, *Seizing Opportunity* went to the library shelves. Economic Development Minister Murray Smith, a small-time businessman from Calgary, had his own ideas about the economy. In 1995, he laid out a strategy. Because the cabinet in which he sat wasn't spending money and was too busy cutting spending, Smith's plan was forgotten. Next came a plan from the Klein-created Alberta Economic Development Authority that released its own *Building On The Alberta Advantage* in 1997.

The technology types had to get in on the action. The Alberta Science & Research Council released its strategy called *Information & Communications Technology: A Strategy For Alberta* in 1998.

With Murray Smith gone to another portfolio, Calgary MLA Jon Havelock took over Economic Development. In 2000, he released another economic development strategy entitled *Get Ready Alberta*. Havelock was gone before the plan was implemented.

By this time, the Athabasca Oil Sands were into their third boom year and few thought about economic diversification. The people who did think about diversification - economists such as Todd Hirsch of the Canada West Foundation, Mike Percy of the School of Business at the University of Alberta, and Paul Boothe, another economist from the University of Alberta - were ignored.

In 2004, Economic Development Minister Mark Norris, thinking about a bid for leadership of the Conservative Party when his boss Premier Klein retired, put together yet another plan to help diversify the economy. All the right things were said: lessen reliance on natural resources and encourage diversification through value-added industries, research, technological innovation and a knowledge-based economy. Its impressive title: *Securing Tomorrow's Prosperity: Sustaining The Alberta Advantage.* While Norris was touting the plan, a Statistics Canada report said that 45% of Alberta's international exports were raw materials.

Premier Klein didn't seem to care about encouraging new industries, not when the energy sector was producing billions for the Provincial Treasury. In 1998, when the government-appointed Alberta Tax Reform Commission recommended tax incentives to encourage knowledge-based industries, his caucus turned it down. Klein's government had promised to avoid the trap of investing in the private sector and it would hold to that promise, except for the small matter of subsidies for oil sands development. In one of those odd twists, they made money available to the motion picture industry, probably because they wanted to see Clint Eastwood and Brad Pitt making cowboy movies in the province again.

TOO MUCH TALK, TOO LITTLE ACTION

A fair question: Why is the Government of Alberta always talking about economic diversification rather than doing something about it?

One somewhat ambiguous answer: energy. Energy is the reason diversification is talked about and energy is the reason diversification is not achieved.

When the price of oil is high and the economy is rolling along nicely, who cares about anything else? It seems that every energy-dominated economic boom is expected to last forever - based on the logic that essentials such as oil and natural gas will always be needed - and besides, energy pays so well.

When energy supplies and prices are in a slump, diversification rears its head around the Legislature Building again. Inevitably someone will ask the question of why, with so much money floating around during the last boom, we weren't smart enough to invest in more stable, more predictable industries.

It all seems so logical: invest in diversification when the money is available so that a diversified economy will prop up the economy when energy is sagging.

Mostly, Alberta must diversify because of the lessons of the 1980s. With the collapse of international oil prices in 1986 and the rise in interest rates, the world economy slipped into recession. Alberta's economy went into a slump for the first time since the Conservatives won power in 1971.

If you believe the somewhat entertaining, but misleading, premise of *Mavericks: An Incorrigible History Of Alberta* by Aritha Van Herk, an economic slump shouldn't have posed a problem in a province full of creative entrepreneurs and innovators, the so-called mavericks who flaunt the rules and are adept at making something out of nothing. The 1980s slump showed quite the opposite: without a vibrant energy industry, the rest of Alberta's economy went into the tank too. When oil prices went south, Alberta had to rely on its own wits and entrepreneurial smarts to pick up the pieces, to boost the economy.

It didn't happen, not even with substantial government help. Premier Getty put about $2 billion directly into private businesses - the names include NovAtel, Gainer's, Alberta Terminals, Northern Steel, MagCan, General Systems Research, Northern Lite Canola, Smoky River Coal, Chembiomed, North Saskatchewan Riverboat Company, Atlas Lumber and many more - and lost most of it. Getty put his confidence and the public's money into private businesses in an attempt to stabilize the economy. Didn't happen. Even with generous public money, many of them went down. Turns out that the private sector wasn't as innovative or as smart as the folklore insisted.

ONLY GOVERNMENT HAS THE POWER TO DIRECT THE ECONOMY

The Government of Alberta's job is to manage the province. Building a more stable economy through diversification is essential. The private sector won't do it because they are too busy taking care of themselves to worry about others.

Only the provincial government has the power and resources to make diversification work. If the government wants the private sector to come, it must show that the private sector is wanted and in the private sector, that means money.

Since the financial fiascoes of the Getty Government, Conservatives continue to say they are very reluctant to dabble in the private sector. Quite frankly, they are afraid to make mistakes and end up like Getty.

What they say and what they do are different. The oil sands 1% royalty rate is a massive subsidy into a private business. The seemingly endless stream of money into the agriculture sector is subsidies. Having gone this far, the extra mile to broaden the general economy shouldn't be that difficult, if done properly.

Venture capital is one way to attract private businesses. The Klein Government sold VenCap, the government-owned venture capital company set up during the Lougheed era, in the cost-cutting frenzy in Klein's first term. Innovative companies are usually risky investments because they are different. Yet, if government wants to encourage innovation, it must be involved because the private sector didn't fill the gap when VenCap was sold and went east.

Second is the sector tax credit. Two reports in the 1990s - the *Alberta Tax Reform Commission* in 1998 and *Barriers to Technology Commercialization in Alberta* in 1996 - cited a research and development tax credit as essential in the development of a technology industry. A tax credit isn't handing out money; it is a credit against taxes owed. Tax credits apply when business makes profits and pays taxes on the profits.

The Alberta Tax Reform Commission spelled it out in clear terms: other provinces offer a tax credit for research and development so if Alberta wants to get into the game, the playing field must be leveled with an Alberta tax credit.

For other ideas, the Conservative Government can dust off any of those half dozen or so economic diversification strategies now on the shelves of the Legislature Library.

ENVIRONMENT: A NEW REALITY

Ralph Klein's first portfolio was Environment, a ministry he asked for because he wanted to be where he thought the action would be. Premier Don Getty figured Klein's personality and salesmanship talents might be better suited for ministries involving tourism and international trade but Klein, seeing himself in a different light, persevered.

He held Environment for just over three years, from 1989 through December 1992 when he won the Conservative leadership race and became Premier of Alberta.

By some measures, Klein was a fine Environment Minister. He took an assortment of laws, set up an elaborate and extensive public consultation process that took two years, and came back with an omnibus bill called the Environmental Protection & Enhancement Act. It was considered at the time to be landmark legislation not only for the public consultation process but for its balance between economic development and environmental protection, clarity and breadth.

Klein stood up for the environment, battling Premier Getty and Forestry

Minister Leroy Fjordbotten who wanted to dot Northern Alberta with environmentally-insensitive pulp mill development to boost an ailing provincial economy.

Standing up to his own Premier helped Klein build a reputation as a serious politician and a fighter, a reputation that took him straight into the Premier's office.

Who suspected that Ralph Klein would be the last Environment Minister in Alberta to take environmental protection seriously? When Klein moved into the Premier's office, he too would put environmental protection on the back burner, sacrificed in the name of economic development and growth of the provincial economy. In 1995, on a trade mission to Texas, Klein told potential investors in the energy sector that every provincial regulation is being reviewed and "we're going to scrap the ones that don't work for business and fix the ones that could work better."

The succession of ministers following Klein in Environmental Protection - Ty Lund, Halvar Jonson, Gary Mar and Lorne Taylor - would be more interested in building the economy than in preserving and protecting the environment. It is a pattern that dominated Alberta politics since the discovery of oil near Leduc in 1948. In Alberta, the economy is always first - always. No exceptions. None. End of argument. Environmental regulation was demoted to demon status when it was seen to impede economic interests.

Albertans have long considered themselves to be entrepreneurs and business people, given to building business and an economy regardless of the consequences. With the province's rich deposits of natural gas and oil, a vibrant economy could be built on natural resources alone. When resource development clashed with environmental protection, the government and the citizens of Alberta had to make a choice - and their choice was always with resource extraction and economic development.

Even after the Conservative Government began to set aside land under the Special Places project - land that by law would be preserved and protected – Ty Lund amended the law to include economic development among its goals. In other words, if land under the Special Places program was discovered to have exploitable deposits of oil, gas or coal beneath the surface, by all means, the land could be exploited. Lund also saw that cabinet got a veto over any attempt to restrict economic or industrial activity on land designated under the Special Places program. The

World Wildlife Fund Canada then gave Alberta a well-deserved failing grade for failing to protect new sites.

Did anyone in the Klein Government speak on behalf of the environment? In 2002, *Insight into Government* reported: "Environmental Protection Minister Lorne Taylor's job is to speak on behalf of environmental issues. His job is to write policy to protect the province's environment. So why does he sound like the Minister of Economic Development? Since the Marrakesh Accord on the Kyoto Protocol was reached in 2002, Taylor has been complaining that the Protocol will ravage the provincial economy and the energy industry. Nobody in the Klein Government, including Taylor, has said a word about the impact of the growth of greenhouse gas emissions on the environment."

Public awareness of the Klein Government's single-minded determination to build an economy at the expense of the environment began shortly after the Liberal Government under Prime Minister Jean Chretien showed an interest in the Kyoto Protocol, an international agreement to reduce greenhouse gas emissions to below 1990 levels. The Kyoto Protocol was based on scientific evidence claiming that the planet was experiencing gradual warming and its impact over time could seriously damage the planet and its ecosystems.

From the beginning late in the 1990s, the Klein Government wanted nothing to do with the Kyoto Protocol or federal government intrusion into the province's affairs. Nor did they have a serious concern with greenhouse gas emissions. If they did, they weren't admitting it. Some, like Stockwell Day of Red Deer North, claimed that global warming was a media stunt. When the Canadian Association of Petroleum Producers (CAPP) told a provincial government committee that the energy industry was prepared to deal with global warming as long as they knew the rules, Day came out of the meeting and told reporters: "I can't believe that CAPP hasn't challenged the media line that climate change is occurring."

A NEW EMISSIONS STRATEGY: CHANGE THE MEASUREMENT

When the Kyoto Protocol appeared to be making progress with revised agreements in Bonn and Marrakech in 2001, Government of Alberta rhetoric reached new levels. Among the economic reasons cited: the Americans refused to participate; and while Alberta's other energy competitors, notably Venezuela and Mexico, did sign on, they did not have compliance requirements.

Taylor told the Legislative Assembly that Kyoto as it stood would have significant cost to Alberta "and the issue is that the federal government has no idea of what those costs might be. Our estimate is that this would cost the industry in Alberta up to $3 per barrel of oil to a total some place in the neighbourhood of $6 billion per year out of our economy."

Environmental reasons didn't bother Alberta. Conservative MLAs looked through the Legislature Building windows and saw sunshine, knew they could drink the water flowing in the rivers, saw no haze over the Rocky Mountains and assumed that all was well environmentally.

Numbers were telling a different story. Statistics from the Government of Alberta's Environmental Protection department and the Pembina Institute showed that greenhouse gas emissions were a runaway train in Alberta. Gross emissions across the province in 1990 were 165 megatonnes and projected to rise to 210 megatonnes in 2000. Without action, gross emissions in Alberta would rise to 280 megatonnes in 2012, almost double Kyoto's target. Alberta's greenhouse gas emissions were going the wrong way - up rather than down.

Clearly, Kyoto's targets weren't possible in Alberta without a drastic change in attitude and direction - not with huge development in the oilsands, development that meant massive amounts of greenhouse gases. If emissions from the oil sands were curbed or capped, it meant that economic development would be capped. If development in the oil sands was capped, the provincial economy would stagnate and perhaps decline. It could be 1985 all over again.

The Klein Government saw economic disaster throughout the province if Kyoto's target became international law.

To counter national and international concerns about greenhouse gas emissions and global warming, the Klein Government decided to do something to make it appear that they were concerned. They tried to dump all over the federal government - Kyoto would be as disastrous to Alberta as the National Energy Program - and when that approach had limited appeal outside the province, Taylor came up with an alternate plan.

In May 2002, Taylor wrote an environmental protection plan by himself, without the benefit of public consultation. Premier Klein, who as Environment Minister prided himself on the consultation process, said nothing. Taylor's plan was based on the belief that global warming could be addressed through technological innovation. He said that his new plan, to be introduced to provincial environment ministers in a few weeks in PEI, "would be centered on actually reducing carbon dioxide. With or without Kyoto makes no difference. Preferably without because the technology will not get us there in time."

How about a broad consultation process to involve citizens in the development of the new plan for the environment, the kind of public consultation Ralph Klein delivered as Environment Minister? Not required. Feedback from 74 Conservative MLAs will suffice, Taylor said.

Alberta politicians had taken this arrogant approach before. Convinced that they are correct on all political matters because they keep winning elections, Alberta's Conservative ministers believe that when ministers from other provinces see the wisdom from Alberta, they will recognize the error of their own ways and immediately fall into line. Thirty-five years of majority government rule is partly responsible for such arrogance. Taylor brought this arrogance to the Environment Ministers' meeting in Charlottetown.

Provincial environment ministers, with an ability to think for themselves, wouldn't discuss a plan foisted on them at the last minute. To his and the province's everlasting detriment, Taylor picked up his plan, resigned as co-chair of the ministers' climate change committee, slammed the door on his way back to the airport, and returned to Alberta.

It was classic Alberta strategy on the national stage. The Government of Alberta doesn't win many political battles with other governments because federal/provincial agreements always come down to practical politics and relationships. Smart politicians, through the art of compromise, shrewdly build a supply of goodwill and maneuver themselves into positions where they can negotiate a better deal. Smart politicians learn early that the way to beat the federal government is through a solid coalition of provinces marching to the same beat. It isn't about being soft: it's about being smart.

The Kyoto Protocol did not become national policy but Alberta companies saw the example set by the provincial government and used it as an excuse for their own performances. TrueNorth, an oil company on the verge of investing in the oilsands, abruptly turned away. Their stated reasons? Not the massive cost of construction, the high cost of natural gas, the labour shortage or skyrocketing electricity costs brought by the Klein Government's confusing electricity deregulation strategies. No, it was fear of the Kyoto Protocol. Energy companies complained that the banks were getting tough with loans - because of Kyoto. Even the Churchill Corporation, a public company in Alberta and one of the Conservative Government's big supporters, blamed "Kyoto-related" reasons for a bad quarter.

Not winning the battles in the public or political domains, the Klein Government and Taylor did the next best thing - change the measurement of greenhouse gas emissions. Since the Kyoto Protocol was all about measuring gross emissions of greenhouse gases, the Government of Alberta could redeem itself by changing the measurement to make it appear as if they were doing something positive about greenhouse gas emissions.

There are lies, damned lies and statistics. Enter the term "emissions intensity". Taylor unveiled the measurement in 2002. As part of the proposed new law on climate change, the Climate Change & Emissions Management Act, Taylor insisted "an emissions intensity objective represents a new way of thinking about our overall objective." Indeed, it was. Where the Kyoto Protocol measured gross emissions, Alberta's plan measured emissions intensity. The concepts are entirely different.

Gross emissions measure the amount of greenhouse gases pumped into the atmosphere. Emissions intensity measures greenhouse gas emissions in relation to the economy. Specifically, emissions intensity is the ratio of gross emissions to Gross Domestic Product (GDP).

By 2005, the Government of Alberta's annual report gushes that "Alberta's greenhouse gas emissions intensity continued to decline in 2002 and is down 2 index points compared to 2001. Much of the improvement, the annual report claims, is due to strong economic growth in low greenhouse gas emission sectors with moderate economic growth in higher greenhouse gas emissions sectors. With 2002 emissions intensity at 15 index points below 1990 levels, Alberta is nearly a third of the way to the 2020 target."

Absolute nonsense. Alberta's plan will continue to be nonsense until it measures what it is supposed to measure - gross greenhouse gas emissions. As it stands now, Alberta's gross greenhouse gas emissions could double in the next ten years and as long as the economy grows by the same percentage, the Conservative Government says it is making progress.

Higher amounts of greenhouse gases in the air is higher amounts of greenhouse gases in the air, no matter what the economy is doing. The Klein Government could have been honest about it.

Unless the latest Conservative Government becomes honest in measuring greenhouse gases, nothing it does on global warming will be credible. Equally suspect will be other attempts to protect the environment. The Government of Alberta has to clean up its act in more than one way.

The world is changing rapidly. The second decade of the new millennium will be different than the first decade.

With its resource-driven economy, Alberta will be under significant pressure to change its environmental ways. The Stelmach Government can resist tougher environmental law, arguing that the federal government way is not the way of Alberta. The Government of Alberta can always do in the environment what it has done before in other areas - wait until the courts force it to act. Alberta refused to act on gay rights and bilingual education until the courts forced the provincial government to comply with the law. Conservative MLAs then run around the province complaining that the courts forced them to act.

The United States is an emerging factor in environmental restraint. With so much interest in a continental energy policy, U.S. politics will become as instrumental in determining how Alberta deals with the environment as Canadian national policy, if not more so. When the Americans start to apply pressure through the power of the marketplace, Alberta will have to listen.

Politics and political attitudes in the United States changed dramatically with the election of Barack Obama as President in 2008. George W. Bush and the Republican Party's lax attitudes toward energy and the environment are history.

Barack Obama assures that the United States Government has a new attitude towards energy and environment. A detailed description of Obama's energy plan must wait for another day, but consider the key terms used in the plan he talked about during the election: clean energy future, energy efficiency, energy conservation, climate change action through a cap-and-trade system, increased uses of alternate energy, greater use of renewable resources to generate electricity, and the development of hybrid vehicles.

As this is written, the American Clean Energy & Security Act is before the

Senate. If it becomes law, there will be an impact of energy production in Canada, including product from the Athabasca Oil Sands.

Obama is a serious man and he means business. Since the United States is such a huge market for Alberta energy, a spill-over effect of American energy and environmental policy is certain. If Alberta resists, Obama can swing a big stick.

The road ahead, I think, is clear. Energy and environmental policy in Alberta will be influenced by forces beyond its borders.

PEOPLE I MET IN POLITICS

ROBIN FORD

F
ew readers of this book know the name Robin Ford. Pity, because he was
a fine man. Robin Ford was a talented, visionary civil servant and a deputy
minister in the Don Getty and Ralph Klein regimes. Yet, when he died in
1999, not a single provincial politician attended the funeral. Only Elaine McCoy,
who was Ford's Minister in the Labour portfolio, attended and she had been out of
politics for six years. I counted no more than five senior public servants of the
hundreds that Robin had worked with. I mentioned the conspicuous absences at
Ford's funeral to Chief Deputy Minister Jack Davis. "Don't read too much into
that," he said. How could I not notice the lack of respect?

In 1992, I was told of a speech given by Labour Minister Elaine McCoy citing
work being done to restructure the department. I called her office but she was out
of town. So I called her deputy, Robin Ford. We had spoken several times previously.
He took the call rather than do what so many other deputy ministers would do -
ship the call to the communications department. Ford gave me the full story of the
revolutionary and almost unnoticed work being done to downsize the Labour

department, to set up separate organizations to do regulatory work, and to privatize other services. Two years later, the Klein Government would copy the ideas and not once give credit to McCoy and Ford.

Robin was a rare gentleman and a cultured man with United Nations experience. If he saw me on the street, he would stop and chat. He always returned my calls and was always helpful without violating government rules on confidentiality.

In 1996, Murray Smith was appointed as Minister of Labour. He was smarting from talk that he had been moved out of Economic Development because he didn't have the courage to downsize the department. Smith and Ford quickly had a falling out and Smith fired Ford on the spot, giving him just hours to clean out his desk.

I saw Robin only once after that. My wife and I were in the airport in Edmonton. Robin and his wife were travelling also. All of us were running to catch flights.

We had just a short chat, enough for us to know that Robin was doing fine, he was looking at several consulting offers, but nothing excited him. We promised to meet when back in Edmonton.

We didn't talk again. He died later that year.

12

OPEN LETTER TO ED STELMACH
MORE OF THE SAME?

Ed Stelmach, Premier
Government of Alberta
Legislature Building
Edmonton, Alberta

Sir:

A friend told me that after you won the Conservative leadership, he heard arguments that because of your low-key political style, you might be another Harry Strom. Your first majority government changed that view. He said the new conventional wisdom is that you may become another Ernest Manning.

Quite frankly sir, everything I hear and read of your administration after 30 months, points to neither Harry Strom nor Ernest Manning. Most of what I hear is that your leadership is more like a continuation of the meandering drift so obvious in the last six years of the Ralph Klein Government. The vision, the leadership and the passion are missing. Listen to the terms often used by friends I trust to describe your government: "mumbling", "bumbling", and "arrogant". Can they be right?

The people who elected you expected better because Ralph Klein left "a lot of messes." Those aren't my words. Peter Lougheed, long retired to the comfort of Calgary's boardrooms, is still a keen observer of the political scene. He was quoted to that effect in the *Globe & Mail's Report On Business* last summer. I agree with him. Your former boss did leave you "a lot of messes." You were expected to clean them up and put the province back on track. Instead, it's more of the same.

That you are a modest, cautious Premier is no surprise to me. Although you served 12 years as a MLA and held four portfolios while I was publishing *Insight into Government*, I saw nothing in your performance to indicate a future premier. Nothing bold, nothing innovative. With Ed Stelmach, every assignment was business as usual. You always travelled well under the radar.

To deal with the issues confronting the province, you have to do better. You have to do better because that's why you won the leadership - to get the province back on track. Are you up to it? Or are your numerous critics correct?

If Premier Klein attacked other issues with the same determination he attacked the deficit and debt, your job wouldn't be so intimidating. But by the beginning of his third term, in 2001, Klein had lost his zest to govern. While he ignored important work in health, education and infrastructure, he was still talking about debt and taxes.

By the beginning of his fourth term, the time for change had arrived and the Conservative Party sensed it long before Klein or the voters did. Cocky, colourful Ralph Klein with his sometimes bizarre public behaviour had become a liability. The Conservative Party membership, small as it was, believed that if Klein stayed much longer, damage to Conservative support across the province might cost the next election. They weren't going to take that chance. It astonishes me still that with so much political power, Ralph Klein achieved so little when he could have done so much. He could have been a real superstar.

When Klein was forced to retire, Jeffrey Simpson of the *Globe & Mail* described the event as "the end of the bozo era." A harsh indictment, yes, but no more harsh than some of the words Klein used on his political opponents. Simpson's description may have been an indication of the way the rest of the country looked at Ralph

Klein's performance in the last five years.

As you know from your decade in Klein's cabinet, no government in Canada ever had it so good. You have it very good too. You lead a province in which wealth does not have to be created; it just has to be managed. The province has been on an economic joyride fuelled by the energy industry. The media is timid. The political opposition is struggling to remain credible. Your MLAs won't have to die to get to political heaven; they're already there.

Yet, you have much to do. You inherited a lengthy list of troubles. Some are standard political problems that can be solved with money and good planning. They include an already hefty infrastructure deficit, a health system that hasn't received the intelligence and patience it so desperately craves, and an education system crying for attention. With a healthy bankroll, you should be able to take care of them sensibly. Politics in Alberta today is such that you can deal with these basic issues and be re-elected easily by playing safe. Or you can choose to be an aggressive leader and get to the substantive issues.

The more substantive issues are neither simple nor did they happen quickly. But they go to the heart of respect for the political institutions and health of a democracy. They are within your ability and responsibility to change.

First is the role of the provincial government. After 14 years of a government that ranged from fiscal conservatism to spendthrift liberalism, Albertans have no idea what to expect of their government or what their government should expect of them, beyond their taxes and unquestioning support in elections. Governing is not as simple as Klein made out. Government is more than a mechanism to collect taxes and energy royalties and distribute the money as politicians see fit.

Secondly, Alberta's political process is falling further and further behind standards set in other provinces and in the federal government. This is not a case where you eventually end up at the head of the pack if you stand in one spot long enough. For more than a half-century, Alberta has not touched its political mechanisms or institutions. The political machinery in Alberta is basically the same as it was when I arrived in 1964 to study at the University of Alberta. The consistently dismal voter turnout may be a reflection of that stubborn resistance to change. Corporate cash still drives Alberta's political parties. Alberta hasn't even begun to think about other methods of electing a government. The political process between elections is hidden behind the locked doors of the Legislature Building.

The result is the most politically apathetic population in the country.

Thirdly, Alberta's role in Confederation is not a sexy topic but it is a vital one. Thanks to the magnificent gift of vast energy reserves, Alberta is the wealthiest province in the country yet its relationship with other provinces and the federal government hasn't been given much thought. Wealth doesn't automatically bring influence and respect; they must be earned. If you are concerned about Alberta's role in the country, you haven't yet told anyone or asked anyone's help. Ralph Klein's rants against all things federal make Albertans believe they will be better off to go at it alone. I don't recall the last time a member of the Conservative Government spoke positively about the country. The absence of a feel for Canada makes me ill.

ROLE OF GOVERNMENT

Ralph Klein and his Conservative caucus ran government as if it were a business. Klein had the ill-founded notion that the private sector was superior to the public sector but I was never able to find out why he, who had never operated or worked in a corporation or met a payroll, believed so fervently in something about which he knew so little.

Few others in his first caucus had successful business experience yet they too thought they knew all about business. None of them suspected that government and private business might have different purposes, that the government sector must do for the public what the private sector will not do.

The stark contrast between the Getty and Klein governments is told by terminology: Getty talked of his concern for "the family"; Klein talked of "clients".

Under Klein and his smaller-is-always-better approach, Alberta's public service was blamed for every problem that befell the Conservative Government. Klein cut its staff numbers, fired deputy ministers who dared question the government line, eroded the public service's jurisdiction by turning some of its functions over to the private sector, and demoralized the remainder. The way to straighten out the public service, Klein and his caucus believed, was to reject the way the public service had been run for most of the century and instead run it like a business. It was a mistake that would come back to haunt him. Without sound policy advice from the public service, Klein drifted for at least five years. This drift was one reason his party rejected him.

The fact is that government is not a business and shouldn't be run like a business. Governments in Canada were never intended to be businesses. Governments are concerned with people and motivated by providing services to people; business is motivated by profit. Government doesn't have to be concerned about profits - it levies taxes that should be sufficient to pay for the public services that citizens demand.

The Government of Alberta likes to brag about low taxes in good times but goes crawling to Ottawa when the economy tilts downward. Alberta has a maddening habit of over-reacting every time the price of oil softens.

In December of 2008, when the oil sands were threatened by low prices, your government, which never credited the federal government for its involvement in the oil sands and habitually blames the federal government for everything that goes wrong in the province, ran to Ottawa asking for tax breaks. More recently, you sent your Finance Minister to Ottawa demanding money. You should have been embarrassed. But I suppose that's good business. Ottawa can no more afford tax cuts than you can. If Klein had socked away much of those huge surpluses, you could afford to give tax breaks yourself. You buckled under public pressure to raise royalties for companies exploiting the oil sands and now you discover that playing to public sentiment was a mistake.

Government and business are alike in one way - they try to maximize their ability to meet their objectives.

The Government of Alberta should take an active role in the growth and development of the province it governs. Premier Klein said early in his first term that government's role was to set a stable environment to allow the private sector to flourish. In effect, he turned Alberta's economic growth and economic direction over to the private sector and to the mercy of free market forces. But the private sector will go only where the risk is minimal and profits can be maximized. The private sector cares nothing for the social or cultural welfare of the people of Alberta.

Alberta's economy continues to be driven by the energy industry, as it has been for 60 years. The ride hasn't always been smooth. When the energy industry went into the tank in the 1980s, largely because oil prices dropped to single digits and interest rates rose to double digits, Alberta had no alternate economy to cushion the shock. The arrogance and confidence that came with the oil boom in the late 1970s - the wisdom of the day was that the boom would last forever because oil would always be needed - disappeared when oil prices collapsed. Albertans discovered that they weren't the innovators and entrepreneurs they thought they were when the energy sector was carrying the load. Alberta in a recession was just like every other province - bewildered, demoralized, and looking for someone to blame. Everywhere in the province was the fear that without the energy industry, Alberta would be just another struggling prairie economy.

To this day, the Government of Alberta hasn't learned from the experience. It believes once again that the energy sector will boom forever. Remember the bumper sticker for the 1980s? "Lord grant us another boom; this time we won't piss it away." It must have crossed your mind when the economy dived in 2009.

The oil sands explosion may last a few more decades. But then again, it may not. Late in 2008, oil prices "collapsed" to the $40 range that, five years ago, would have been a very healthy price.

Why would you take such a gamble on a volatile resource when the future of the people of Alberta is riding on it? Why would you allow the endless, but certain, boom-and-bust cycles of the oil economy to dictate the well-being of the people you govern? Why would you allow Alberta's economy and the welfare of its people to continue to be slaves to the vagaries of international oil prices?

Should oil prices collapse again, oil sands investment will go in the same direction. The oil sands carry considerable environmental risk. Emissions from plants pollute the air, lakes and rivers, and the plants consume huge amounts of water and valuable natural gas. To burn one resource - natural gas - to exploit another - oil - makes little sense. Everywhere around you, politicians and citizens know that radical steps to preserve and protect the environment are right around the corner. Your government may fiddle with the measurement (emissions intensity rather than gross emissions) to mask its unwillingness to combat greenhouse gas emissions but at some point, you will have to accept the inevitable. The question is not "if" but "when" tough action to protect the environment will be mandatory. Even the energy companies know they must change.

To protect the province from over-reliance on the oil sands, the economy must be broadened. Twenty-five years ago, Peter Lougheed talked about diversifying the economy. Don Getty did too. Very little came of their efforts, as meager as they were. Under Klein, there was talk of building a "value-added" economy but, like so much of the talk during Klein's era, nothing came of that either.

In the 1990s alone, I counted seven different economic development strategies. That none were vigourously pursued is on the public record. Just as the Klein Government sought a magical solution in health care, it also sought magic in economic development and economic diversification. The magic didn't happen. Too many cooks spoiled the soup. On one hand, the Department of Economic Development was responsible for economic and trade issues. A separate Alberta Economic Development Authority, staffed with many of Klein's friends from Calgary, was also working on economic development. Too often, they worked at cross-purposes.

I see that you have another new energy strategy, outlined in December 2008. Is your government serious about it, or is it merely another process to divert attention when the government doesn't know what to do? It says that Alberta aspires to be a "global energy leader." Greg Melchin, an Energy Minister under Klein, used those exact words in May 2005.

Alberta still exports far too much in raw materials. Processing raw materials in the province would create thousands of jobs and add a vital new dimension to the province's economy. Why would the Government of Alberta not have an Alberta-first policy when it comes to big purchases? Why would the Government of Alberta not use its fiscal might to build such an economy?

Economic diversification is a long, gradual road that requires intelligence and money. It requires commitment in good times and in bad times. Your government must create an economic climate to encourage investment in new industries. Venture capital money will help attract innovative new businesses. The vastly underutilized Heritage Savings Trust Fund could be used as a venture capital centre. Tax incentives will encourage research & development. If you have been paying attention to statistics coming out of your own public service, you would know that research & development investment in Alberta is among the lowest of all provinces. The federal government that Klein despised so much put more research money into Alberta's universities than the Government of Alberta did. For those who scream that the government shouldn't be investing in such things, you can point out that the oil sands investment explosion came only when the province reduced royalties to a mere 1% while the companies still carried capital debt from the project. That's a subsidy with a capital S. Without the subsidy, the oil sands would remain a bit player and the Alberta economy would be as vibrant as Saskatchewan's.

History says that if the Government of Alberta doesn't establish a welcoming environment, new industries won't come on their own. Tax incentives are available throughout North America and if Alberta doesn't attempt to compete, it won't succeed. With ample money, it is time for the government to finally act.

An attractive tax regime is only the first step.

An economic environment that will attract new business includes a reliable, efficient infrastructure network. High-speed rail linking Calgary, Edmonton, Grande Prairie and Fort McMurray will allow the efficient movement of people and products in and out of those centres. High-speed rail will take the pressure off roads that, in a climate such as Alberta's, are very costly to maintain. As an essential public service, public transport should run efficiently but doesn't have to be profitable. I was in Spain in 2008 and rode a high-speed rail link between Madrid and Toledo. A second high-speed rail line runs from Madrid to Barcelona. If Spain can see the merits, why not Alberta? If Alberta waits for the private sector to build a high-speed rail line, it will wait for a long time. The Americans are looking at high-speed rail lines in a number of metro areas. Time for Alberta's government to behave like a leader.

Firms considering establishing themselves in Alberta will want their employees to have a satisfying quality of life in stable, safe communities. Should government be an active player in the social and cultural life of the province? This is more problematic. The question is whether a cultural life is self-sustainable. In most cases, cultural facilities - theatres, libraries, art galleries, and museums - can't survive without government assistance. Without government assistance, their fees would be so high that a significant proportion of the population couldn't afford the services. That is not acceptable. Yet, without a vibrant cultural life, business will think twice about coming to Alberta and they could go elsewhere.

It is time, sir, for the Government of Alberta to start thinking about the people of the province, and not just the money. You can't eat money, drink it or smoke it. Money by itself won't protect you from the cold. Money stuffed in the mattress is old-time thinking. Money has value only when it is used wisely. Money spent wisely goes into programs that make life better for citizens: public education, public health, public buildings, roads, recreation and community development.

THE POLITICAL PROCESS

Albertans are not engaged in the politics of the province. More than half of the eligible voters don't cast their ballot in provincial general elections. Even fewer vote in local elections. A small minority belongs to a political party. The majority pays little attention to provincial politics, a fact verified by scant newspaper attention. Politics is not a popular topic anywhere in the province. This is not a sign of a healthy democracy. Either the citizens of Alberta don't care or have lost faith in their political institutions.

To engage people in politics, political parties must make an effort to communicate with them. Under current conditions where corporate money makes up the majority of money received by most parties, the parties have no incentives to build a membership. You know that corporate money has been banned in federal politics and in some of the provinces. Their political systems haven't collapsed. The federal Conservatives are showing that ample money can be raised from individual contributions. At the same time, they communicate with the donors. In the U.S., the Democrats raised tens of millions, $5 at a time, most of it through the internet. It is good politics, good business and healthy in a democracy.

Klein said that he was getting out from under the Dome, meaning he wasn't spending time in the Legislature Building, but with citizens of the province. Laws are written in the Legislature Building. If Klein wasn't writing them, who was? Time to open the doors and windows of the Legislature Building, sir, so the voters of the province can see what is going on inside it. Time to start asking Albertans what they want between elections, rather than telling them at election time.

ALBERTA IN CONFEDERATION

You should be concerned that other Canadians will start to look at Alberta as the Europeans look at the United States - with envy and loathing. Envy because of the wealth, loathing because of the behaviour of Alberta's provincial politicians in recent years. The envy is understandable but loathing is a different matter entirely. So far, the loathing is confined to politicians representing the Government of Alberta but if things don't change, the feeling will spread.

Ralph Klein had no sense of Alberta in the context of the country. He used other premiers to coerce money and power from the federal government. If he had national thoughts, he didn't say. He didn't contribute to the national debate on what the country should be, where it was going, and Alberta's place in it. In Klein's world, governing was all about debt, taxes and patronizing the private sector. And forever reminding the federal government that Alberta owned its natural resources.

Small events tell a larger story. The Government of Alberta has its own offices in places where it has a strategic interest including the United States, Asia and Europe. But the Government of Alberta has no office in Ottawa, the seat of the federal government in its own country. When the Alberta was opening its office in Washington D.C., Klein was shutting down the office in Ottawa. This was grudge politics, not smart politics. How did Alberta know what the federal government was doing? Did the Premier and his cabinet trust the newspapers to tell them?

Peter Lougheed, who says you and he talk occasionally, was an active player on the national scene. He was tough with Ottawa on issues relating to natural resources but he was active on all matters affecting the province. He was vocal and he was a builder. He worked at making Alberta a more powerful and influential member of the federation. He even used the Heritage Fund to help other provinces.

Dare I say it - Lougheed never walked out of a national conference to gamble in a casino. By that single simple act, Klein did more to damage Alberta's relationships with other provinces than can be imagined. If the provinces didn't get Klein's drift, Lorne Taylor, his Environment Minister, walked out of a federal meeting when the other provinces wouldn't debate his plan on greenhouse gas emissions. On his way out the door, Taylor resigned as co-chair of a national committee. These examples are not smart politics or leadership. Such behaviour diminishes everyone and everything political in the province.

Check the record: when Klein ranted, the rest of the country turned off. The Alberta agenda has gone exactly nowhere in other provinces. Alberta set up a single-rate personal income tax regime; no other province paid attention. Alberta deregulated parts of the electricity system; no other province will touch it. Alberta privatized the retail liquor business; no others are interested. Alberta vigorously fought the Kyoto Protocol while the other premiers sat back and watched. Alberta did its own health care report - the Premier's Advisory Council On Health chaired by former Deputy Prime Minister Don Mazankowski - and released it in advance of the Romanow and Kirby reports, both federal government-sponsored reports on health care, because Klein hoped to influence them, but nobody was listening. When other provinces couldn't be convinced, the government that commissioned the Mazankowski report began to ignore it. Few provinces sympathized with Alberta over greater privatization in health care, the gun registry, or Canada's position on Iraq. When no other province slashed spending to balance their budgets as Alberta did, Klein's response was more crude language.

Some of these examples are good policies that might work in other provinces but none of them wanted to be seen following Alberta's lead.

Alberta has no natural political alliances with other provinces. Klein's politics were personal. He had personal relationships with Mike Harris in Ontario and, to a lesser degree, with Jean Charest in Quebec. When Harris was gone, Klein lost his only friend amongst the premiers.

Relationships with the rest of Canada must be rebuilt, not just with Ottawa but with the provinces. That might be tricky because with so much wealth, other provinces envy - perhaps resent is a better word - Alberta. But the wealth is a fact and it must be dealt with.

How should Alberta do it? Is Alberta equal - or more equal because of its wealth? Wars were fought and blood spilled to preserve the ideal that in matters of governance, all persons are equal regardless of wealth or position. Big money buys influence in the private sector, not the public sector.

I don't remember the last time that the Government of Alberta talked about the relationship of Alberta with other provinces. The interprovincial strategy seems to be based on the fear that the federal government is trying to steal the Heritage Savings Trust Fund or skim part of the oil royalties through taxation. They seem to know more of what they don't want than what they do want. And what they don't want is the federal government telling them what to do.

The Government of Alberta can't continue to define itself in the context of battling the federal government. Alberta has the talent and the means to be a national leader. Money doesn't automatically mean leadership and influence. It is time for Alberta to be part of the nation rather than identifying itself by what makes it different. Time for mature politics.

There is much to be done. I hope you will see the potential before you and that you will use the power Albertans have given you for the good of Alberta and Canada.

Sir, you can be another Ernest Manning or even a Peter Lougheed. Or you could face a leadership review and suffer the same fate as Ralph Klein.

The choice is yours. Political conditions are in your favour: a huge majority government, ample money, a small opposition, and no existing political alternative. It is up to you to seize the advantage to make Alberta a better place to work and live. If you don't, if you are content to be a caretaker leader, if you continue to stumble along, sometime in the next few years an enterprising journalist will sit down at his desk, turn on the computer and start to write about the Stelmach era. His first line will be: *Ed Could Have Been a Superstar.*

Sincerely,

Rich Vivone

REFERENCES

200 Days of Change, Nancy Betkowski campaign for leadership of the Alberta
    Conservative Party, 1992

Alberta Views

Alberta Tax Review Commissions, 1994, 1998, Government of Alberta

Banksters & Prairie Boys, Monier Rahall, Monopoly, 1997

Building On Values: The Future of Health Care in Canada, Roy Romanow
    Commissioner, Commission on the Future of Health Care in Canada,
    Government of Canada, 2002

Calgary Herald

Calgary Sun

Children's Advocate annual reports, Government of Alberta

Children's Forum reports, 2000 et la, Government of Alberta

Democracy Derailed, Kevin Taft, Red Deer Press, 2007

Dr. Death or Dr. Dud, Ian Gray, *Insight into Government*, 2004

Edmonton Journal

Edmonton Sun

Globe and Mail

Health of Canadians: The Federal Role (a.k.a. Kirby Report), Michael Kirby, Senate
    Standing Committee on Social Affairs, Science & Technology, Government
    of Canada, 2002

Honest Politics: Seeking Integrity in Canadian Political Life, Ian Green and David
    Sugarman, Lorimer, 1997

Insight into Government, Rich Vivone & Associates, 1986-2005

Integrity in Government in Alberta: Toward The 21st Century, Allan Tupper Chair,
    Government of Alberta 1996

Investigation into Allegations Involving Hon. Peter Trynchy, Minister of
    Transportation & Utilities, Ethics Commissioner, Government of Alberta,
    December 14, 1994

Investigation into Allegations involving the Honorable Premier, Ethics
    Commissioner, Government of Alberta, November 10, 1995

Investigation into Allegations involving the Honorable Premier, Ethics
    Commissioner, Government of Alberta, December 19, 1996

Investigation into Allegations involving the Honorable Premier, Ethics
  Commissioner, Government of Alberta, April 21, 1997

King Ralph: The Political Life and Success of Ralph Klein, Don Martin, Key
  Porter, 2002

Klein Revolution, The, Mark Lisac, NeWest Press, 1995

Kyoto Protocol, United Nations Framework Convention on Climate Change, Kyoto,
  Japan, 1997

Kyoto Protocol, Marrakesh Accords, United Nations Framework Convention on
  Climate Change, Marrakesh, Morocco, 2001

Last Amigo: Karlheinz Schreiber and the Anatomy of a Scandal, The, Stevie
  Cameron and Harvey Cashore, Macfarlane, Walter & Ross, 2001

Lougheed Legacy, The, David Wood, Key Porter, 1985

Mavericks: An Incorrigible History of Alberta, Aritha van Herk, Penguin Canada,
  2001

Ministerial Error and the Political Process: Is there a duty to resign?, Stuart James
  Whitely, Sheldon Chumir Foundation for Ethics in Leadership, Calgary,
  2007

Not Without Cause: David Peterson's Fall From Grace, Georgette Gagnon and
  Dan Rath. Harper and Collins, 1991

On The Take: Crime, Corruption & Greed In The Mulroney Years, Stevie
  Cameron, Seal Books, 1995

Ottawa Inside Out, Stevie Cameron, Harper Collins, 1990

Our Fair Share, Report of the Alberta Royalty Review Panel, Government of Alberta,
  September 2007

Peter Lougheed: A biography, Alan Hustak, McClelland & Stewart, 1985

Political Financing in Canada: Achieving a Balance, International Foundation for
  Electoral Systems White Paper Series, Diane Davidson, Elections Canada

Premier's Advisory Council on Health Report, Don Mazankowski Chair,
  Government of Alberta, 2002

Ralph Klein: A Maverick Life, Frank Dabbs, Douglas & Macintyre, 1995

*Reinventing Government: How the Entrepreneurial Spirit is Transforming the Public
  Sector*, David Osborne and Ted Gaebler, Addison-Wesley, 1992

Report of the Learning Commission, Government of Alberta, 2003

261

Return Of The Trojan Horse: Alberta and the New World (Dis)Order,
Trevor W. Harrison, editor, Black Rose Books, 2005

Shredding The Public Interest: Ralph Klein and 25 Years Of One-Party Government,
Kevin Taft, Parkland Institute, 1997

Start Young, Start Now! Report of the Task Force On Children At Risk, Government
of Alberta, 2000

Strategy for Children and Families, Edmonton Social Planning Council, 2008,

Statement On Public Disclosure Of Interest, Premier Peter Lougheed, 1973,
Legislative Assembly of Alberta

Tar Sands: Dirty Oil and the Future of a Continent, Andrew Nikiforuk, Greystone
Books, 2008

Trojan Horse: Alberta and the Future of Canada, The, Gordon Laxer and Trevor
Harrison, editors, Black Rose Books, 1996

Unfinished Business, Sir Roger Douglas, Random House, 1993

Voters and non-voters, research report, Leger Marketing, Elections Alberta, 2008

We Can Do Better: Toward an Alberta Child Poverty Reduction, Edmonton Social
Planning Council, 2008

INDEX

M

MacBeth, Nancy 19, 20, 28, 42, 47, 179, 190, 191, 197, 198 (see also
    Betkowski, Nancy)
Macdonald, Alex 192
MacNichol, Vance 138
Magnesium Company of Canada 77, 235
Manning Centre for Building Democracy 51
Manning, Ernest 221, 247, 257
Manning, Preston 19, 100, 192, 209
Mar, Gary 116, 128, 129, 130, 131, 132, 140, 180, 189, 237
Martin, Don 17, 38, 54, 59, 172
Martin, Paul 80
Martin, Ray 75
Martini's 54, 61, 122
Mavericks: An Incorrigible History of Alberta 89, 235
Mazankowski Council 126, 129, 130, 141, 143 (see also Premier's Advisory
    Council on Health)
Mazankowski Council report 46, 132 (see also Premier's Advisory Council on
    Health)
Mazankowski, Don 127, 128, 256
McCaig, Bud 134
McClellan, Shirley 15, 80, 111, 134, 145
McCoy, Elaine 104, 163, 164, 214, 245, 246
McGuinty, Dalton 131
Melchin, Greg 253
Millar Western 77, 81, 82
Miniely, Gordon 169
miracle on the prairies 17
Mitchell, Grant 24, 41, 107, 191, 192, 196, 197, 199, 201, 202, 206
MLA conduct 167, 169, 170, 171
MLA housing allowance 179
MLA pension plan 14, 15, 30
Moore, Marvin 12, 20, 43, 125, 129
Moore, Sherrold 30
Mortgage Properties Inc. 76
Morton, Ted 218
Muir, Leilani 33
Mulder, Michelle 156
Mulroney, Brian 16, 81, 166
MultiCorp 80, 117, 118, 174, 175, 176
Municipal grants 110

To order your copy of

Ralph Could Have Been a Superstar
Tales of the Klein era

go to
www.vivone.com

YOUR WRITING AND RESOURCE NOTES